T0244160

Bitcoin Supercycle

Bitcoin Supercycle

HOW THE CRYPTO CALENDAR CAN MAKE YOU RICH

MICHAEL TERPIN

Skyhorse Publishing

Copyright © 2024 by Michael Terpin

Skyhorse Publishing books may be purchased in bulk at special discounts for sales promotion, corporate gifts, fund-raising, or educational purposes. Special editions can also be created to specifications. For details, contact the Special Sales Department, Skyhorse Publishing, 307 West 36th Street, 11th Floor, New York, NY 10018 or info@skyhorsepublishing.com.

Skyhorse® and Skyhorse Publishing® are registered trademarks of Skyhorse Publishing, Inc.®, a Delaware corporation.

Visit our website at www.skyhorsepublishing.com.

10 9 8 7 6 5 4 3 2

Library of Congress Cataloging-in-Publication Data is available on file.

Cover design by Ravin Dave

Cover photo created by Form-u.la with humans and robots using Midjourney and Adobe

Author photo courtesy of Greg Doherty Photography

Print ISBN: 978-1-5107-8215-0
Ebook ISBN: 978-1-5107-8217-4

Printed in the United States of America

I dedicate this, my first published work of nonfiction, to the memory of my father, Walter Terpin (1923–2020), who instilled in me the work ethic and moral fabric to succeed in life, and my mother Jeanne Elizabeth Jackson Terpin (1928–1979), who, along with her sister, my beloved aunt Helen Chaffee (1929–2013) and maternal grandmother, Macie VanOrman Jackson (1898–1992) fostered in me and my brothers Mark and Christopher Terpin (both very much alive and well and living in Buffalo, New York) a passion for creativity, the arts, and, in my case, a lifelong passion for writing.

I also dedicate this book to the two most important women in the storyline of my own adult life:

My former wife, Maxine Hopkinson, who encouraged me to pick up a suitcase and travel the world in pursuit of bitcoin knowledge and evangelism starting in 2013, when she noticed the industry wanted to hear from me and was offering to fly me around the world. "Go where you are loved," she said.

And last, but certainly not least, this book is dedicated to my current partner and love, the beautiful and brilliant Joyce Chow, a tireless, devoted soulmate and fellow crypto degen, who has been a constant source of inspiration, boundless energy, and personal fulfillment.

Contents

Introduction

April 20, 2024, 4:09 a.m. GST (00:09 UTC)

It's a beautiful late night in Dubai, with sultry trade winds blowing into the manmade harbor. Just three days earlier, the region was pummeled by an unprecedented storm of near-biblical proportions, dumping a record ten inches of rapidly falling rain—more than two years' worth in one day—onto a bustling boomtown of three million people that essentially has no municipal drainage system to cope with such a storm. Complicating matters further, nearly 50,000 people came to Dubai this week, the newest mecca for the cryptocurrency world, to attend four hundred events and to observe (through a stroke of genius planning or extraordinary good luck) the quadrennial event that in many ways defines and drives an industry and an economy that has grown from nothing to more than $2.5 trillion dollars—the bitcoin halving.

I stayed up late so I could once again watch the blocks tick by online. "Nine more blocks, eight more blocks, seven more blocks . . ." announced the various sites and watch parties occurring around the world. I was on the deck of former Bitcoin Foundation chairman Brock Pierce's DNA Fund yacht, which was still lively with afterparties as 4 a.m. approached. I was counting down the minutes with a small group, including prolific crypto startup investor Brian MacMahon of Expert Dojo, who flew in from Los Angeles for the occasion. I engaged in online *chatter from around the world, as the last blocks of the Fourth Bitcoin Cycle were created and sealed. Finally, the halving was here, with Happy Halving greetings online and on the yacht. I was hoping someone would have shot off fireworks above the harbor full of bitcoiners, but all that I heard was the light breeze and chatter of people on the yacht's upper decks as they finally headed back to their hotels.*

The Bitcoin halving is simple and elegant, yet widely misunderstood by those who are not intimately involved in the industry. "Does this mean I now have twice as much bitcoin, like a stock split?" asked one of my attorneys. Thankfully, he was not a crypto attorney but one who has dealt with enough issues in this realm that his question surprised me. "No," I explained. "The halving simply means that the supply of new bitcoin is issued at half the rate of the prior four-year period. This is more akin to OPEC cutting oil production, which generally pushes the price of oil upward."

The Bitcoin "halving" is quite simply the algorithmic mechanism that pseudonymous Bitcoin creator Satoshi Nakamoto put into place to reward early active participants in building the network with a larger share of the rewards than later participants. Think Amway or Mary Kay. Here, early bitcoin "miners" earn newly minted bitcoin directly from the chain through what Satoshi referred to in the Bitcoin white paper as "mining," a term used to describe the process of running software that independently verifies transactions between any two entities on earth without the need for governments, lawyers, bankers, or any type of third-party counterparty. This verification process, referred to as consensus, employs voluntary third parties with no stake in the transaction to independently confirm that a certain amount of bitcoin leaves one digital wallet and is accepted by another without any attempts to spend it twice. These miners are rewarded for turning on their computers and running this program all day and all night (hence, "proof-of-work") with a small fee for each completed transaction. More importantly, they receive fresh bitcoin from the bitcoin exchange "coinbase" (not to be confused with the American exchange, Coinbase). The Bitcoin coinbase is the algorithmic source that generates new bitcoin on a fixed schedule of 21 million bitcoin over 132 years for solving a cryptographic equation whose difficulty assures that the power of computers on the network is sufficiently strong to defeat any attack that would dismantle the permanent record of these transactions. Satoshi dubbed this linked chain of permanent financial records a blockchain. It is literally a chain of blocks, each containing a ledger of all transactions confirmed in the prior ten-minute period. We now have a permanent record, viewable by anyone on earth with access to the internet, of all transactions dating back to the Genesis Block (the initial building block), which kicked off the existence of Bitcoin on January 3, 2009. That initial block carried the inscription "The Times 03/Jan/2009 Chancellor on brink of second bailout for banks" as both a time stamp and political commentary. More on this in my chapter on the Bitcoin white paper.

My purpose in writing this book is multifold:

1) I have been looking for narratives to explain the fundamental value and continual growth of bitcoin since it was $66 in 2013. How often do you find an asset class comprising both value and growth? Since 2015, when the effects of the first halving cycle had run its course

and the second halving cycle was being established, I began using the phrase "Four Seasons of Bitcoin" to describe the four discrete components of every four-year cycle:

a. Spring, when the "seed" of the new Bitcoin halving occurs;

b. Summer, when the seed of spring blossoms into parabolic growth and a new all-time high;

c. Fall, when the new cycle's bubble pops and unsteady, weak hands race for the exits; and

d. Winter, when pessimism is at its most extreme, yet the buying opportunity is always the greatest.

These cycles have repeated like clockwork for fifteen years, and I believe they have at least three more cycles until we have reached a more mature market where the majority of the world's population holds at least some bitcoin, directly or indirectly, and the peaks and troughs of each cycle's price are more in line with far more established asset classes, like gold and bonds.

2) I desired a platform to address a more mainstream audience about the short- and long-term financial opportunities presented by bitcoin and cryptocurrency, from the perspective of an industry insider instead of a nonpartisan journalist. Most traditionally published books on bitcoin to date have been written by journalists. It's one thing to write about a war from an outside perspective, interviewing hundreds of sources; it's another having actually lived through the firefights in the foxhole.

3) I'm seeking to initiate and/or support new narratives within the financial and corporate communities that require an understanding of the past, present, and future of bitcoin (the mothership) and of the increasing array of interesting, often disruptive, cryptocurrency projects that form a completely different narrative and opportunity than the Bitcoin protocol itself. I spend one chapter discussing the differing perspectives of the Bitcoin "maximalist" community and the broader "multichain" perspective that includes all other cryptocurrencies. Bitcoin maximalists consider bitcoin to be the "one true God," and all other attempts are poor copies or frauds. Multicoiners believe bitcoin is great for an immutable store of value, but newer chains with more advanced technology are better at solving other challenges, including smart contracts, decentralized finance, and blockchain gaming. Newer chains are also faster and have lower fees but are less decentralized and less secure.

Bitcoin Supercycle is divided into twenty-one chapters (one for each of the 21 million bitcoins in existence), with the chapters organized into five sections (which I refer to as books).

"Book One: Bitcoin Is Internet-Based Hard Money" begins with a history of the prior attempts to create digital money, dating back to the Cypherpunks (for a truly comprehensive view of the history of money and why Bitcoin is the most complex form of money ever invented, I highly recommend reading *The Bitcoin Standard*, by Dr. Saifedean Ammous, which has sold more than a million copies since it first hit the bookshelves in 2018).[i] I limit my narrative to the past fifty years instead of the five thousand years or more that humankind has sought to quantify value beyond simple barter. However, I delve briefly into the concept of hard money and its evolution, setting up the current battle between bitcoin and the world's central banks, which are no longer backed by gold or any other physical asset, and racing one another to see who can print enough money to stay in power. An increasingly digital and educated population is quickly discovering that money printing without economic development is a quick path to the impoverishment of nations. Finally, I cue up the road map provided by the Bitcoin white paper, which was issued on October 31, 2008, at the depths of the financial crisis now known as the Great Recession. Steeped in Austrian economics and libertarian ethics, the concepts in the white paper served as the basis for the growth of the entire multitrillion-dollar bitcoin and cryptocurrency asset class in less than fifteen years.

"Book Two: Understanding the Bitcoin Cycles" follows each of the five cycles of bitcoin's history to date. There will be thirty-three four-year cycles until the final fraction of a bitcoin will be issued in 2140. I spend an entire chapter footnoting Satoshi's nine-page white paper, *Bitcoin: A Peer-to-Peer Electronic Cash System*, as it is critical to understanding how Bitcoin works. From there, I spend one chapter for each four-year cycle, beginning with the First Cycle (2009–2012) prior to the first halving, which provided the highest gains of any asset class in history before reaching a fraction of 1 percent of today's valuation. The Second Cycle (2012–2016) is when Bitcoin grew from $12 to $1,200 and became alternately famous (when it reached $1,000, which was more than 1,000,000 times its first recorded price) and infamous (the Silk

Road illicit drug markets and the implosion of Bitcoin's first centralized exchange, Mt. Gox). Cycle Three (2016–2020) saw the rapid rise of Ethereum as a contender to Bitcoin's dominance as the Initial Coin Offering (ICO) frenzy disrupted the way startups raised money by bypassing venture capitalists and angels altogether and selling anonymously to the crypto public at large (at least until regulators clamped down). That important cycle also saw the creation of Bitcoin Cash and Bitcoin SV, which were contentious hard forks of Bitcoin, threatening to divide the community in a competition for the "true" Bitcoin (which the original Bitcoin won). Cycle Four (2020–2024) followed the third halving, and it was best known for the creation of three new narratives:

1) decentralized finance (DeFi), which provided yield and lending to cryptocurrency;
2) non-fungible tokens (NFTs), which allowed for each unit of cryptocurrency to be marked up, either in a comment field or smart contract, to create unique digital assets; this category exploded in popularity with meme-related collectibles like Bored Apes and Crypto Punks, then faded as quickly as it had risen; and
3) the metaverse, a virtual world scenario incorporating tokenized avatars, virtual reality (VR), and augmented reality (AR).

Finally, I address the new cycle (2024–2028) and why I believe it will bring on a supercycle, both in terms of faster price movements but also in global usage. The term "Supercycle" first came into usage during the Great Depression of the 1930s, following the publication of a series of papers and books by

Ralph Nelson Elliott, later known collectively as the "Elliott Wave" theory, in which most financial cycles consist of five waves (more on this in Chapter 15), but a broader Supercycle exists lasting decades. Since then, the term Supercycle has been used to describe various rapid growth phenomena, including new technology markets, which tend to grow from 8 to 80 percent in ten to twelve years. It has also been used intermittently to describe broader financial and technological epochs, such as the Industrial Age, the Computer Age, and the Internet Age. Many believe we are now at the dawn of another epoch, which is defined by the rapid growth of artificial intelligence (AI) and digital assets.

The term "bitcoin super-cycle" was first used (from best I can tell) in January 2019 by crypto influencer Alex Saunders in a video about "the Bitcoin and Litecoin Super-Cycle," where he predicted rapid growth in the 2020–2024 halving cycles. Bitcoin educator and influencer Dan Held wrote a post in 2020, followed by interviews and podcasts in 2020–2021, where he posited that the emergence of COVID-19 and increased money printing by the United States would bring on a Bitcoin supercycle within that cycle that could lift the price per bitcoin as high as $800,000. As it turns out, both predictions were premature, and of course, my theories are simply that: my own theories, although I spend a full chapter detailing why I believe the 2024–2028 halving cycle is where a true Supercycle finally kicks off.

"Book Three: The Four Seasons of Bitcoin"

At the core of this book is a detailed explanation of how the Four Seasons of Bitcoin work in practice and how following "the Crypto Calendar" has provided dramatically better investment returns than buy-and-hold strategies alone or even dollar-cost averaging (DCA).

Here's a preview:

Bitcoin Spring begins the day of the halving. It's when the "seed" of an entire new cycle is planted. On this day, most bitcoin miners become temporarily unprofitable, as they typically operate at 20 percent profit margins (some are much higher, some are less; this is largely dependent upon the price of electricity per kilowatt and the "hashing power" of the bitcoin miners). At the moment of the halving, the bitcoin reward per block gets cut in half. On November 28, 2012, it went from 50 bitcoin per block to 25; three cycles later, on April 20, 2024, it went from 6.25 bitcoin to a mere 3.125 BTC per block. In the early days of Bitcoin, prior to the first halving, the majority of mining was done by individuals (known as "solo mining"), running the original mining software that came with each Bitcoin QT wallet downloaded from the bitcoin.org website. About midway through the first cycle, GPU mining took off (popularized by Laszlo Hanyecz, who famously spent 10,000 of his bitcoin to buy a pizza), increasing the difficulty levels to the point that CPU mining became ineffective. By early 2013, field programmable gate array (FPGA) chips were built to do nothing but mine bitcoin, and they were far more powerful than GPUs. This increased the difficulty to the point that "home mining" was no longer an option (at least for bitcoin) by the end of that cycle. Solo mining was replaced by industrial bitcoin mining farms, each competing for the fractions of a bitcoin that would be prorated by mining pools. Each new halving makes the majority of miners unprofitable until the difficulty levels adjust and/or new mining equipment arrives. Helping the profitability in the current cycle is the advent of Bitcoin Ordinals and Runes, NFT-like products built on Bitcoin that command higher fees than ordinary bitcoin transactions.

Bitcoin Summer takes place the day the former all-time high (ATH) of the prior cycle is exceeded. For the first halving (2012), it took only four months to break the first cycle's high-water mark of $30. After the second halving (2016), it took six months to exceed the existing ATH of $1,236. For the third halving (2020), the wait extended to seven months to surpass the 2017 high of $19,188. What has been unique to the 2024 cycle is that the all-time high price from 2021 was breached one month prior to the halving. This has never happened before, and it is a potential signal of a supercycle ahead.[ii] There are also pundits who claim it simply means a quicker cycle, as most cycles have reached new all-time highs within nine to eleven months of the prior all-time high being achieved (nine months in 2013, eleven months in 2017, and ten months in 2020–2021). If this dynamic played out again, the ultimate ATH for the 2024–2028 cycle would come between December 2024 and February 2025. This dynamic is counter to the other repeating trend in all-time highs: they have so far always occurred in the fourth quarter of the year after the halving. I have a different perspective, that the March 2024 ATH belongs to last cycle, meaning this Bitcoin Summer has not yet occurred.

Bitcoin Fall is quite simply the season when prices fall. Prices in the bull market of Bitcoin Summer tend to overheat as a new class of retail investors are brought in with quick riches in mind, and they keep doubling down on their profits as though this were an endless summer. Bitcoin Fall begins the day after the all-time high, when buying demand is beginning to wane and experienced whales take some profits off the table to reinvest at the start of Bitcoin Winter. It surprises many traditional investors when I point out that the price of bitcoin to date has been at least as predictable as the real estate and stock market cycles, with the third year of each cycle thus far (2014, 2018, 2022) being the *only* years one lost money, with the other twelve years being solidly in the black to the tune of double, triple, even quadruple digits of gains. This is not a coincidence; the next "red" year will likely be 2026, following a Bitcoin Summer high in late 2025.

Bitcoin Winter begins the day of capitulation, which is often difficult to recognize until it's in the rearview mirror. Capitulation is not simply a massive drop in price, as there have been 30 and 40 percent pullbacks even in a bull market. Capitulation is where there are literally no sellers left, as all weak hands have folded their cards and gone home. In the most recent 2022 winter, many thought the bottom was reached when the price dropped below $30,000 after Terra Luna imploded or when it fell below $20,000 when Celsius began its descent into bankruptcy. Indeed, it was the scandalous implosion of FTX, at the time the world's second-largest crypto exchange, which sent the price of bitcoin down to $15,700, with hungry bears projecting it had much further to fall.[iii] Yet, when the Genesis crypto lending division of CoinDesk and Grayscale parent company DCG declared bankruptcy a few weeks later, there was nary a drop in bitcoin price, specifically because there were no sellers left—just "hodlers" (Bitcoin slang for long-term holders from an early meme). This was the buying opportunity of a lifetime, just as the days after the contentious fork of Bitcoin Cash (itself a contentious fork of Bitcoin) into Bitcoin SV marked the bottom of the 2018–2019 Winter, and the implosion of early bitcoin exchange Mt. Gox marked the bottom of the 2014–2015 Winter. Buyers of bitcoin at each market bottom were handsomely rewarded for their unshakable belief.

"Book Four: Mastering the Bitcoin Cycles"

In this section, I break out various strategies for maximizing gain during each cycle, as well as what a supercycle means for these strategies. Areas I cover include:

1) *Maximizing profit while minimizing risk.* Here, I lay out my personal strategy for cycle trading. Unlike day trading or algorithmic trading, which have mixed results compared with cycle trading and take up exponentially more time and resources, the basis of cycle trading of bitcoin and other crypto markets is fairly simple. My thesis is that each cycle has a relatively predictable top and bottom. The goal is to load up on new bitcoin at the market bottoms (as well as promising altcoins if that's within your risk profile and philosophy) and sell them at the market tops. While one can never (or at least rarely) pick the market tops to the day, the "season" of the tops and bottoms have been very predictable within a ninety-day window for each cycle thus far. Whether one deployed this strategy for bitcoin alone or mixed it in with altcoins, it has created monumentally better returns than the stock market or traditional commodities. This strategy has also substantially outperformed the "set it and forget it" mantra of the hodlers.

2) *Asset allocation.* In Chapter 18, I look at strategies to maximize gains (e.g., staking mid-cycle; understanding

altcoin cycles; buying real estate, stocks, or commodities with profits from the top of the cycle to reinvest in bitcoin about one year later at the cycle's bottom). One key strategy is to understand that traditional assets often work on ten-year cycles, whereas Bitcoin and crypto work on four-year cycles. Arbitraging these cycles can compound your bitcoin profits.

3) *Ethereum, Solana, and the race for the new protocols.* Bitcoin maximalists can skip this chapter, but as a bitcoin-first multichain believer, I am always on the lookout for new protocols that can disrupt markets. I was fortunate enough to work with the Ethereum team prior to their crowdsale and launch, and I've seen multiple other protocols grow 100x or more in price in less than a year, so they should not be discarded without examination.

4) *Altcoins, memecoins, Web3 gaming, and NFTs.* I go further down the altcoin rabbit hole in this chapter, as each cycle has had new trends that have outperformed bitcoin in appreciation. Altcoins with an AI narrative grew in value more than four times as fast as bitcoin in the year leading up to the most recent halving, while top new memecoins like Bonk, Brett, and Dog Wif Hat performed even better. This is a high-risk, high-reward territory, but no comprehensive view of the crypto markets in 2024 should ignore these categories as a topic.

5) *Staking, lending, and liquidity providing for income.* Warren Buffett famously didn't like gold or bitcoin because it did not provide income or dividends. Staking, lending, and liquidity providing, which is

primarily in the field of Ethereum, Solana, and hundreds of altcoins, has proven to be another portfolio driver, with relatively low-risk returns of up to 15 percent (and higher-risk returns as high as 50–80 percent).

"Book Five: Million-Dollar Bitcoin"

I wrap up this book with a discussion of the spread of Bitcoin throughout the Global South as a preferred form of payment and a counter to the hyperinflation destroying those economies. In the final chapter, I analyze various scenarios to reaching the Holy Grail of cryptocurrency: $1 million bitcoin, which will provide the earliest buyer of bitcoin with a 1,000,000,000,000 (that's one trillion) times return on the earliest 2009 investment. What will power the million-dollar bitcoin? The estimated market cap of gold as of the writing of the 2024 bitcoin halving is $15.7 trillion. Million-dollar bitcoin, presuming 20 million bitcoin are already mined (the final million bitcoin will take more than 100 years to extract), equals a $20 trillion market cap. In the last chapter, I project a few scenarios where I believe this price can be achieved as early as 2030 and no later than 2045, reflecting a return of more than 15x over the 2024 halving price. Bitcoin bulls including Michael Saylor and PlanB have speculated bitcoin price as high as $10 million per bitcoin or more upon its mass adoption.

Finally, I speculate a bit on the next 100 years beyond initial critical mass (2040–2140) and what a world looks like where bitcoin is ubiquitous and the asset class is larger than gold, eventually passing stock markets and perhaps real estate. Programmable money will interoperate with the AI programs of the future to automate most of our financial lives to an extent never before imagined. As always in human history, there will be threats and obstacles to this crypto utopia, but one thing remains clear. There will only ever be 21 million bitcoins, and if every millionaire in the world wanted to own just one bitcoin, there aren't enough to go around. Enjoy the read, and please let me know what you think.

Book One
Bitcoin Is Internet-Based Hard Money

Chapter One

What Bitcoin Is, Why It Is Important, and How to Use It

Give me control of a nation's money supply, and I care not who makes its laws.
   —Mayer Amschel Rothschild (1744–1812),
   founder of the Rothschild banking dynasty[iv]

If you don't believe me or don't get it, I don't have time to try to convince you, sorry.
   —Satoshi Nakamoto, creator of Bitcoin[v]

To put it simply, Bitcoin is digital cash.

Bitcoin is a peer-to-peer system that transfers value between any two people on Earth (eventually into outer space, as long as there is an internet connection) in a manner that requires no permission from a gatekeeper or custodian. This is referred to as a "permissionless" system of transactions. The creation of this protocol did not happen overnight; it required the creation of the internet and sophisticated forms of cryptography. All of these essential elements came together on Halloween 2008 when the pseudonymous cryptographer

Satoshi Nakamoto released a nine-page white paper outlining his vision of how exactly this system could be launched and scaled. He then programmed the software, and the Bitcoin blockchain came to life on January 3, 2009, when Bitcoin issued its first block on what Satoshi referred to as a "blockchain"—literally a chain of cryptographic blocks representing the total lifetime ledger of all transactions in the history of Bitcoin. He referred to this initial block as the Genesis Block.

Bitcoin was the first truly permissionless system that did not involve banks, custodians, or third-party counterparties of any kind. The genius of Bitcoin was in its "proof-of-work" dimension, wherein "miners" run a software program that provides a decentralized form of payment processing. The theory of bitcoin mining was that if more than one person runs a program that independently validates a peer-to-peer transfer of value from one party to another and the result is agreed upon by another independent miner, then it is likely a valid transaction. When three more miners agree, it is even more valid. When 100 or 1,000 miners agree on the same transaction, it is mathematically impossible to refute. Importantly, the whole process is completely anonymous; none of these miners have knowledge of either party transacting nor any financial interest in stopping a valid transaction.

The incentive for miners (a phrase that refers symbolically to the mining of physical gold) is twofold:

1) Miners are rewarded a small fee for their part in the confirmation of each transaction. This fee is far less than traditional banking or credit card fees, and it is split among all of the miners confirming each transaction using the Bitcoin mining algorithm. Initially, this

miner fee was in pennies. Today, it's a few dollars for transactions of unlimited value.

2) Most importantly, miners earn 100 percent of all new bitcoins created, totaling 21,000,000 bitcoins issued over a 132-year period. That period consists of 33 four-year cycles, with each cycle issuing half the bitcoin of the cycle prior.

Bitcoin is also the first digital *asset*, whereas everything prior to its creation was a digital *file*. Why is this important? Digital files were revolutionary when they first appeared, with clear advantages over analog data. An analog photograph required the use of physical film, a physical darkroom, and silver nitrate to process a physical print. A digital camera can take and process unlimited pictures, restricted only by storage space. These pictures can then be copied endlessly with no degradation in quality. This is a superior format for data.

However, this ability to instantly replicate is not a good format for an asset. As presented in Chapter 2, one of the key characteristics of money is scarcity; if one could replicate gold, silver, or dollars infinitely, they would have little to no value. They would (or should) cease to be an asset. But thanks to the protocol outlined above, bitcoin and other cryptocurrencies allow for the reliable, verifiable transfer of ownership. When I send a bitcoin to you, it provably shifts its ownership from my wallet to yours. There is no duplication involved. Since it exists only digitally, it retains the benefits of digital data, including the ability to be transmitted across the globe in seconds through the marvel of the internet. This makes Bitcoin a new type of asset, an asset that is at once scarce and valuable and exists only in digital form.

What You Will Learn in This Book

My ultimate goal in this book is to demonstrate four things:

1) As I pointed out in my still popular TEDx Talk from 2014, Bitcoin with a Big B is the protocol, and bitcoin with a small b is the currency.[vi] Together, they represent one of the most significant technological developments in the history of modern civilization, at least equal to the creation of the microprocessor that enabled the PC revolution and the creation of the internet.

2) Bitcoin is not a scam or a fad, nor is the blockchain technology it created. Blockchain has survived many early obstacles to become a proven technology now used by most of the Fortune 500. Meanwhile, Bitcoin has become a significant asset class that has provided superior returns to investors, speculators, and savers alike compared with any other asset class over nearly any time frame since its inception. This year's approval of the Bitcoin exchange-traded fund (ETF) by eleven major traditional financial institutions has thus far exceeded expectations in its sales trajectory, further pushing its narrative into the mainstream.

3) We are in a unique period where bitcoin adoption and value is poised to explode, leaving most people forever behind. The Bitcoin Supercycle that is the title of this book refers to both the great appreciation in value I forecast over the next twenty years but also the technological definition of a supercycle, wherein adoption tends to grow exponentially once it reaches 8 percent penetration, which we are on the cusp of achieving globally and have exceeded already in many

nations. Bitcoin's growth has almost completely mimicked the growth of the internet, which grew from 2.6 million users in 1990 to more than 5.4 billion users in 2024, passing one billion users in 2005.[vii]

4) There are proven cycles one can follow to determine when to buy bitcoin and when to sell. These cycles are as reliable and relatively predictable as those in the stock market and real estate. Still, they are shorter cycles (four-year instead of ten-year or eighteen-year cycles, respectively). The bulk of this book goes through the actual performance of each four-year cycle and the trends it has identified (see Chapters 5–9). These trends are the basis for my "Four Seasons of Bitcoin" theories, which I detail at length in Chapters 10–13.

Use Cases for Bitcoin: A Simple Explanation

In general, those who will tell you that Bitcoin is worthless and that it accomplishes nothing have, in fact, never tried using it. US Senator Elizabeth Warren, who famously proclaimed that she was gathering an "anti-crypto army" to eviscerate bitcoin usage in the United States and said buying bitcoin was like "buying air," as it had no value whatsoever beyond pure speculation, has clearly never tried using it.[viii] Those of us who have come to depend upon bitcoin as a fundamental part of our portfolio and use daily know otherwise. I will lay out the most important use cases for bitcoin, which (like money itself) vary depending on one's financial status and which country one lives in.

Use Case Number 1: Investment. As noted earlier, bitcoin has been one of the best investments one could have made for most of the past fifteen years. Its average annual return has been more than 200 percent per year, and even in the past five years, the average annual return has been 140 percent. In fact, of the fifteen years bitcoin has existed, there have only been three years that one could have lost money during a full calendar year (2014, 2018, and 2022, each year representing the third year of each cycle). As I demonstrate in the Four Seasons of Bitcoin chapters, there is a system for knowing when to buy and sell to maximize long-term gains and minimize the prospect of any short-term loss.

For anyone looking to build a career in technology or finance, the opportunities afforded by the nascent, rapidly growing crypto industry are also exponential. Crypto-related venture capital jumped from 0.3 percent of the global venture capital market in 2017 to 12.62 percent in 2022, with the percentage for US-based crypto funds at 21.81 percent, according to the *Vision Track 2024 Institutional Hedge Fund & Venture Report*.[ix] Crypto hedge funds also grew to $15.2 billion by the end of 2023, reporting an average return for the year of 66.57 percent, with the top quartile earning a remarkable 350.8 percent return. Bitcoin mining is also rapidly growing.

Use Case Number 2: Friction-Free Finance. Has your bank rejected a transaction, particularly an international wire? How about turning down a loan for which you had sufficient collateral? Frustrated by "banking hours" when you need to receive or transmit funds in the evening or over a weekend or holiday? With bitcoin, you literally become your own bank, but with much better policies. You can transact with anyone in the world twenty-four hours a day, seven days a week, 365 days a year. There are no "account holds" or frozen transactions. The transaction goes through as long as you correctly enter the recipient address and have sufficient funds for the transaction and the small miner fee.

I appreciate that I can send $100,000 or even $1,000,000 or more to someone globally to buy or invest in something, and the receipt and settlement is instant. You wish to book a private jet on a Friday night? Good luck, unless you're using bitcoin. That is a key reason that more and more private jet brokers accept bitcoin: it works perfectly when the banks are closed, as well as when the banks require a few days to complete a transaction, but you have immediate, legitimate needs for payment. There are also thousands of international e-commerce sites that will not accept US-issued credit or debit cards, but they can settle instantly with bitcoin.

Use Case Number 3: Accept Bitcoin as Payment. In the early days of Bitcoin, the narrative was that everyone should be able to buy a cup of coffee or a cheeseburger with bitcoin. Certainly, a number of early bitcoiners did well by accepting and then holding on to bitcoin as a form of payment in those early days. The founder of US-based bitcoin and cryptocurrency exchange Kraken, Jesse Powell, once quipped upon the closure of Room 77, a small café in Berlin that accepted bitcoin as payment when bitcoin prices were in the single digits, that he "will never forget the taste of that $87,000 hamburger" (the price of bitcoin is now about four times the price when he tweeted that remark).[x]

As for me, I have long practiced what I preach, accepting bitcoin for my marketing and consulting services as far back as 2013, when a $20,000 retainer was roughly two hundred bitcoin. Whether you're a store owner, a consultant, a winery, an author, or simply have a few side hustles, let it be known that you accept bitcoin. Then, keep that bitcoin instead of immediately converting it. It's unlikely that the percentage of your total sales in bitcoin will equal your overall profit margin, so consider it an investment in your future wealth.

Use Case Number 4: Legacy and Inheritance. Many of the early bitcoiners I know have yet to sell a single bitcoin, which is an impressive act of self-discipline and confidence. While I have always believed in the future of bitcoin, I also diversified my bitcoin capital gains into real estate, technology companies, and other more traditional investments. As it turns out, I would have done better having kept everything in bitcoin, even when those investments gained 10x in seven years (the venture capitalist's ideal) because bitcoin appreciated more than 100x from 2014 to 2021.

Since most nations tax on realized capital gains, the joys of "hodling" include the ability to pass increasingly more valuable bitcoin investments to the next generation. Given that the average American household has less than $21,000 in annual discretionary income, this cycle may likely be the last one where the average person can realistically afford to buy one whole bitcoin.[xi] Compounding this is the fact that if every one of the 24.5 million US millionaires (not to mention the 59 million millionaires in the world) wanted to own one bitcoin, they could not do it, given there are less than 20 million bitcoin issued, so far, with the last million bitcoin taking 116 years from now to be mined. Considering that an estimated four million to five million bitcoin are likely lost[xii] and a total of nine million bitcoin have not moved in the past three years, it's unlikely that even five million bitcoin can be purchased in the next few decades without a massive price jump.

Bitcoin legend Michael Saylor disagrees with the concept of a balanced portfolio, which he refers to as selling a superior asset in order to invest in an inferior one. He thoroughly analyzed where to invest his large corporate treasury at public company Microstrategy in 2020 as the world plunged into a pandemic, where he was confident that massive money printing would cause inflation and debase the US dollar. Saylor's main product line is business intelligence software, and he decided in August 2020 to make a massive bet on bitcoin at around $11,500 per bitcoin. This bet has paid off handsomely, and Microstrategy stock has outperformed not only its peers but the price of bitcoin itself as Microstrategy has pivoted into being a bitcoin development company and has increasingly used its balance sheet to issue new stock as collateral to buy more bitcoin. Most investors today look at Microstrategy stock (NASDAQ: MSTR) as a leveraged investment on the price of bitcoin.

Saylor is incredibly bullish on bitcoin's future, once appearing in a video that went viral suggesting an all-in strategy on bitcoin (the original video is on YouTube):

"Take all of your money and buy bitcoin. Then take all of your time to figure out how to borrow more money to buy more bitcoin, then take all your time to figure out what you can sell to buy bitcoin, and if you absolutely love the thing that you don't want to sell it, go mortgage your house and buy bitcoin with it."

Saylor has continued to follow this strategy at MicroStrategy, repeatedly buying bitcoin regularly. As of June 20, 2024, the company held 226,331 bitcoins, which is more than 1 percent of the total bitcoin supply, according to CoinDesk.[xiii] This is a remarkable feat for a company that has been buying bitcoin for less than four years.

Use Case Number 5: Banking the Unbanked. Most middle-class citizens of the Western world do not need bitcoin for daily payments. In developed nations, most people have access to credit and debit cards, ATMs, and bank accounts. Yet, even in the United States, an estimated 5.9 million households do not have any family members with either a checking or savings account as of 2021, according to the FDIC National Survey of Unbanked and Underbanked Households.[xiv] This puts these households in a world of predatory lending, including so-called payday loans, which charge annualized interest of more than 500 percent for loans based on the collateral of one's next paycheck. This can lead to a downward spiral as each new paycheck pays off the prior exorbitantly high-interest loan, and one never gets out of the vicious cycle of poverty despite working one or more regular jobs.

Bitcoin has rewarded savers with an average of more than 100 percent per year appreciation over the past twelve years, and the worst it has done over a four-year cycle from cycle low to next cycle low has been more than 400 percent. While each cycle is subject to diminishing returns through the law of large numbers, it is unlikely to provide a lower return than bank interest for quite some time. Bitcoin does not require a minimum balance to open an account, nor does it require any fees to keep the account open. There are no tellers, no bank presidents to approve a large transaction. You are effectively your own bank. You are in control of your financial life.

Use Case Number 6: Remittance and Cross-Border Payments. Global remittance payments, which are international payments sent between individuals, were most recently reported at $732.62 billion and are expected to pass $1.031 trillion by 2029, according to the 2024 Remittance Market report by

ResearchandMarkets.com.[xv] The majority of these payments flow between family members in first-world nations to their poorer relatives in the third world. Remittance fees through traditional financial organizations such as banks and specialized providers like Western Union average 10 percent of the transaction and can often be as high as 20 percent or more, depending on where the transaction initiates and where it is received.

Bitcoin solves this problem by allowing permissionless remittance globally for fees that average $0.77 as of August 15, 2024, for nearly any size transaction.[xvi] Most nations now have "last mile" solutions to convert bitcoin into cash or stablecoins for daily spending, and third-world participants are rapidly becoming aware that the more they can save their bitcoin, the quicker they can rise out of poverty. In Chapter 20, I address some growth solutions in Africa and Latin America.

Cross-border payments, which reflect business-to-business international payments, are a less mature market than remittances. However, it is still estimated at $160 billion as of 2023, with growth to $345.42 billion by 2033, according to the Brainy Insights report. There is no clear leader in this market, most of which is dominated by banks, fintech payment platforms, and other traditional financial institutions. Bitcoin can eviscerate fees and save massive amounts of time, given that some corporate payments can take up to 90 days to facilitate from purchase order to fulfillment. This is a key area for innovation as bitcoin and other cryptocurrencies, particularly stablecoins, become more accepted for payments.

Use Case Number 7: Payment for Politically Unpopular Causes. WikiLeaks would most likely not exist today without

Bitcoin. The permissionless manner in which any amount of bitcoin can be sent enabled the ultimate defenders of a global free press to continue their crusading mission long after the group's ability to accept credit and debit cards dried up in 2011. The famed Canadian trucker protests over restrictions also turned to bitcoin when it found they could not process contributions due to political pressure from the Canadian government. Many other instances are seen where politically unpopular speech, products, or actions where traditional finance has put a chokehold on commerce are freed up by bitcoin, including online casinos and legalized marijuana.

Yes, bitcoin has also been used for illegal purchases. Still, it has been proven that the percentage of transactions today for buying drugs, weapons, or other illicit activities is a tiny percentage of the overall commerce in bitcoin. According to Chainalysis, the leading blockchain data and forensic analysis firm, only 0.34 percent of all on-chain transactions had suspected links to crime.[xvii] Of those transactions, 75 percent were in tokens other than bitcoin (mainly stablecoins pegged to the US dollar), according to their *2024 Crypto Crime Trends* report. This is also a lower amount than traditional banks, which have been fined for allowing it (when drug barons are caught, they usually have suitcases of cash, not bitcoin storage devices).

The initial dark web marketplace, Silk Road, was an eBay-like marketplace for illegal drugs and weapons. Its existence led to the initial parabolic bitcoin price run-up from pennies to $30 (and subsequent crash back to $1) in 2011 after the consumer tech blog *Gizmodo*[xviii] wrote about it, and it was then recirculated online through the popular headline aggregator, Slashdot. When law enforcement officials finally tracked down and arrested Silk Road creator Ross Ulbricht in late 2013, he was convicted and sentenced to life imprisonment without the possibility of parole (a controversial sentencing that has been subject to many unsuccessful appeals). Pro-crypto US presidential candidate Donald Trump said in May 2024 that he would commute Ulbricht's sentence for time served on his first day in office.

The 29,655 bitcoins seized in the Silk Road arrest were auctioned off in 2014 and purchased for an estimated $19 million (roughly $640 per bitcoin, which was over the market average at the time). Venture capitalist Tim Draper contends he has yet to sell any of that bitcoin, which, as of May 12, 2024, was worth more than $1.8 billion, nearly 100x the purchase price.

Use Case Number 8: Digital Store of Value. Remember the stories of the old man who would store his cash in a mattress (a horrible store of value, given inflation)? How about tales of people burying gold in their backyard? Bitcoin also allows its holders to self-custody their investment in a digital commodity whose value has not only beaten inflation but by a large margin. This is particularly important in third-world nations where runaway inflation occurs, including Argentina (288 percent), Lebanon (222 percent), Sudan (92 percent), and Venezuela (76 percent).[xix] Even Turkey, a country on the verge of first-world status, had 67 percent inflation in 2023.

It is more important than ever for citizens of nations whose money printing and irresponsible fiscal and banking policies have resulted in disastrous hyperinflation rates to embrace bitcoin. It is the path to financial freedom, including the ability to send and receive funds from anywhere in the world.

Chapter Two

The Lessons of Hard Money

Money is only a tool. It will take you wherever you wish, but it will not replace you as the driver.
— Ayn Rand, *Atlas Shrugged* (1957)[xx]

When I was young, I thought that money was the most important thing in life; now that I am old I know that it is.
— Oscar Wilde, *A Woman of No Importance* (1893)[xxi]

Money is our madness, our vast collective madness.
— D.H. Lawrence, *Pansies* (1929)[xxii]

No man's credit is as good as his money.
— John Dewey[xxiii]

What exactly is money?

Money has evolved as a concept from the earliest civilizations to represent one's ability to create commerce with one's neighbors that goes beyond simple barter and to save and invest that currency or commodity to build wealth. All money, as generally defined, must have the following features:

- *Unit of account.*
- *Store of value.*
- *Medium of exchange.*

Let's unpack each of these:

Unit of account. Perhaps the most readily identifiable characteristic of money, a unit of account, defines the value of a currency or commodity into standardized, fungible units. When you hear the terms US Dollar, Euro, Chinese RMB, or United Arab Emirates dirham as your national currency, you can immediately relate its value to items you own or would like to purchase. You can buy a T-shirt for ten US dollars or a Lamborghini for two hundred thousand. If you deal in multiple national currencies, you can calculate quickly that one US dollar can be exchanged for roughly 93 cents of euros, $1.36 of Canadian dollars, 3.67 UAE dirhams, or 7.8 Hong Kong dollars. In modern times, these ratios are far from fixed, and trillions of dollars are traded daily in foreign exchange markets (FOREX) to facilitate international trade and speculation.

The "unit of account" determines the world order in many ways. At the end of World War II, forty-four nations came together at a small resort town in New Hampshire and negotiated the Bretton Woods Agreement, under which the US dollar became the reserve currency for the world. All other currencies were pegged against the US dollar, which was backed by gold at a fixed $35 per ounce.

When Nixon removed the backing of US dollars by gold, replacing it with "the full faith and credit" of the United States government, he effectively enabled the US government to issue an IOU to pay its debts in increasingly larger amounts. This monetary system is known as "fiat currency"—the backing of the currency is by the fiat of the nation issuing it. Its value comes from the mandate that its citizens must accept the currency as legal tender instead of demanding payment in gold or silver. It is also the only currency acceptable for the payment of taxes. Today, zero nations are embracing a gold standard—not even those producing and exporting gold.

By removing the convertibility of US dollars to gold to settle trade deficits (Roosevelt had already removed its convertibility by its citizens), the Bretton Woods Agreement came to an end. Yet, the United States continued to promote its reserve currency status, including the negotiation of a petrodollar policy in 1973, wherein all purchases of oil globally needed to be made in US dollars. This not only strengthened the US dollar, but it flooded these strong US dollars into the Middle East, creating a golden economic age for the region. The petrodollar policy is now under attack on multiple fronts, as is the US reserve currency status.

While it is unlikely that Bitcoin could replace the US dollar as a global reserve currency anytime soon, it certainly could become part of a basket of currencies and commodities used in lieu of a single reserve currency standard. El Salvador was the first nation to name bitcoin as one of its national currencies, for which it was attacked by the International Monetary Fund and the World Bank, both legacy institutions created by the Bretton Woods Agreement.

"I think we are selling ourselves short, only looking to become a store of value like gold," said Vinny Lingham, a serial entrepreneur known as the "Oracle of Bitcoin" who first predicted that bitcoin would reach $1,000 in 2013. "I believe we should be going for units of account."[xxiv]

Store of value. To create savings, a unit of account must have recognized value and durability. One of the many issues with a barter economy that makes it hard to scale is the lack of durability and fungibility. If you're a cobbler, you can only make one pair of custom shoes at a time, although one could build an inventory of basic shoes in advance and hope they represented the right range of sizes and styles. A chef, however, cannot stock inventory in advance for items that spoil. Similarly, a barber can only cut hair on one head at a time. An advertising executive can only write one piece of copy or draw one design at a time, and so on. With products, some inventory perishes, from food to medicine to advertising inventory and hotel rooms for a particular night. Hence, the concept of credit began to arise around barter, given that barter has an uncorrelated coincidence of wants. I may need eggs from the farmer today but not tomorrow. The farmer can only keep today's eggs for so long, but he can often receive credit based on trust and reputation for the eggs he promises to deliver a month from today.

Money, particularly cash, removes the trust factor around the person paying you. Once you have established that the gold coins or paper currency you have been tendered are, in fact, genuine, you do not require any further trust from the seller—other than the trust he or she will deliver the goods and not rob you of the money they just gave to you. This is where contracts and the rule of law come in, but in most simple transactions, the payment and delivery settle instantly and with permanence. I give the pet store $300 for a puppy on an "as is" basis, and I pay with cash. The pet store owner now owns that cash, and I now own the puppy, even if that puppy gets sick and dies tomorrow.

Money as a store of value is also fundamental to the concepts of savings and investment. If my gold coins or US dollars are durable, I can save them up from the proceeds of my labor and/or my investments and then use them to buy a car, a luxury vacation, or a home.

Compound interest, which legendary investor Warren Buffett once called "the seventh wonder of the world," enables money to compound and grow through the productive lending of it to creditworthy individuals or entities, often making them all the more trusted through the pledge of collateral to secure the loan.[xxv] This is how banks are supposed to work, although they don't quite work in as simple a fashion as they did at the dawn of the twentieth century. Moreover, if accrued interest is less than the rate of inflation, real purchasing power has not actually grown.

Pure barter generally necessitates credit for goods that expire, and credit can go unfulfilled for a variety of reasons, including the death of the maker of these goods and services or their rogue behavior in not delivering on their side of the agreement. Money, on the other hand, is designed to be immortal, even if its actual value in any given market fluctuates. This is why gold was widely accepted as the ultimate form of money for more than six thousand years. Along with silver, gold was minted as coins to ensure the authenticity of its backing and the purity of its contents, i.e., that it was not debased with less valuable metals.

For thousands of years, gold also served as the backing for paper money. As noted previously, the Bretton Woods Agreement was based not only on the United States as the strongest currency, but on its full backing by gold. This was enabled largely by the audacious Executive Order 1061 by President Franklin D. Roosevelt, who in 1933 seized gold from its citizens under the pretense of helping the country recover from the Great Depression.[xxvi] The executive order had teeth, with the threat of ten years in prison for those who did not comply. Everyone had to turn in their gold coins, bars, and certificates and were paid the "fair market value" of $20.67 per ounce. As soon as the gold was collected, Roosevelt repriced the dollar's backing to a much higher rate of $35 per ounce (the amount used in Bretton Woods), stripping the average American of nearly 60 percent of the value of their gold.

This controversial policy—some would call it outright theft—took place on April 5, 1933. Many believe that the birthday of Satoshi Nakamoto, listed as April 5, 1975, was a hidden "Easter egg" reference to the day FDR took away Americans' right to own gold and 1975, a reference to the year when that right was restored by President Gerald M. Ford. It's one of many reasons why Bitcoin is called digital gold.

We will delve into why Bitcoin is a superior form of hard money to gold in the next chapter. Suffice it to say that the massive appreciation of bitcoin as a digital currency since its initial issuance in 2009, beating every other asset class over the past fifteen years, ten years, five years, and in the most recent complete calendar year of 2023, is sufficient evidence of its store of value thus far. The argument that one can find shorter periods when buying at a market top and selling at the market bottom invalidates this proposal is specious, as one can find similar periods in the S&P, NASDAQ, bond markets, gold, and silver where those assets also lost money. We will extensively chart this out in the body of this book.

Today's grand bet is that governments backed by fiat currency can simply print their way to liquidity. They will spend enough newly debased paper money to provide social programs for the poor while providing asset bubbles and arbitrage opportunities for the rich. It's an insidious game that is not well understood by the vast majority of the world's population, which spends most of its time eking out a subsistence living, living paycheck to paycheck, focused mainly on currency in its role as a medium of exchange.

Medium of exchange. As its ardent enthusiasts will tell you, one bitcoin will always equal one bitcoin. Those who mined or bought one thousand bitcoin in 2010 for five cents per bitcoin and held on to them still have the same amount. However, its fiat money equivalent has gone from $50 to over $60,000,000. The same can be said for buying ten ounces of gold in 1975 at $140 an ounce and selling today at more than $2,400 per ounce. The medium of exchange is typically conducted in a unit of account. Many "bitcoiners" (as bitcoin holders will often refer to themselves) will only accept bitcoin for certain transactions. For example, there were T-shirts for sale at the first Bitcoin Foundation conference in May 2013 for $20 apiece, but payment was only accepted in bitcoin. Given the price that day was $120 per bitcoin, each T-shirt cost one-sixth of a bitcoin. Presuming the seller, known as "Shirtoshi," held on to that bitcoin, he effectively sold those T-shirts for more than $10,000 apiece.[xxvii]

There has been an argument made that due to the continual appreciation of bitcoin over time, it cannot be considered a reliable medium of exchange. Ironically, many pundits claim the opposite: that because the quoted daily price of bitcoin is also subject to volatility and can as easily drop 10–20 percent in a day as it can jump by that amount, no sane person would transact in that currency. The truth is that one generally transacts in bitcoin at a price based on one's native currency, and if they do not convert it, calculate the additional capital gains or losses when they do finally sell.

Therefore, while the unit of account may remain fixed for fiat currencies, its purchasing power has been decimated in the past hundred years. This loss of purchasing power began with a series of events that occurred in rapid succession around World War I and the first great global pandemic, the Spanish Flu. In 1913, a secretive meeting of prominent US bankers and one US senator took place on Jekyll Island, South Carolina, resulting in the creation of the Federal Reserve (which, as the joke goes, is neither Federal nor a Reserve). Most Americans believe "the Fed" is a branch of the US government since its chair is appointed by the US president. But it's largely a private bank—a "central" bank, which in itself was a modern invention, resurfacing after failing twice in the early 1800s. That is when President Andrew Jackson (a distant relative of mine) halted it, saying that central banks were "unauthorized by the Constitution, subversive to the rights of States, and dangerous to the liberties of the people." [xxviii]

The concept of central banks (and of fractional banking overall) is the antithesis of sound money policy. While not an exact analogy, it's the philosophical differences between Keynesian and Austrian economics, between printing money to stimulate demand compared with fiscal restraint based on balanced budgets, since everything must be settled in gold or other hard money. Since the creation of the Fed one hundred years ago, the purchasing power of the US dollar has decreased by a shocking 96 percent. This compares with the prior hundred-year period without a central bank, where everything was backed by gold and the government printed currency based on those gold stockpiles. During that century, inflation was negligible.

Despite its volatility (mainly to the upside), bitcoin is a far more reliable medium of exchange than hyperinflating national currencies in Africa and South America, and this has been borne out by the much higher adoption rates of bitcoin and stablecoins (a form of cryptocurrency that is either backed by or tracking the US dollar or other more "stable" major fiat currencies). In these nations, bitcoin has been a life raft, as it was in 2013 for Cypriots and in 2019 for Greeks dealing with frozen bank accounts and bank runs due to currency crises in those countries. For much of the third world, particularly western Africa and much of South America, hyperinflation is a daily challenge of life, and those are the nations with the highest adoption of bitcoin. I cover this more fully in Chapter 20.

Chapter Three

The Science and Philosophy Behind Bitcoin

The problem, to be clear, is centralization and the corruption it creates. The solution is decentralization. . . . Decentralization must be incentivized and supported.
—David Chaum, creator of ecash, the original digital money before Bitcoin[xxix]

Bitcoin is perhaps the most misunderstood asset class in history.

At its core is cryptography, an ancient science dating back thousands of years to Egyptian pharaohs and other early civilizations. "Secret writing" was used in ancient India to deliver encoded messages between spies. Julius Caesar used an algorithm to encrypt and decrypt messages to his armies on the battlefield, hereafter known as the Caesar cipher. In the 1500s, Mary Queen of Scots is believed to have used more than 100 ciphers to protect information during her reign.[xxx] Most of these early systems were based on simple rules (such as moving letters of the alphabet to a set number of positions).

Unfortunately, those ciphers were worthless once the code was cracked.

In the twentieth century, the Enigma machine was created by German engineer Arthur Scherbius[xxxi] near the end of World War I. This innovation added a mechanical component by physically rotating the output of a keyboard, which would later be decrypted by typing the message on an identical machine using the reverse settings. This system was heavily used by the Nazi armed forces during World War II, yet it, too, was ultimately cracked by Polish and British cryptographers.

Prior to the last fifty years, encryption was used mainly to guard military secrets. Later, it became popular with corporations wishing to protect proprietary information from competitors. In the 1970s, IBM formed a "crypto group" (long before the phrase meant cryptocurrency). In 1973, the National Standards Board (now called NIST) created a Data Encryption Standard (DES)[xxxii] that was cracked by the late 1990s. The search for a more perfect privacy continued.

Why should individuals care about cryptography?

First, history is filled with stories of kings and governments shielding information from the masses. Reading books was once a privilege reserved for scribes, priests, and royalty. This was smashed by Johannes Gutenberg's creation of movable type and the printing press in the mid-1400s. More recently, the combination of post-9/11 intrusions into personal privacy and fundamental liberties by governments worldwide has heightened these concerns. Big Tech plus Big Government plus AI could mean the End Times for personal freedom and any right to privacy in a hyperconnected world.

In the 1970s, some of America's most brilliant and talented mathematicians and free thinkers clustered around a handful of elite universities and began to imagine and then invent the new world we now live in.

Berkeley, Stanford, and MIT were the epicenters of this movement. While still an undergraduate student, Ralph C. Merkle created a scheme for communication over an insecure channel that he named Merkle's Puzzles,[xxxiii] and it became the basis for public-key cryptography, which is one of the core technologies behind Bitcoin. After graduating with both his bachelor's and master's degrees from Berkeley and a PhD from Stanford, he then joined the iconic Xerox PARC, where his colleagues were busy inventing the mouse, the laser printer, Ethernet, and the Windows-based graphical user interface (GUI). For his part, Merkle had a profound effect on the advancement of modern cryptography, creating the Merkle-Damgård construction and Merkle tree structure that enables the complex mapping of data from variable-length inputs to fixed-length output known as cryptographic hashing. "Hashing" is a key component of the "proof-of-work" consensus mechanism that makes Bitcoin work in a trustless, permissionless manner, at scale and globally.

On the other side of the country, a trio of young MIT professors, Ron Rivest, Adi Shamir, and Leonard Adleman, invented the RSA cryptosystem (named after the first letters of their last names). RSA revolutionized modern cryptography by creating the first usable system for public-key cryptography. Their work later won a Turing Award, the computing industry's highest honor. Rivest went on to found Verisign, while Shamir created Shamir's Secret Sharing protocol, which was later used to protect Bitcoin wallet addresses.

Enter the "Cypherpunks"

Philosophically, many of these early innovators began to share a belief that privacy was key to an open and free society, and they began to write their thoughts and share ideas as well as code. In 1982, graduate student David Chaum wrote a breakthrough paper for his PhD dissertation at UC Berkeley called "Computer Systems Established, Maintained, and Trusted by Mutually Suspicious Groups,"[xxxiv] outlining many concepts fundamental to creating a permissionless cryptocurrency. It was later observed that Chaum's thesis contains every significant component of the Bitcoin white paper (written twenty-seven years later), other than proof-of-work. He also coined the word "cryptocurrency," invented the blind signature, and pioneered the concept of "zero-knowledge proof," which is the core of today's privacy coins and protocols.

Chaum created a company, DigiCash[xxxv], which developed the first working cryptocurrency called "Ecash." That pioneering early project ultimately failed, largely because it had traditional financial partners. Chaum resurrected it many years later as Ecash 2.0, which was adapted by IBM as a private network. In addition, Ecash[xxxvi] 2.0 is now the inspiration and basis for his 2023 white paper, *Better than Money*[xxxvii], where he envisions a world with "inter-fungible" tokenized assets. He is also considered the founding father of the "cypherpunk" movement, which united hundreds of like-minded mathematicians, intellectuals, and libertarians who believed that modern computer science, coupled with the internet, could create a golden age of freedom from state oppression by giving individuals the literal keys to their own communication and, ultimately, their own monetary system.

Three of the key spiritual leaders of the cypherpunks were:

John Gilmore, who became wealthy enough as the fifth employee of Sun Microsystems that he was able to retire early and pursue his passions, which included cofounding the Electronic Freedom Foundation (EFF) and creating the controversial Alt.* hierarchy on Usenet. He is perhaps best known for his quote, "The Net interprets censorship as damage and routes around it." [xxxviii]

Eric Hughes, a cryptographer and coder who wrote and hosted the first anonymous remailer, also authored the *Cypherpunk Manifesto*[xxxix] in 1993, which states the case for privacy as a human right:

> *Privacy is necessary for an open society in the electronic age. Privacy is not secrecy. A private matter is something one doesn't want the whole world to know, but a secret matter is something one doesn't want anybody to know. Privacy is the power to selectively reveal oneself to the world. . . .*
>
> *Therefore, privacy in an open society requires anonymous transaction systems. Until now, cash has been the primary such system. An anonymous transaction system is not a secret transaction system. An anonymous system empowers individuals to reveal their identity when desired and only when desired; this is the essence of privacy.*

Timothy C. May (aka Tim May) was a Berkeley-trained cryptographer who retired from Intel at age thirty-five and remained a recluse until his death at age sixty-six in 2018. He wrote the dark but eerily prescient essay "The Crypto Anarchist Manifesto"[xl] in 1994, in the infancy of the dial-up Web and fifteen years before Bitcoin. Thus far, nearly everything in his essay has come true:

Computer technology is on the verge of providing the ability for individuals and groups to communicate and interact with each other in a totally anonymous manner. Two persons may exchange messages, conduct business, and negotiate electronic contracts without ever knowing the True Name, or legal identity, of the other. Interactions over networks will be untraceable via extensive re-routing of encrypted packets and tamper-proof boxes which implement cryptographic protocols with nearly perfect assurance against any tampering . . .

The technology for this revolution—and it surely will be both a social and economic revolution—has existed in theory for the past decade. The methods are based upon public-key encryption, zero-knowledge interactive proof systems, and various software protocols for interaction, authentication, and verification. . . . And the next ten years will bring enough additional speed to make the ideas economically feasible and essentially unstoppable.

Enter Bitcoin

This is meant to be a partial list of contributors to the evolution of digital money. I intend to show that Bitcoin, the first *peer-to-peer* digital money, as well as the first digital money system that succeeded, did not arise out of a vacuum. It had nearly forty years of digital blueprints and building blocks enabling its creation, many of whose authors are credited in the Bitcoin white paper, which I reprint in its 2,736-word entirety (it fits on a T-shirt), along with my comments and explanations around every concept, in Chapter 4.

Other important influences on the creation of bitcoin include:

Wei Dai, a computer scientist from Washington State, states in a white paper that he was "fascinated" by Tim May's Crypto Anarchist Manifesto and decided to spec out a program called "b-money" in 1998 to achieve the shared vision. He never attempted to build it, but Satoshi credited Dai in the Bitcoin white paper.[xli]

Hal Finney[xlii] was an accomplished cryptographer and videogame designer who created the first reusable proof-of-work, a fundamental part of the bitcoin operating system. Besides being an avid cypherpunk, he subscribed to most of the leading cryptography mailing lists, including the one where Satoshi introduced the Bitcoin white paper on October 31, 2008. Finney was the most proactive person responding to the white paper, repeatedly encouraging Satoshi to build the program he outlined. On January 3, 2009, Satoshi launched the bitcoin blockchain with the "Genesis Block," and nine days later, the Bitcoin architect sent fifty bitcoins to Finney, representing the first bitcoin transfer. A reliable early contributor to the Bitcoin protocol, tragedy struck Finney when, barely a year after the creation of Bitcoin, Finney was diagnosed with ALS, also known as Lou Gehrig's disease, which took his life on August 28, 2014.

Nick Szabo,[xliii] who keynoted my second CoinAgenda conference in 2015, has widely been suspected of being Satoshi (as have Wei Dai and Hal Finney, among others). If so, he left several "Easter egg" clues. His birthday is the same as the one listed by Satoshi, April 5. His initials are the same as Satoshi Nakamoto's but reversed. He is also the only prominent cryptographer from the cypherpunk era who did not receive bitcoin from Satoshi. Whether or not he is Satoshi, as proposed by Nathaniel Popper in his excellent book *Digital Gold*, he created the first white paper explicitly describing a proof-of-work system in a cryptocurrency, calling it bit gold. Szabo also created the first "smart contract," in which the code executes a contract. This later became the basis for the Ethereum Virtual Machine and many other protocols.

Why Should You Care About Bitcoin

Bitcoin, now and at the very beginning of its existence, has several unique properties that should appeal to every investor and saver who cares enough to understand their alternatives:

- It's decentralized. There are no leaders and no rules other than those committed to the Bitcoin code.
- It's a hard asset with digital qualities.
- It has a fixed supply. No more than 21 million bitcoins can ever exist.
- It has a reliable monetary policy, set in code for 132 years.

Let's review what makes Bitcoin a unique and important development in the history of technology, finance, and, ultimately, civilization.

- Bitcoin was created by a pseudonymous founder, Satoshi Nakamoto, with a nine-page white paper that dropped amid the 2008 global financial crisis. Yet, it has become the best-performing asset class—by orders of magnitude—over gold, silver, stock markets, and real estate.

- Bitcoin is the original blockchain. Satoshi coined the word, referring to an immutable, time-stamped series of blocks containing a digital ledger of transactions. These blocks can be traced back in sequence to the original "Genesis Block" from January 2009.
- Bitcoin is an immutable blockchain that creates a sealed permanent set of records every ten minutes. Each record provides mathematical proof of the completed digital asset transfer between two parties without any third-party permission.
- Bitcoin "mining" uses software that independently verifies these transactions in return for new bitcoin issued every ten minutes as a reward for those miners running the machines and expending electricity. The work of the miners confirms each transaction by hundreds of disinterested parties. It also cryptographically proves there has been no double spending of these assets and then inscribes a permanent transaction record. This is a fundamental economic breakthrough that would inevitably win a Nobel Prize if Satoshi were not anonymous.

"Cryptocurrency" is a term coined by Cypherpunk David Chaum, who remains a vibrant force in the sector, in 1983. Today, this term encompasses all public blockchains, from the pioneering Bitcoin to innovations like Ethereum's smart contracts and multichain blockchains such as Cosmos. The cryptocurrency market has surged to over $2.2 trillion, with Bitcoin alone accounting for over half of this value. This represents a phenomenal leap from its humble beginnings, with the entire asset class valued at less than $1 million in 2010. Cryptocurrencies' unprecedented growth and transformative potential signal a new era in finance and technology.

Like many new technologies, early adopters behave very differently than the "early majority," as profiled in the technology business cycle books *Crossing the Chasm* and *Inside the Tornado* by author and iconic Silicon Valley venture capitalist Geoffrey Moore. In the case of Bitcoin, the earliest adopters were a mix of cryptographers and libertarian dreamers, some of them even adapting the moniker of anarcho-capitalists or, in the spirit of Tim May, crypto anarchists. Wei Dai felt that crypto anarchy was indeed a higher calling, very different than all forms of anarchy preceding it:

> *Unlike the communities traditionally associated with the word "anarchy," in a crypto-anarchy, the government is not temporarily destroyed but permanently forbidden and permanently unnecessary. It's a community where the threat of violence is impotent because violence is impossible . . . because its participants cannot be linked to their true names or physical locations.*[xliv]

Many of today's leaders in the Bitcoin ecosystem got their first introduction through libertarian outlets like Free Talk Radio and the Free State Project in New Hampshire. Satoshi Roundtable founder Bruce Fenton and Bitcoin Center NY founder Nick Spanos were avid supporters of libertarian presidential candidate Ron Paul. Spanos went as far as setting up live peer-to-peer bitcoin trading and a bitcoin ATM next door to the New York Stock Exchange, thumbing his nose at the most iconic symbol of Wall Street. My first bitcoin public speaking appearance was at a New York City conference in July 2013, discussing whether the First Amendment protected digital currency as a form of free speech.

The earliest Bitcoin advocates and acolytes had the advantage of fierce loyalty to the protocol, so many of them became fabulously rich without much investment by simply holding on to the hundreds or even thousands of bitcoins they received for a few pennies or dollars each. I am friends with many of these people, and they are happily retired in their thirties or forties, but they still support libertarian and freedom-centric causes. When the time comes for key decisions to be made about the future of Bitcoin in an environment where lobbyists and political donations matter, they will show up. At the recent Bitcoin 2024 conference in Nashville, leading presidential candidate Donald Trump delivered a keynote address showcasing his support for the bitcoin industry and held a private fundraiser and roundtable dinner that charged $833,600 per person. It sold out.

Chapter Four

The Bitcoin White Paper

Bitcoin is absolutely the Wild West of finance, and thank goodness. It represents a whole legion of adventurers and entrepreneurs, of risk takers, inventors, and problem solvers. It is the frontier. Huge amounts of wealth will be created and destroyed as this new landscape is mapped out.
— Erik Voorhees[xlv]

Bitcoin is a swarm of cyber hornets serving the goddess of wisdom, feeding on the fire of truth, exponentially growing ever smarter, faster, and stronger behind a wall of encrypted energy.
— Michael J. Saylor[xlvi]

Bitcoin never sleeps. We need to move quickly and grow quickly and do everything sooner rather than later.
— Roger Ver, also known as Bitcoin Jesus[xlvii]

In this chapter, I have decided to reprint—and annotate—the original Bitcoin white paper by Satoshi Nakamoto for several reasons:

1) I don't believe one can truly grasp Bitcoin in its entirety without reading the white paper, as it lays out the original intent and the manner in which Satoshi explains his new system.

2) I wanted to make sure that everyone who reads my book can also answer "yes" to the question of whether they've read the Bitcoin white paper.

3) It's a good guide to evaluating other blockchain systems in the future. Bitcoin maximalists believe there is no room for assets other than Bitcoin. In contrast, multichain advocates believe some blockchain functions are solved faster, better, and/or cheaper by newer chains.

Here is the original white paper, complete with my notes:

Bitcoin: A Peer-to-Peer Electronic Cash System

Satoshi Nakamoto
satoshin@gmx.com
www.bitcoin.org

Abstract. A purely peer-to-peer version of electronic cash would allow online payments to be sent directly from one party to another without going through a financial institution. Digital signatures provide part of the solution, but the main benefits are lost if a trusted third party is still required to prevent double-spending. We propose a solution to the double-spending problem using a peer-to-peer network. The network timestamps transactions by hashing them into an ongoing chain of hash-based proof-of-work, forming a record that cannot be changed without redoing the proof-of-work. The longest chain not only serves as proof of the sequence of events witnessed, but proof that it came from the largest pool of CPU power. As long as a majority of CPU power is controlled by nodes that are not cooperating to attack the network, they'll generate the longest chain and outpace attackers. The network itself requires minimal structure. Messages are broadcast on a best effort basis, and nodes can leave and rejoin the network at will, accepting the longest proof-of-work chain as proof of what happened while they were gone.

[Terpin: In 179 words, Satoshi laid out the technological blueprint for what is today a trillion-dollar asset class. Each

of these components is fundamental to Bitcoin working: 1) each party who wishes to interact does so independently, using digital signatures to verify they have they have the funds required to make a transaction; 2) no central counterparties means these transactions cannot be stopped through legal or political action, and 3) proof-of-work demonstrates the system is secure and permanent as long as no party overtakes the longest chain, which would require more CPU power than the rest of the network combined, known as a 51 percent attack.]

1. Introduction

Commerce on the Internet has come to rely almost exclusively on financial institutions serving as trusted third parties to process electronic payments. While the system works well enough for most transactions, it still suffers from the inherent weaknesses of the trust based model. Completely non-reversible transactions are not really possible, since financial institutions cannot avoid mediating disputes. The cost of mediation increases transaction costs, limiting the minimum practical transaction size and cutting off the possibility for small casual transactions, and there is a broader cost in the loss of ability to make non-reversible payments for non-reversible services. With the possibility of reversal, the need for trust spreads. Merchants must be wary of their customers, hassling them for more information than they would otherwise need. A certain percentage of fraud is accepted as unavoidable. These costs and payment uncertainties can be avoided in person by using physical currency, but no mechanism exists to make payments over a communications channel without a trusted party.

What is needed is an electronic payment system based on cryptographic proof instead of trust, allowing any two willing parties to transact directly with each other without the need for a trusted third party. Transactions that are computationally impractical to reverse would protect sellers from fraud, and routine escrow mechanisms could easily be implemented to protect buyers. In this paper, we propose a solution to the double-spending problem using a peer-to-peer distributed timestamp server to generate computational proof of the chronological order of transactions. The system is secure as long as honest nodes collectively control more CPU power than any cooperating group of attacker nodes.

[Terpin: Satoshi elegantly demonstrates the problems inherent with financial institutions inserting themselves in between two willing parties. When all purchases were made in person, cash was the easy answer, perhaps accompanied by bodyguards. Once payments needed to be made across the miles—first by mail, then by phone and fax, then by the Internet—cash became impractical without a third party ensuring the funds were good and the products or services were delivered. This legal and regulatory overhead raised the cost of each transaction, adding significant costs to all transactions done this way, as well as making it impractical to process small purchases at all.]

2. Transactions

We define an electronic coin as a chain of digital signatures. Each owner transfers the coin to the next by digitally signing a hash of the previous transaction and the public key of the next owner and adding these to the end of the coin. A payee can verify the signatures to verify the chain of ownership.

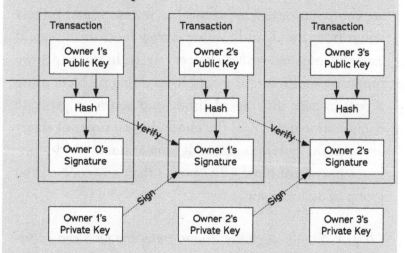

The problem of course, is the payee can't verify that one of the owners did not double-spend the coin. A common solution is to introduce a trusted central authority, or mint, that checks every transaction for double-spending. After each transaction, the coin must be returned to the mint to issue a new coin, and only coins issued directly from the mint are trusted not to be double-spent. The problem with this solution is that the fate of the entire money system depends on the company running the mint, with every transaction having to go through them, just like a bank.

We need a way for the payee to know that the previous owners did not sign any earlier transactions. For our purposes, the earliest transaction is the one that counts, so we don't care about later attempts to double-spend. The only way to confirm the absence of a transaction is to be aware of all transactions. In the mint-based model, the mint was aware of all transactions and decided which arrived first. To accomplish this without a trusted party, transactions must be publicly announced [1], and we need a system for participants to agree on a single history of the order in which they were received. The payee needs proof that at the time of each transaction, the majority of nodes agreed it was the first received.

[Terpin: One rarely hears Bitcoin described as a "chain of digital signatures"—but that's exactly what it is. In order for those signatures to have authority to validate a transaction without a third party, it must prove that it was the first to receive valid funds. Satoshi's solution was the time-stamped server, described below, to prove the order of publicly identifiable transactions for the entire chain.

3. Timestamp Server

The solution we propose begins with a timestamp server. A timestamp server works by taking a hash of a block of items to be timestamped and widely publishing the hash, such as in a newspaper or Usenet post [2-5]. The timestamp proves that the data must have existed at the time, obviously, in order to get into the hash. Each timestamp includes the previous timestamp in its hash, forming a chain, with each additional timestamp reinforcing the ones before it.

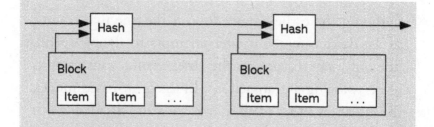

4. Proof-of-Work

To implement a distributed timestamp server on a peer-to-peer basis, we will need to use a proof-of-work system similar to Adam Back's Hashcash [6], rather than newspaper or Usenet posts. The proof-of-work involves scanning for a value that when hashed, such as with SHA-256, the hash begins with a number of zero bits. The average work required is exponential in the number of zero bits required and can be verified by executing a single hash.

For our timestamp network, we implement the proof-of-work by incrementing a nonce in the block until a value is found that gives the block's hash the required zero bits. Once the CPU effort has been expended to make it satisfy the proof-of-work, the block cannot be changed without redoing the work. As later blocks are chained after it, the work to change the block would include redoing all the blocks after it.

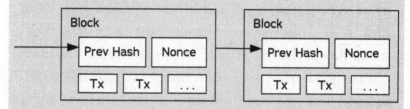

The proof-of-work also solves the problem of determining representation in majority decision making. If the majority were based on one-IP-address-one-vote, it could be subverted by anyone able to allocate many IPs. Proof-of-work is essentially one-CPU-one-vote. The majority decision is represented by the longest chain, which has the greatest proof-of-work effort invested in it. If a majority of CPU power is controlled by honest nodes, the honest chain will grow the fastest and outpace any competing chains. To modify a past block, an attacker would have to redo the proof-of-work of the block and all blocks after it and then catch up with and surpass the work of the honest nodes. We will show later that the probability of a slower attacker catching up diminishes exponentially as subsequent blocks are added.

To compensate for increasing hardware speed and varying interest in running nodes over time, the proof-of-work difficulty is determined by a moving average targeting an average number of blocks per hour. If they're generated too fast, the difficulty increases.

[Terpin: There are several interesting components to this section. First is the concept of "one CPU, one vote," as it's the ultimate representational democracy; bad actors find a much harder time colluding with CPUs than with people. The increase in CPU power as more people use bitcoin makes it exponentially harder to undo a valid transaction, as the proof-of-work already established would need to be redone for all subsequent blocks. Satoshi also introduces the concept of difficulty, which requires more power as the network grows to add more security.]

5. Network

The steps to run the network are as follows:

1) New transactions are broadcast to all nodes.
2) Each node collects new transactions into a block.
3) Each node works on finding a difficult proof-of-work for its block.
4) When a node finds a proof-of-work, it broadcasts the block to all nodes.
5) Nodes accept the block only if all transactions in it are valid and not already spent.
6) Nodes express their acceptance of the block by working on creating the next block in the chain, using the hash of the accepted block as the previous hash.

Nodes always consider the longest chain to be the correct one and will keep working on extending it. If two nodes broadcast different versions of the next block simultaneously, some nodes may receive one or the other first. In that case, they work on the first one they received, but save the other branch in case it becomes longer. The tie will be broken when the next proof-of-work is found and one branch becomes longer; the nodes that were working on the other branch will then switch to the longer one.

New transaction broadcasts do not necessarily need to reach all nodes. As long as they reach many nodes, they will get into a block before long. Block broadcasts are also tolerant of dropped messages. If a node does not receive a block, it will request it when it receives the next block and realizes it missed one.

6. Incentive

By convention, the first transaction in a block is a special transaction that starts a new coin owned by the creator of the block. This adds an incentive for nodes to support the network, and provides a way to initially distribute coins into circulation, since there is no central authority to issue them. The steady addition of a constant amount of new coins is analogous to gold miners expending resources to add gold to circulation. In our case, it is CPU time and electricity that is expended.

The incentive can also be funded with transaction fees. If the output value of a transaction is less than its input value, the difference is a transaction fee that is added to the incentive value of the block containing the transaction. Once a predetermined number of coins have entered circulation, the incentive can transition entirely to transaction fees and be completely inflation free.

The incentive may help encourage nodes to stay honest. If a greedy attacker is able to assemble more CPU power than all the honest nodes, he would have to choose between using it to defraud people by stealing back his payments, or using it to generate new coins. He ought to find it more profitable to play by the rules, such rules that favor him with more new coins than everyone else combined, than to undermine the system and the validity of his own wealth.

7. Reclaiming Disk Space

Once the latest transaction in a coin is buried under enough blocks, the spent transactions before it can be discarded to save disk space. To facilitate this without breaking the block's hash, transactions are hashed in a Merkle Tree [7][2][5], with only the root included in the block's hash. Old blocks can then be compacted by stubbing off branches of the tree. The interior hashes do not need to be stored.

A block header with no transactions would be about 80 bytes. If we suppose blocks are generated every 10 minutes, 80 bytes * 6 * 24 * 365 = 4.2MB per year. With computer systems typically selling with 2GB of RAM as of 2008, and Moore's Law predicting current growth of 1.2GB per year, storage should not be a problem even if the block headers must be kept in memory.

[Terpin: While most of this past section is technical and not required for understanding bitcoin, it's fascinating to see Satoshi recognize that blockchain size could one day be an impediment to growth. Indeed, block size became a political issue among varying factions in the Bitcoin ecosystem in late 2017 when the first significant fork, called "Bitcoin Cash," was implemented to save on transaction fees through the use of a more accommodating block size.]

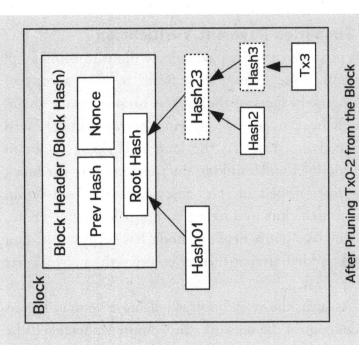

After Pruning Tx0-2 from the Block

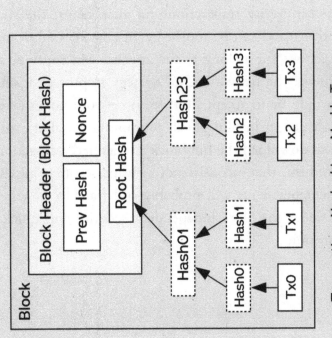

Transactions Hashed in a Merkle Tree

8. Simplified Payment Verification

It is possible to verify payments without running a full network node. A user only needs to keep a copy of the block headers of the longest proof-of-work chain, which he can get by querying network nodes until he's convinced he has the longest chain, and obtain the Merkle branch linking the transaction to the block it's timestamped in. He can't check the transaction for himself, but by linking it to a place in the chain, he can see that a network node has accepted it, and blocks added after it further confirm the network has accepted it.

As such, the verification is reliable as long as honest nodes control the network, but is more vulnerable if the network is overpowered by an attacker. While network nodes can verify transactions for themselves, the simplified method can be fooled by an attacker's fabricated transactions for as long as the attacker can continue to overpower the network. One strategy to protect against this would be to accept alerts from network nodes when they detect an invalid block, prompting the user's software to download the full block and alerted transactions to confirm the inconsistency. Businesses that receive frequent payments will probably still want to run their own nodes for more independent security and quicker verification.

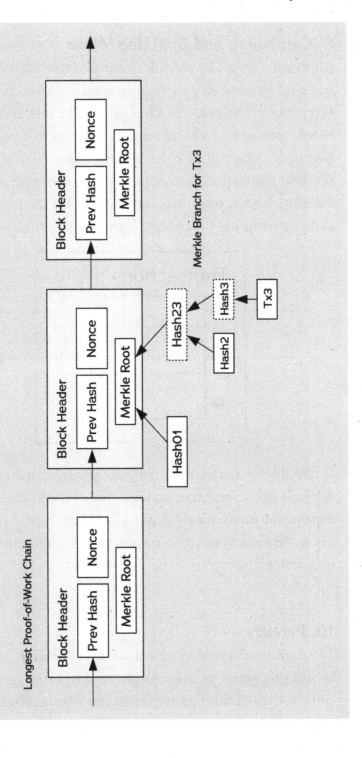

9. Combining and Splitting Value

Although it would be possible to handle coins individually, it would be unwieldy to make a separate transaction for every cent in a transfer. To allow value to be split and combined, transactions contain multiple inputs and outputs. Normally there will be either a single input from a larger previous transaction or multiple inputs combining smaller amounts, and at most two outputs: one for the payment, and one returning the change, if any, back to the sender.

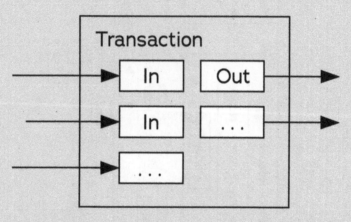

It should be noted that fan-out, where a transaction depends on several transactions, and those transactions depend on many more, is not a problem here. There is never the need to extract a complete standalone copy of a transaction's history.

10. Privacy

The traditional banking model achieves a level of privacy by limiting access to information to the parties involved and the trusted third party. The necessity to announce all transactions publicly precludes this method, but privacy can still be maintained by breaking the flow of information in another place: by keeping public keys anonymous. The public can see that someone is sending an amount to someone else, but without information linking the transaction to anyone. This is similar to the level of information released by stock exchanges, where the time and size of individual trades, the "tape", is made public, but without telling who the parties were.

As an additional firewall, a new key pair should be used for each transaction to keep them from being linked to a common owner. Some linking is still unavoidable with multi-input transactions, which necessarily reveal that their inputs were owned by the same owner. The risk is that if the owner of a key is revealed, linking could reveal other transactions that belonged to the same owner.

[Terpin: In this section, Satoshi explains the pseudonymous nature of bitcoin addresses, where the identity of the sender is not publicly identified but transactions can be traced using what has become known as chain analysis. This is the part of the white paper where the average reader sees too many math equations ahead and stops reading. The Calculations section simply provides validation for his theory that dishonest actors seeking to invalidate the longest chain would have a difficult time. It's good to recognize that this white paper was primarily meant for fellow cryptographers to read. Unless you're also a math nerd or have questions about how the network deals with attackers, it's fine to skip ahead to the Conclusion without missing much.]

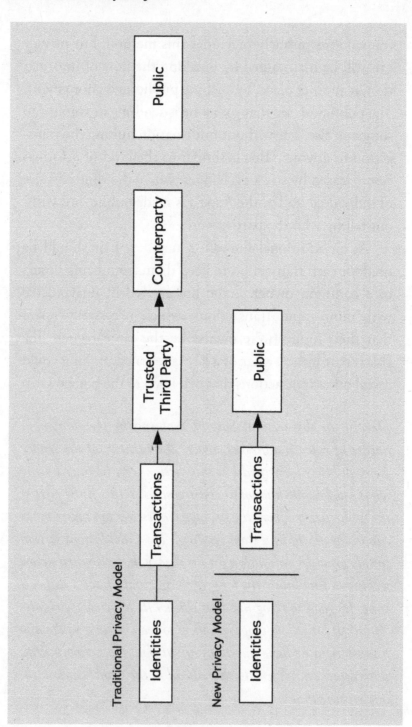

11. Calculations

We consider the scenario of an attacker trying to generate an alternate chain faster than the honest chain. Even if this is accomplished, it does not throw the system open to arbitrary changes, such as creating value out of thin air or taking money that never belonged to the attacker. Nodes are not going to accept an invalid transaction as payment, and honest nodes will never accept a block containing them. An attacker can only try to change one of his own transactions to take back money he recently spent.

The race between the honest chain and an attacker chain can be characterized as a Binomial Random Walk. The success event is the honest chain being extended by one block, increasing its lead by +1, and the failure event is the attacker's chain being extended by one block, reducing the gap by -1.

The probability of an attacker catching up from a given deficit is analogous to a Gambler's Ruin problem. Suppose a gambler with unlimited credit starts at a deficit and plays potentially an infinite number of trials to try to reach breakeven. We can calculate the probability he ever reaches breakeven, or that an attacker ever catches up with the honest chain, as follows [8]:

p = probability an honest node finds the next block

q = probability the attacker finds the next block

q_z = probability the attacker will ever catch up from z blocks behind

$$q_z = \begin{cases} 1 & \text{if } p \le q \\ (q/p)^z & \text{if } p > q \end{cases}$$

Given our assumption that $p > q$, the probability drops exponentially as the number of blocks the attacker has to catch up with increases. With the odds against him, if he doesn't make a lucky lunge forward early on, his chances become vanishingly small as he falls further behind.

We now consider how long the recipient of a new transaction needs to wait before being sufficiently certain the sender can't change the transaction. We assume the sender is an attacker who wants to make the recipient believe he paid him for a while, then switch it to pay back to himself after some time has passed. The receiver will be alerted when that happens, but the sender hopes it will be too late.

The receiver generates a new key pair and gives the public key to the sender shortly before signing. This prevents the sender from preparing a chain of blocks ahead of time by working on it continuously until he is lucky enough to get far enough ahead, then executing the transaction at that moment. Once the transaction is sent, the dishonest sender starts working in secret on a parallel chain containing an alternate version of his transaction.

The recipient waits until the transaction has been added to a block and z blocks have been linked after it. He doesn't know the exact amount of progress the attacker has made, but assuming the honest blocks took the average expected time per block, the attacker's potential progress will be a Poisson distribution with expected value:

$$\lambda = z\,\frac{q}{p}$$

To get the probability the attacker could still catch up now, we multiply the Poisson density for each amount of progress he could have made by the probability he could catch up from that point:

$$\sum_{k=0}^{\infty} \frac{\lambda^k e^{-\lambda}}{k!} \cdot \begin{cases} (q/p)^{(z-k)} & if\ k \le z \\ 1 & if\ k > z \end{cases}$$

Rearranging to avoid summing the infinite tail of the distribution . . .

$$1 - \sum_{k=0}^{z} \frac{\lambda^k e^{-\lambda}}{k!}\left(1 - (q/p)^{(z-k)}\right)$$

Converting to C code . . .

```c
#include <math.h>
double AttackerSuccessProbability(double q, int z)
{
        double p = 1.0 - q;
        double lambda = z * (q / p);
        double sum = 1.0;
        int i, k;
        for (k = 0; k <= z; k++)
        {
                double poisson = exp(-lambda);
                for (i = 1; i <= k; i++)
                        poisson *= lambda / i;
                sum -= poisson * (1 - pow(q / p, z - k));
        }
        return sum;
}
```

Running some results, we can see the probability drop off exponentially with z.

```
q=0.1
z=0        P=1.0000000
z=1        P=0.2045873
z-2        P=0.0509779
z-3        P=0.0131722
z=4        P=0.0034552
z=5        P=0.0009137
z=6        P=0.0002428
z=7        P=0.0000647
z=8        P=0.0000173
z=9        P=0.0000046
z=10       P=0.0000012

q=0.3
z=0        P=1.0000000
z=5        P=0.1773523
z=10       P=0.0416605
z=15       P=0.0101008
z=20       P=0.0024804
z=25       P=0.0006132
z=30       P=0.0001522
z=35       P=0.0000379
z=40       P=0.0000095
z=45       P=0.0000024
z=50       P=0.0000006
```

Solving for P less than 0.1% . . .

```
P < 0.001
q=0.10     z=5
q=0.15     z=8
q=0.20     z=11
q=0.25     z=15
q=0.30     z=24
q=0.35     z=41
q=0.40     z=89
q=0.45     z=340
```

12. Conclusion

We have proposed a system for electronic transactions without relying on trust. We started with the usual framework of coins made from digital signatures, which provides strong control of ownership, but is incomplete without a way to prevent double-spending. To solve this, we proposed a peer-to-peer network using proof-of-work to record a public history of transactions that quickly becomes computationally impractical for an attacker to change if honest nodes control a majority of CPU power. The network is robust in its unstructured simplicity. Nodes work all at once with little coordination. They do not need to be identified, since messages are not routed to any particular place and only need to be delivered on a best effort basis. Nodes can leave and rejoin the network at will, accepting the proof-of-work chain as proof of what happened while they were gone. They vote with their CPU power, expressing their acceptance of valid blocks by working on extending them and rejecting invalid blocks by refusing to work on them. Any needed rules and incentives can be enforced with this consensus mechanism.

[Terpin: This excellent summary is the first and only time Satoshi mentions the word consensus, which is perhaps the most important reason the system works. It's also important to note that, like the internet itself, the chain is not disrupted by participating nodes being added or removed from the network, since they have already left their proof-of-work as permanent record, which is perpetuated by the security of the system that comes from its use of CPU power.]

References

[1]   W. Dai, "b-money," http://www.weidai.com/bmoney.txt, 1998.

[2]   H. Massias, X.S. Avila, and J.-J. Quisquater, "Design of a secure timestamping service with minimal trust requirements," In *20th Symposium on Information Theory in the Benelux*, May 1999.

[3]   S. Haber, W.S. Stornetta, "How to time-stamp a digital document," In *Journal of Cryptology*, vol 3, no 2, pages 99-111, 1991.

[4]   D. Bayer, S. Haber, W.S. Stornetta, "Improving the efficiency and reliability of digital time-stamping," In *Sequences II: Methods in Communication, Security and Computer Science*, pages 329-334, 1993.

[5]   S. Haber, W.S. Stornetta, "Secure names for bit-strings," In *Proceedings of the 4th ACM Conference on Computer and Communications Security*, pages 28-35, April 1997.

[6]   A. Back, "Hashcash - a denial of service counter-measure," http://www.hashcash.org/papers/hashcash.pdf, 2002.

[7]   R.C. Merkle, "Protocols for public key cryptosystems," In *Proc. 1980 Symposium on Security and Privacy*, IEEE Computer Society, pages 122-133, April 1980.

[8]   W. Feller, "An introduction to probability theory and its applications," 1957.

Book Two

Understanding the Bitcoin Cycles

Bitcoin: First Cycle 2009 - 2012

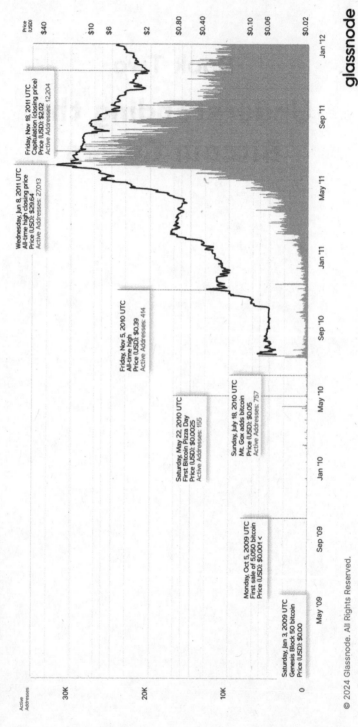

Active Addresses

Price (USD)

Saturday, Jan 3, 2009 UTC
Genesis Block 50 bitcoin
Price (USD): $0.00

Monday, Oct 5, 2009 UTC
First sale of 5,050 bitcoin
Price (USD): $0.001 <

Saturday, May 22, 2010 UTC
First Bitcoin Pizza Day
Price (USD): $0.0025
Active Addresses: 155

Sunday, July 18, 2010 UTC
Mt. Gox adds bitcoin
Price (USD): $0.05
Active Addresses: 757

Friday, Nov 5, 2010 UTC
All-time high
Price (USD): $0.39
Active Addresses: 414

Wednesday, Jun 8, 2011 UTC
All-time high closing price
Price (USD): $29.64
Active Addresses: 27,013

Friday, Nov 18, 2011 UTC
Capitulation (closing price)
Price (USD): $2.02
Active Addresses: 12,204

glassnode

Chapter Five

The Genesis Block and First Bitcoin Cycle

And God said, 'Let there be light,' and there was light.
                    —Book of Genesis, Verse 1:3[xlviii]

Every new beginning comes from some other beginning's end.

                              —Seneca[xlix]

The Times 03/Jan/2009 Chancellor on brink of second bailout for banks.
          —Text headline inscribed in Genesis Block[l]

Running Bitcoin.
          —Hal Finney, on Twitter, January 9, 2009[li]

There are three "holidays" celebrated in the Bitcoin world: October 31, 2008, when Satoshi released the Bitcoin white paper; January 3, 2009, the day the Bitcoin blockchain was created and launched with the Genesis Block; and May 22, 2010, Bitcoin Pizza Day, when the first known transaction was made to purchase a physical item using bitcoin.

Of these events, the most important is surely the Genesis Block, as it was the first block in the first blockchain, which recently passed 840,000 blocks at the fourth halving on April 20, 2024, at 1:09 UTC. During this time, more than one billion transactions have taken place, each of which is linked back to the original block, the Genesis Block.

Much has been written about the timing and motivation for creating Bitcoin. During the past few chapters, I've demonstrated that Bitcoin was not created in a vacuum but a gradual evolution of both technological breakthroughs, philosophical manifestos, and geopolitical trends. The breaking point that may have pushed Satoshi into action was the financial crisis of 2008, now known as the Great Recession, where a rolling wave of failed banks and corporate bankruptcies led to the largest bailout package in US history, with the UK and other nations following suit. As is often the case, this disaster had its roots in Fed policy, inspiring Jim Cramer's epic "THEY KNOW NOTHING!" rant on CNBC,[lii] where he correctly predicted the potential size and impact of the meltdown almost a year before it happened.

The Times 03/Jan/2009 Chancellor on brink of second bailout for banks.

Government bailouts were unnecessary before the creation of fiat money, as all money was backed by gold for thousands of years. Satoshi's choice of the above Easter egg to place in the coinbase of the first Bitcoin block was profound. Inscribing the headline from *The Times of London* simultaneously proved that the block was created on or after the day it said it was. It also served as a geopolitical commentary that in the brave new world of Bitcoin, no bailouts would be required.

Other interesting elements about the Genesis Block:

- Also known as "Block 0" (in Bitcoin or in any block-chain using proof of work), the Genesis Block is unique in that it has no block prior to it as a point of reference, so it uses 0x0. Every other block refers in its code to the address of the block prior to establishing an unbroken chain of blocks going back to the beginning, which is the Genesis Block.
- The purpose of blocks is to store and prove transactions via multiple miner confirmations. The Genesis Block did not have any transactions, and Satoshi was at that point Bitcoin's only miner. Hal Finney announced he was running the Bitcoin software eight days after the creation of the Genesis Block. By then, more than 1,000 blocks had been added in sequence to the Genesis Block, and Bitcoin was on its way. While the number of bitcoins per block is cut in half every four years, the number of blocks per day remains constant at around 144 (bitcoin blocks are created and sealed roughly every ten minutes, 24 hours a day).
- Coins from the Genesis Block cannot be spent. Whether by accident or design, the initial block in the Bitcoin blockchain contains 50 bitcoins that cannot be spent. Every other block in the chain after the Genesis block creates a miner reward of 50 bitcoins for being the first to "solve the block" (i.e., to answer a math equation designed to add additional security to the network by requiring the level of CPU power suffi-cient to answer it).

- The Genesis Block created the standard for all blocks that followed it, with each block containing the following elements:

1) the number of transactions approved inside of each block,
2) the transaction fees collected, to be redistributed to miners,
3) block height, which refers to the number of blocks preceding each block;
4) a timestamp, in Unix code, proving the order of the block in a sequence in addition to the block height,
5) block difficulty, which determines how hard the math puzzle to be solved should be in order to earn the block reward of cryptocurrency,
6) the nonce (a "number used only once"), which is at the heart of the difficulty equation to solve the block, and
7) data, which can be anything from the Times headline of the Genesis Block to today's Ordinals inscriptions.

- Whomever has the private key to the Genesis Block is Satoshi (or stole his private key). Satoshi mined most of the early bitcoin himself, along with other early cryptographers such as Hal Finney. Satoshi's main wallet contains some 1.1 million bitcoins, making it the largest wallet in the history of Bitcoin. Yet not one satoshi (the smallest portion of a bitcoin, equal to 1/100,000,000th of a bitcoin) has ever left Satoshi's wallet. At a recent price of $60,000 per bitcoin, the coins in Satoshi's wallet are worth around $66 billion, making him one of the richest people on earth. When the price of bitcoin reaches $1 million, he potentially would become the world's first trillionaire.

2009: The Experimental Era

By the end of 2009, there were fewer than one hundred people mining bitcoin, yet they collected nearly 2,500,000 bitcoins as mining rewards, all of it at the lowest possible difficulty rating—level one. Bitcoin started out very slowly, with a handful of cryptographers, goldbugs, geeks, and libertarians who thought this avant-garde system of code could indeed change the world. Hal Finney calculated that the unit price would either go to zero or, if it succeeded to its fullest extent, could reach as much as $10 million per bitcoin, which would put the overall value of all bitcoin at roughly ten times the market capitalization of gold at the time.

What kept the difficulty ranking so low? After all, the difficulty level today is around 90 trillion—meaning that it takes ninety trillion times the computing power to solve the computer problem as it did fifteen years ago—and yet the reward is only 1/16th the amount of bitcoin (3.125 BTC every ten minutes instead of fifty). For starters, not only were there very few miners in the beginning but there were also very few users. Therefore, many blocks in 2009 were sealed with zero transactions in them (in reality, "empty blocks" still have one transaction: the one that sends the miner reward from the coinbase to the winning miner or mining pool).

All mining in 2009 was still done with CPUs—ordinary personal computers, often laptops, pushing their math processors to the point of heating up as difficulty eventually rose.

GPUs came in 2010 and Satoshi pleaded with the GPU miners to stop the arms race, as he thought it was too early to take mining out of the hands of the average, less technical user.

A few key milestones of this flagship year:

- Bitcoin.org[liii] website and BitcoinTalk.[liv] The domain name Bitcoin.org was registered on August 18, 2008, more than two months before the white paper's appearance. It then launched shortly after the publication of the white paper. The website's development was aided by a young Finnish college student, Martti Malmi, who offered to help Satoshi write copy for the fledgling enterprise in exchange for bitcoin. He also agreed to mine twenty-four hours a day, so there would be at least two computers on the network at all times.[lv]
- BitcoinTalk (www.bitcointalk.org) is a traditional, moderated online forum for message threads about Bitcoin and various bitcoin-related subtopics. *BitcoinTalk* is where many firsts occurred, including conversations leading up to the first bitcoin exchange. It is also where the deal to buy two pizzas for ten thousand bitcoin was initiated.
- The first bitcoin exchange. New Liberty Standard (2009–2011) was the first centralized bitcoin exchange, using PayPal to sell bitcoin for cash[lvi]. Since there was very little price discovery available in this nascent market, the exchange itself did an analysis of mining costs, tacked on a small profit, and came up with a fair market value of 1,309.03 bitcoin for each US dollar, less than 1/10th of a penny per bitcoin.

- On October 5, 2009, the first sale of bitcoin took place on New Liberty Standard, where Martti Malki sold 5,050 of the bitcoin he was paid by Satoshi for his help for $5 on PayPal. That amount of bitcoin is worth more than $300 million as of the writing of this chapter.

2010: Of Pizzas and GPUs

On May 18, 2010, nineteen-year-old Laszlo Hanyecz of Jacksonville, Florida, posted on BitcoinTalk that he was willing to pay ten thousand bitcoins for two pizzas ("like maybe two large ones so I have some leftover for the next day"). Hanyecz had a stash of one hundred thousand bitcoins from his expertise in bitcoin mining, which included figuring out how to use more powerful GPU chips instead of CPUs to mine bitcoin. Four days later, Jeremy Sturdivant, known as "Jercos" on BitcoinTalk and also nineteen years old at the time and living in the UK, agreed to call up a Papa John's pizza near Laszlo and order two large cheese pizzas for about $30 in total. Laszlo faithfully sent Sturdivant ten thousand bitcoins, which he spent on his living expenses and a trip to the United States with his girlfriend. According to both parties, neither one has any bitcoin remaining.

Apparently, neither party was a "true believer" in Bitcoin, the type that never plans to sell. However, one must remember that selling or spending a $30 investment, especially when it then goes up in price to $300 or higher, does not seem irresponsible or crazy. Yet, had either of these teenage men held on to those ten thousand bitcoins, they'd be worth more than $600 million just eleven years later. One should also take into account the millions of bitcoins mined during that era, with ten million mined from January 2009 until the first halving in November 2012 alone. There are likely thousands of silent multimillionaires out there "hodling" their bitcoins. According to the Bitcoin Rich List, of the forty-seven million bitcoin addresses currently in existence, 115,292 hold more than $1 million in bitcoin and 10,867 hold more than $10 million in bitcoin. This number will only grow as bitcoin prices hit $100,000 and higher. At some point, the majority of the world's billionaires could be from bitcoin.

In July 2010, programmer Jeb McCaleb learned about Bitcoin from the following post on the user-generated tech news aggregator, Slashdot, by a contributor named Teppy:

> How's this for a disruptive technology? Bitcoin is a peer-to-peer, network-based digital currency with no central bank, and no transaction fees. Using a proof-of-work concept, nodes burn CPU cycles searching for bundles of coins, broadcasting their findings to the network. Analysis of energy usage indicates that the market value of Bitcoins is already above the value of the energy needed to generate them, indicating healthy demand. The community is hopeful the currency will remain outside the reach of any government.[lvii]

McCaleb, another Berkeley-trained coder who had previously developed the peer-to-peer file-sharing site eDonkey and an exchange for Magic the Gathering trading cards called Mt. Gox, decided bitcoin needed a more formal exchange than the PayPal-settled marketplace New Liberty Standard and began adopting the code to sell bitcoin in addition to trading cards.

Mt. Gox became the first bitcoin exchange to incorporate price-quoting, meaning users could have real-time parameters for issuing and executing buy and sell orders instead of the static listings by New Liberty Standard. The addition of Mt. Gox increased the volume of bitcoin trading for cash—and with it, the price. Mt. Gox, which had been in operation since 2006 for trading online playing cards, added bitcoin to its exchange on July 18, 2010. Within less than four months, the price of bitcoin rose from about five cents to a new all-time high of 39 cents on November 5 before setting back to 30 cents on December 31. This would not be the last time that the year's high was in the fourth quarter.

As Bitcoin wrapped up its second year of existence, its success was still by no means assured. In October 2010, a bug was found that allowed a hacker to create 182 billion new bitcoin through an "integer overflow" exploit. Fortunately, one of the core developers (then and now), Jeff Garzik, caught the anomaly and helped reverse it by forking the blockchain fifty-three blocks after the rogue transaction. This quick action likely saved Bitcoin. There have been no successful hacks of the protocol since.

2011: Silk Road and the Early Entrepreneurs

In many ways, 2011 was the most important year in the history of bitcoin. It's the year when bitcoin went from programmer play money to a real-world asset used in commerce regularly. It's the year when the first fiat-to-bitcoin payment systems were set up, with twenty-one-year-old Charlie Shrem starting BitInstant. Slovenians Necz Kodrič and Damijan Merlak founded BitStamp that year, later moving it to London, regulated out of Luxembourg. Acquired by public company Robin Hood in June 2024, it remains the oldest continuously operating bitcoin exchange.

This was also the year when Roger Ver (also known as "Bitcoin Jesus" for his fierce advocacy of bitcoin adoption in these early days) discovered the Bitcoin white paper and tried for three days and three nights to disprove it, to the point of being so exhausted over lack of sleep that the young, in-shape martial arts expert living in Japan needed to be hospitalized. When he was released, he bought 250,000 bitcoin for $1 apiece on Mt. Gox. I've heard Roger, who also attended the very first BitAngels meetup in early 2013, tell this story in person, and it's always enthralling to hear him relate that life-changing experience.

2011 is also when the nefarious "Silk Road" came into being as an eBay for illegal drugs, all paid for in bitcoin. Silk Road worked well, with user reviews and merchant rankings, and its existence helped build up an early narrative about Bitcoin's eventual use cases that led to its first 100x pump. Law enforcement ultimately caught the site's young founder, Ross Ulbricht, and he is currently—and controversially—serving multiple life sentences without the possibility of parole for operating that exchange.

On January 1, 2011, bitcoin was still at 30 cents. By June, when the aforementioned Slashdot reposted an article from the tech blog *Gizmodo* about Silk Road, speculators bid up the nascent asset to $30 on the Mt. Gox exchange. Troubles with users getting their funds out of the exchange dropped the price back under $1 before rebounding to five dollars by year's end (see chart). This would be an ongoing theme with Mt. Gox, leading up to its bankruptcy after missing funds and hacks were discovered in 2014. I had the unprecedented opportunity to sit down and meet with Mt. Gox owner Mark Karpelès prior to interviewing him on the big stage at Korea Blockchain Week in September 2024, just as this book was being typeset. He revealed that a hack on nearly 80,000 bitcoin occurred the very day he bought the site from McCaleb on March 1, 2011, and that he kept it quiet, hoping he could make it up with trading profits. As the price of bitcoin moved up from that day's closing price of 86 cents to $1,236 by December 2013, what started as a small cash liability of less than $70,000 the day of the hack ballooned to nearly $100 million by the time Mt. Gox was facing insolvency. Karpelès related to me that he had personally mined 200,000 bitcoin in 2010, and that he lost them all by storing them on Mt. Gox. (The occasion of my fireside chat was his surprising announcement that he was going to be launching a new exchange and wallet, Ellipx.) Ten years later, Japanese bankruptcy trustees are finally set to repay the remaining funds in bitcoin.

2012: Year of the First Halving

Leading up to the first halving, things were relatively stable in Bitcoin during the presidential election year of 2012. Bitcoin started the year around $4.50 and ended the year at $13.50. While 200 percent profit would be unthinkable in the traditional stock markets, gold or silver, it was a ho-hum year for Bitcoin after the prior year's 100x low to high fluctuation.

More entrepreneurs came onto the scene, each wave more buttoned-down than the prior, and it seemed like each year of development in Bitcoin was like a decade in traditional markets. Tradehill (2011–2013) was the first US exchange, but it was ill-equipped as a bootstrapped startup with no institutional backing to wrestle with the regulators and the banking industry, despite their beautiful offices that I visited in the San Francisco financial district shortly before they shut down.

Coinbase, the first American exchange to survive and scale, was cofounded by Brian Armstrong, an Airbnb software engineer, and Fred Ehrsam, a Goldman Sachs trader. Their professionalism, dedication to compliance, and pursuit of traditional venture capital was rewarded with a $100 billion IPO just nine years after its founding, making Armstrong a multibillionaire and Coinbase the second-largest exchange in the world, only behind Binance (more on them later).

As the year neared an end, excitement for the first halving was palpable. Would the code work? What would happen when, in one day, the supply of new bitcoins was cut in half, making the majority of miners unprofitable? Would it endanger the Bitcoin network itself if the majority of miners shut down all at once?

Halving dynamics were always a big part of Satoshi's plan:

> *The fact that new coins are produced means the money supply increases by a planned amount, but this does not necessarily result in inflation. If the supply of money increases at the same rate that the number of people using it increases, prices remain stable. If it does not increase as fast as demand, there will be deflation and early holders of money will see its value increase. Coins have to get initially distributed somehow, and a constant rate seems like the best formula.*[lviii]

The world saw how Satoshi's theory worked upon the issuance of Block 210,000 on November 28, 2012, and the four years that followed.

Early Bitcoin Culture

A few of the enduring memes that have survived from early Bitcoin culture, which inform its fundamentals and helped spur continuous faith in the protocol surviving during its darkest days, include the following:

HODL. A post on BitcoinTalk, a Reddit-like forum for bitcoiners started by Satoshi himself in 2009, featured a hilarious rambling post from a drunken young man who was depressed and upset but vowed not to sell his bitcoin in December 2013 when the market started crashing (albeit after a 100x run-up that year). This post has become an iconic meme that coined one of the most memorable phrases in bitcoin lore.

HODL (pronounced "Hod-dle") has now become a verb; it has been said that it is an acronym for "Hold on for Dear Life," and people who never sell bitcoin are referred to as hodlers. In recent years, people who put themselves to productive work, building new bitcoin or crypto projects during a bear market, have been called "buidlers" in appreciation of this original meme.

To the Moon Guy

Another iconic meme over time has been the pictogram issued every time a bullish market trend occurred in bitcoin. The account simply known as "To the Moon Guy," would react with this drawing:

To the moon!!! └(°0°)┘

Moon (used as a noun or as a verb) refers to parabolic gain in value. One popular bitcoin channel on YouTube today is called Carl the Moon.

Wen Moon, Wen Lambo

Another early bitcoin meme poses the question, "wen moon?, "wen lambo?"—in this case, "wen lambo" refers to the day that one bitcoin will buy one Lamborghini sports car. The phrase started to gain traction after entrepreneur Peter Saddington, cofounder of VinWiki, bought a $200,000 Lamborghini in 2015 with funds from the sale of 45 BTC he had purchased a few years earlier for $115.[lix] Early bitcoin programmer and serial entrepreneur Jim Blasko has a Nevada license plate "40 BTC," representing the price he paid for his Lambo. Previously, a user of the social media platform 4Chan bought a Lamborghini Gallardo for 216 bitcoin. During the bull market of 2021, when a Lambo could be purchased for a little over three bitcoin, Lamborghini reported its highest-ever sales. Similar to benchmarks like $100, $1,000, $100,000, and one million dollars, the day one can buy a Lamborghini with a single bitcoin will be an epic day for followers of the meme, as well as for bitcoin as an asset, as it will have reached a fully diluted value (FDV) of more than $4 trillion.

Video Memes

The rapid spread of video memes has resulted in enhanced recognition of bitcoin in some circles. Michael Saylor's bullish video commentaries have been turned into meme videos.

These include his "No Second Best" diatribe, quoted in part in the prior chapter, as well as his most recent commentary on CNBC that he has a name for people who invest in fiat currencies: "We call them poor." Each of these video fragments has been mixed and remixed, yeilding millions of views. Memes will be an important part of the adoption of Bitcoin going forward, particularly among younger audiences who spend a lot of time on YouTube and TikTok.

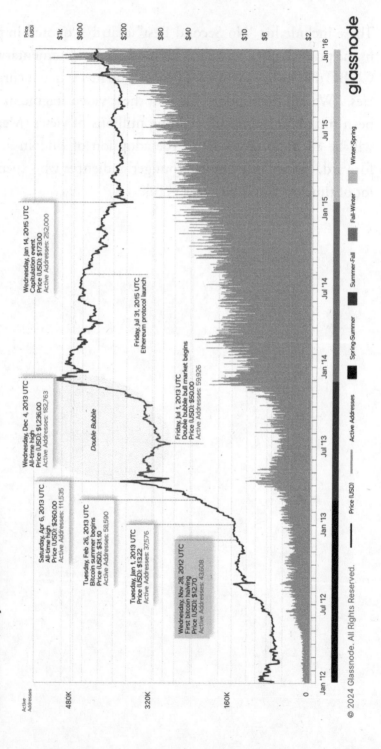

Bitcoin: Second Cycle 2012 - 2016

Saturday, Apr 6, 2013 UTC
All-time high
Price (USD): $260.00
Active Addresses: 111,535

Tuesday, Feb 26, 2013 UTC
Bitcoin summer begins
Price (USD): $31.10
Active Addresses: 58,590

Tuesday, Jan 1, 2013 UTC
Price (USD): $13.22
Active Addresses: 37,576

Wednesday, Nov 28, 2012 UTC
First bitcoin halving
Price (USD): $12.70
Active Addresses: 43,608

Wednesday, Dec 4, 2013 UTC
All-time high
Price (USD): $1,236.00
Active Addresses: 182,763

Double Bubble

Friday, Jul 31, 2015 UTC
Ethereum protocol launch

Friday, Jul 1, 2013 UTC
Double bubble bull market begins
Price (USD): $60.00
Active Addresses: 59,926

Wednesday, Jan 14, 2015 UTC
Capitulation event
Price (USD): $173.00
Active Addresses: 252,000

Active Addresses

480K

320K

160K

0

Jan '12   Jul '12   Jan '13   Jul '13   Jan '14   Jul '14   Jan '15   Jul '15   Jan '16

Price (USD)

$1k
$600
$200
$80
$40
$10
$6
$2

Price (USD) ——   Active Addresses ——

Spring-Summer   Summer-Fall   Fall-Winter   Winter-Spring

glassnode

Chapter Six

The 100x Cycle of 2012-2016

Booms start with some tie-in to reality, some reason which justifies the increase in asset values, and then—and this is the critical feature of speculative mood—the market loses touch with reality.

—John Kenneth Galbraith[lx]

Money is better than poverty, if only for financial reasons.
—Woody Allen[lxi]

The first Bitcoin cycle was fantastic, a journey started by an audacious white paper from a pseudonymous and arcane cryptographer with visions of disrupting the global economic system from the bottom up through cryptography and willing participants. By the time its self-enforcing first cycle ended, it had gained several thousand users, spread across more than 40,000 wallet addresses. Most importantly, the Bitcoin blockchain distributed its first ten million bitcoins, working exactly as Satoshi envisioned. It had created passionate advocates who believed, even when its value was pennies, that this finally was the blueprint for the separation of money and the state, a path to financial freedom for anyone who took the time to learn. Meanwhile, 99 percent of the world had never even heard of Bitcoin. This was all about to change.

We begin the second of thirty-three bitcoin cycles with the first Bitcoin halving on Wednesday, November 28, 2012, six days after the American holiday of Thanksgiving. Weeks earlier, US president Barack Obama was elected to a second term in office, easily defeating Republican challenger Mitt Romney by more than one hundred electoral college votes. The world was relatively at peace, as the Iraq and Afghanistan conflicts were nearing an end and the Ukraine and Gaza wars had yet to begin. The world had pulled itself away from the brink of global depression through its high-risk bailout measures, fueled by what at the time appeared to be massive money printing by the US government, but now looks like a blip compared to later programs during the global COVID-19 pandemic. Importantly, it worked for the time being, as global stock markets recovered by 50 percent or more since their depths in January 2009.

So, where was Bitcoin? Unbeknownst to nearly everyone, the first significant cryptocurrency was about to go off on an epic tear, rocketing up 20x in just four months to $260, retreating to $50, then racing to an all-time high of $1,236. The incredible 100x run-up in the first eleven months of 2013 finally caught the attention of mass media, and the Bitcoin narrative entered the mainstream, albeit skeptically. By year's end, the long crash precipitated by the implosion of the world's largest exchange, Mt. Gox, had turned the bullish frenzy into a slow bloodbath that only let up as 2016 arrived and the prospect of a new cycle and new leaders to fix these problems.

Note: Prices are reported differently by various exchanges, and even the market cap aggregators often report slightly different averages depending on their weighting, as well as whether they report the high for the day or the closing price. I generally use CoinGecko[lxii] closing numbers, except when reporting all-time highs, cycle lows, and the halving prices. For those prices, I typically look for the best documented number, having lived through these times and remembering tracking the prices myself. For historical numbers in the early days, I used Glassnode.[lxiii] For the all-time high price for 2013, I used CoinDesk,[lxiv] which is generally the most reliable source of midday historical numbers.

2013: The First Great Bull Market

Even though there were parabolic increases in the price of bitcoin in 2010 and 2011, they were quick and unsustainable, more of a bull blip than a classic bull market. The year 2013 was different, and it set the parameters for cycle behavior that informs my Four Seasons of Bitcoin thesis. First, it was the first year with a "double bubble" in a parabolic run-up. It was also the first bull market caused primarily by the halving supply shortage, coupled with new users, just as Satoshi predicted would happen.

As I explain in Chapters 10–13, which cover my Four Seasons of Bitcoin thesis in detail, halvings cause shortages of new coins, which causes the first leg of new demand as prices go up. Once prices go up, something called the Veblen Effect, named after early twentieth-century economist Thorsten Veblen, kicks in. This theory dictates that certain goods attain a luxury status that makes them more valuable *because* of their higher price, making them a status symbol, as opposed to classic economic theory, where rising prices will lower demand as consumers look for more affordable alternatives. Examples of Veblen goods include Hermès handbags, Patek Philippe watches, and Manolo Blahnik shoes. With a Veblen *asset*, the higher price makes it more exclusive and, therefore, less attainable, which justifies its higher price. This is sure to play out in the fifth Bitcoin cycle when owning a single bitcoin grows out of reach of the average consumer, but it had its beginnings in the second cycle when the price shot up so quickly there was a frenzy to buy bitcoin regardless of the price . . . as long as it kept going up.

I've spoken about Bitcoin as a Veblen asset for quite some time. Still, it was gratifying to see an accomplished academic share similar views, as Dr. Diego Vallarino recently posted an article on Medium, "The Veblen Effect on Bitcoin: Will It Become a Luxury Good after Halving?"[lxv]

Four Seasons of Bitcoin, Season One

The run-up to the first halving had very different dynamics than every cycle since. For the first eighteen months, there were virtually no sales of bitcoin other than the 5,050 bitcoin sale by Martti Malki for five dollars. In fact, a BitcoinTalk member named SmokesTooMuch offered to auction off 10,000 bitcoins in March 2010 for a $50 minimum bid. He withdrew the offer when nobody bid the minimum reserve (even New Liberty Standard only bid $25). As we observed in the last chapter, the dynamic of price going up solidly every year as more users bought or mined bitcoin prevailed, with only the very brief parabolic rise in June 2011 around the

Slashdot reposting of the *Gizmodo* article on Silk Road[lxvi] driving a massive pump and subsequent dump. (Note: when I use the terms "pump" and "dump," it does not necessarily mean a manipulated market. Prices going up rapidly are often referred to in crypto as a pump, and they are generally followed by a quick decline retracing the entire gain, known as a dump, borrowing similar language from Wall Street.)

In 2013, the price started at $13.51 on January 1, only a slight uptick relative to the halving price five weeks earlier. This has turned out to be normal behavior immediately after a halving, as there is always uncertainty about how miners will react (e.g., will they turn off their miners or will they sell more of their bitcoin to keep the lights on until the difficulty levels adjust to the point the average miner can be profitable again). The real parabolic behavior only kicks in once the high of the prior cycle is reached, which is where Bitcoin Spring (which starts on the day of the halving) turns to Bitcoin Summer. In the case of 2013, that day was February 26, when the price opened and closed at $30.40.

Barely one month after the first Bitcoin Summer began, the price soared on April 6th to $260, according to *Brave New Coin*, on reports that Russians in Cyprus were using bitcoin as a way to move funds out of the troubled banking system there. The speculative impact of the story is now generally believed to be bigger than the actual demand shock, and the price then went through a massive correction all the way back to $68 within nine days. Part of the retrace was the familiar plotline of troubles at Mt. Gox in handling the demand repeating itself. At this point, several new exchanges with much better back-end security and more professional teams appeared on the scene, including Bitstamp, Coinbase, ItBit (now part of

Paxos), and Kraken. By the end of 2013, there were dozens of functioning bitcoin exchanges. Nonetheless, more than 60 percent of global volume still went through Mt. Gox. In addition, on April 10, the Chinese government declared bitcoin to not be a currency and banned banks from handling it.

Another key reason that 2013 was important in the history of bitcoin was its first significant mainstream media attention, when the price hit $100, then $200, then crashed, and ultimately reached $1,236. When the price of one bitcoin reached $1,000, it became the first asset to have an appreciation of more than one million times its initial price. Whereas in 2009–2010, one could buy 1,000 bitcoins for one dollar, it now took $1,000 to buy just one bitcoin. In December 2013, Wall Street analyst firm Wedbush Securities wrote the first investor report[lxvii] on bitcoin as an asset class, projecting it could ultimately reach $98,500, with a 0.5 percent chance it would reach $1 million per bitcoin. This and the price run-up had bitcoin squarely in the news, daily fodder at CNBC and other financial outlets, as this puzzling anomaly was somehow making techies rich.

This narrative nicely coincided with the nascent Bitcoin Foundation's first public conference in May 2013, timed to celebrate the third anniversary of Bitcoin Pizza Day, which I detailed in the prior chapter. Prior to this conference, there had never been a public gathering of more than 75 people to discuss Bitcoin, which was in New York in 2011. Bitcoin 2013 gathered more than one thousand Bitcoin enthusiasts from around the globe at the San Jose McEnery Convention Center, which was also the exact location of the first major internet conference nineteen years earlier. Most of the big names in the space attended: Brian Armstrong announced

Coinbase's venture funding as Brian handed out T-shirts in their 10 x 10 booth (I still have mine). Erik Voorhees gave a popular keynote on bitcoin and the history of money. Ripple also announced its venture funding and had a presence on the show floor. BitPay, Blockchain.com, and other nascent leaders were all in attendance, as were founding members of the Bitcoin Foundation: Charlie Shrem, the twenty-one-year-old who founded BitInstant, which allowed anyone to buy bitcoin with cash at a local convenience store; Peter Vessenes, a Seattle-based entrepreneur who was the initial president of the foundation; Jon Matonis, a London-based fintech entrepreneur; and Gavin Andresen, the Bitcoin chief scientist who was entrusted with the keys to the bitcoin core code by Satoshi after he mysteriously disappeared from the Bitcoin ecosystem in 2011.

The second leg of the "double bubble" 2013 bull market began with its midyear low of $66 in early July. This price plummet was caused by a market reaction to the State of California asking the Bitcoin Foundation for a money transmitter license, confusing the Foundation with the decentralized protocol. The Bitcoin Foundation responded that as a nonprofit, they don't transmit any money, they take donations, largely to pay the core developers. From that fear-inspired pullback, which was based on nothing as California never followed up on its false assumption, the bitcoin price rocketed up to a $1,236 all-time high on December 4, according to CoinDesk.

The atmosphere in late 2013 was heady, as centralized exchanges were suddenly running out of bitcoins to sell. Global arbitrage in between exchanges took too long to move liquidity through international banks prior to the introduction of the stablecoin one year later with Tether. I was already very active as a trader and angel investor in this cycle, and I remember the wild daily price oscillations. I recall August starting by finally moving back over $100, a nice recovery from $66 just a few weeks earlier. August 1 was also the first day of the first initial coin offering (ICO), Mastercoin, paid in bitcoin, which I will address later in the book. By the end of October, the price of bitcoin had doubled to $200. A few weeks later, it doubled again to $400, and a few weeks after that, bitcoin hit an unimaginable high of $1,236. At that point, Bitcoin was all over the news, and retail investors began to panic buy into bitcoin at the top, as many Thanksgiving meals had tales of a cousin or sibling making a recent killing buying bitcoin any time in the prior six months (see chart).

However, what goes up must come down, and the 100x bubble popped in early December, starting the first Bitcoin Fall. On the Bitcoin blockchain, one could see older wallets cashing out enough bitcoin to buy a home or pay for their luxurious living expenses for the next four years. Bitcoin Fall would last a little over a year, from its all-time high to its final capitulation date in January 2015 (the final nadir of the cycle, when nearly all retail traders have taken their losses and left the arena). That date is the start of what I call Bitcoin Winter, which is the best time each cycle to *buy* bitcoin, as it has nowhere further to drop after all of the sellers have left. It is also at the bottom of other technical analysis indicators that I will address in Chapter 13.

On December 31, 2013, the year ended with bitcoin priced at $749.24, more than 60x where it was one year earlier. Many pundits thought the price was just taking a breather and was on its way to $5,000 a year later. They were wrong, but the cycle theory was too young to steer them away from the cliff. This is why Bitcoin Summer is so powerful: once you reach a prior all-time high, there is absolutely no technical resistance above you, enabling the parabolic gains of the first cycles. How long can this continue? Read on, dear reader, read on.

2014: Bitcoin's First Fall

My general cycle theory is that scarcity is more important than all other factors (short of protocol failure or a decrease in the number of users). The programmatic deflation of new coins, which thus far has always been a smaller percentage than the addition of new users each year, inevitably causes more demand than supply. While this slowly builds, the secondary conditions (news cycle, global money supply, macroeconomic conditions, interest rates, geopolitical tensions) have not yet been a more extensive influence than scarcity. If that were the case, bitcoin would be at a lower price than it was in 2020, which it most assuredly is not.

When the 2013 bubble popped at the start of December 2013, most buyers thought it was still a bull market and continued to "buy the dip" throughout 2014, which was a disastrous strategy. Buying the dips only works in a bull market. In a bear market, you're simply dollar-cost averaging into an ever-declining price, so it's best to wait until capitulation seemingly has occurred. Traditional technical analysis techniques can also be useful here, just as they help guide day traders through the equities and commodities markets. What appears to be a recurring theme in the four-year cycle is that the worst news possible tends to come out in the third year of the cycle, just when prices have started to nose-dive. The simplest explanation for this is that bull markets hide a multitude of sins, as few question why prices are increasing. When they go down, everyone points fingers and looks for explanations and villains.

The simple scapegoat to explain both the excessive pump and reactive dump was our old friend, Mt. Gox. By the end of 2013, Jeb McCaleb was entirely out of the picture, and Mark Karpelès appeared to be in way over his head to run the world's largest bitcoin exchange. He spent his days choosing teas for his teahouse and pampering his cat. Many articles and books have been written about the rise and fall of Mt. Gox, so I won't go into massive detail here. Suffice it to say that a substantial amount of bitcoins were missing from the exchange, possibly as far back as 2011, when Karpelès himself stated that the accounts were short 80,000 bitcoins when he took over the business, he planned to make up for it with trading profits. By the February 14, 2014 bankruptcy filing in Japan, roughly 650,000 bitcoins were stolen, lost, or otherwise unaccounted for. (Note: as this book is going to print, I am getting ready to interview Karpelès on the main stage of Korea Blockchain Week, which should be a newsworthy event given his silence over the years following the exchange's collapse.)

The Mt. Gox bankruptcy was a sufficient catalyst to scare off many bulls, who took their still substantial gains (the price was $605.24 that day) and went home. Others, resolute that the price of bitcoin would recover and not wanting to sell at a 50 percent discount to the recent all-time high, held . . . all the way down to the year-end price of $320 and beyond. For a hodler, this is fine, as those bitcoins are now worth $66,000 each today. Still, followers of the swing trading philosophy I detail in future chapters would have already sold a few weeks earlier in the $900–1,200 range, then bought back in at or near the early 2015 capitulation point and received 3–5x the amount of bitcoin as their original investment.

Despite the depressed period of more than two years in between the December 2013 high and the January 2016 reclaiming of four-digit status, Bitcoin survived its first brutal bear market. Its participants innovated with what was then called Bitcoin 2.0 but now is simply referred to as altcoins. The first wave of altcoins took place in the first Bitcoin cycle with the development of Litecoin by Charlie Lee, who called it "silver to bitcoin's gold" (his brother Bobby Lee started the first bitcoin exchange in China, BTCC). There were other early experimental forks to bitcoin, generally based on better mining efficiency. These included Feathercoin, Namecoin (which had the functionality of letting one claim bitcoin-based domain names), Devcoin, and Peercoin, the first token to utilize proof-of-stake as part of its consensus mechanism.

The 2014 wave of innovation included the launch of Ethereum, which I was fortunate enough to be involved in, debuting a skinny nineteen-year-old named Vitalik Buterin to the media at CES 2014, then again presenting the Ethereum white paper formally at the North American Bitcoin Conference a couple of weeks later. Its ICO at 30 cents provided a second chance at stratospheric returns for those who missed out on $1 bitcoin. The seeds were slowly being planted for the bull market that followed the next halving in the summer of 2016. But there was a year of additional pain to follow.

2015: Living through Bitcoin's First Extended Bear Market

The year 2015 continued bitcoin's longest bear market, with the long-awaited capitulation event taking place on January 14 at $173, according to CoinDesk (I personally recall that day as one of panic in the air as to whether it might retrace all the way back to $12, which after all was the price just two years earlier). This indeed was the start of Bitcoin Winter, which is not the period that prices fall (that's Bitcoin Fall); it's the year of slow recovery, of waiting patiently for the next Bitcoin Spring.

Like all other Bitcoin Winters, it was a period of price appreciation, with the price of bitcoin nearly quadrupling between the date of this cycle's capitulation, January 14, at $173,[lxviii] and the next Bitcoin Spring price of $670. Yet for the calendar year of 2015, it was an unusually slow upward trend, with the opening price on January 1 at $314.25 and the closing price on December 31 at $430.57.[lxix] Most of the year, bitcoin was priced in the mid-$200s, which in retrospect was a remarkable time to accumulate. I had advised a number of friends and colleagues to double down on buying bitcoin that year, and they were rewarded handsomely when bitcoin went up to nearly $20,000 two years later. Innovation was slow as funding sources dried up, with crypto investors seeking to hold on to their bitcoin and many venture capitalists shunning the sector as a failed experiment.

2016: Run-up to the Second Halving

In the case of 2016, it acted like the tail end of most Bitcoin Winters, with a slow acceleration of price just prior to the halving. The year started at $434.33 and was up more than

50 percent by the July 9th halving at $670. The year ended with a slow pursuit of the next Bitcoin Summer, inching its way up to the prior all-time high as well as the psychological barrier of $1,000, which it had not seen since late 2013 and the preceding bull market. The closing price for bitcoin on December 31, 2016, was $963.74—close to $1,000, but no cigar. It would take only another three days to cross that mark as we entered the new bull market year of 2017 and, most likely, another parabolic Bitcoin Summer.

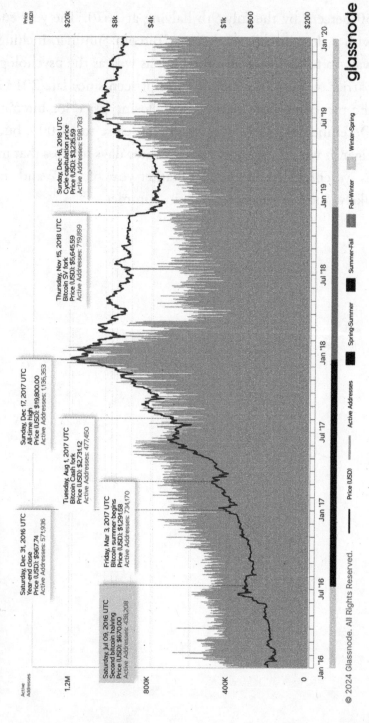

Bitcoin: Third Cycle 2016 - 2020

Saturday, Jul 09, 2016 UTC
Second bitcoin halving
Price (USD): $670.00
Active Addresses: 438,208

Friday, Mar 3, 2017 UTC
Bitcoin summer begins
Price (USD): $1,291.58
Active Addresses: 734,170

Tuesday, Aug 1, 2017 UTC
Bitcoin Cash fork
Price (USD): $2,731.12
Active Addresses: 477,450

Saturday, Dec 31, 2016 UTC
Year-end close
Price (USD): $961.74
Active Addresses: 571,936

Sunday, Dec 17, 2017 UTC
All-time high
Price (USD): $19,800.00
Active Addresses: 1,136,353

Thursday, Nov 15, 2018 UTC
Bitcoin SV fork
Price (USD): $5,645.59
Active Addresses: 719,899

Sunday, Dec 16, 2018 UTC
Cycle capitulation price
Price (USD): $3,239.59
Active Addresses: 598,783

Active Addresses

1.2M

800K

400K

0

Price (USD)

$20k

$8k

$4k

$1k

$600

$200

Jan '16   Jul '16   Jan '17   Jul '17   Jan '18   Jul '18   Jan '19   Jul '19   Jan '20

Price (USD)   Active Addresses

Spring-Summer   Summer-Fall   Fall-Winter   Winter-Spring

glassnode

Chapter Seven

Bitcoin Forks and ICO Mania

A house divided against itself cannot stand.
—Abraham Lincoln[lxx]

We choose mania over boredom every time.
—James Gleick[lxxi]

History doesn't repeat itself, but it often rhymes.
—Mark Twain (attributed)[lxxii]

The Second Bitcoin Cycle (2012–2016) was quite the ride. Unlike the first cycle, it began to have a structure, building the basic elements for at least some repetitive behaviors that technical analysis (often referred to as T.A.) can track and compare with other sets of data to bring meaning to these seemingly disconnected behaviors. The stock market has digested many investing philosophies, some based on broad generalizations (such as portfolio diversification, growth, or value investing), and some focused on repeating trends, including "Sell in May and Go Away"[lxxiii] or the "Santa Claus Rally."[lxxiv]

My thesis about the Four Seasons of Bitcoin began to take shape when I projected in 2015 that there would be a significant increase in price leading up to the 2016 halving from the 2015 bottom. Many pundits at the time proclaimed that Bitcoin was dead and headed to zero. My projection was correct, and the bitcoin price more than tripled between the last cycle's bottom in January 2015 and the second halving the following July. I theorized that there would be another run-up after this second halving until the level became unsustainable again. My estimate of how high it could run was $10,000 by the end of the bull run, which seemed wildly bullish at the time, but turned out to be conservative, as the 2017 high came within a few hundred dollars of $20,000.

While it would take me another cycle to define the parameters of each season (most importantly, the duration and mini-cycles within a bull market), I started calling these seasons by name:

- Bitcoin Spring, when the seed of the halving was planted;
- Bitcoin Summer, when the parabolic run-up occurs;
- Bitcoin Fall, when prices fall—when the bubble pops and prices drop; and
- Bitcoin Winter, when the few remaining believers struggle to regain their narrative.

Let's now go back in time to 2016. At the start of the year, Hillary Clinton seemed assured of a landslide victory over Jeb Bush, with many bemoaning the fact that it would be the fifth time in eight elections either a Clinton or Bush would be president (and the other two terms started with a Clinton as secretary of state). Then an upstart "joke" candidate named Donald Trump slowly knocked out front-runner Jeb Bush and other Republican contenders one by one, finally achieving the GOP nomination and inevitable defeat by historic proportions to the well-oiled Democratic machinery supporting Hillary Clinton. The problem was nobody told this to the voters, who elected Trump in the biggest upset victory since the end of World War II. The next four years were among the most contentious in US history, with massive protests and uprisings as shocked Democrats, predominantly supporting a "woke" and "green" agenda, battled in the streets with MAGA (Make America Great Again) supporters. Near the end of the Trump presidency (and Third Bitcoin Cycle) was the added turmoil of Black Lives Matter protests surrounding the death of George Floyd at the hands of a Minneapolis policeman and the rapid onset of the global COVID-19 pandemic.

What was the response of Bitcoin, moving from the second to the third Bitcoin cycle? Proving once again the importance of scarcity coupled with user adoption as a catalyst for parabolic post-halving growth, the price of bitcoin rose from $670 in July 2016 to eclipse the prior all-time high from back in December 2013 of $1,236 by early March 2017. That breaking of the prior all-time high once again served as a fuse on the bomb of pent-up demand, as the price doubled to more than $2,500 by early June, then doubled again to $5,000 by early October. At this point, the price appreciation of bitcoin seemed unstoppable, doubling again to $10,000 by the end of November. Just a few weeks later, the price reached its all-time high for the cycle of $19,800 on December 17, 2017. Not coincidentally, this date was the first day the Chicago Mercantile Exchange (CME) was allowed to trade futures on bitcoin. Retail investors rushed in, confident that the addition of big institutions to bitcoin trading would drive massive volume and be the dawn of a new day for bitcoin appreciation, launching the price into the tens of thousands.

Well, yes, that happened eventually, but not in 2017. What happened was, in retrospect, predictable. Old wallets opened up and took advantage of all this new liquidity provided by an uninformed surge of new retail investors to cash out on their parabolic gains from the prior months. These seasoned bitcoin investors knew they could return in a year or two and buy back in at a steep discount during the next market panic. The oldest steady hands (often referred to in crypto culture as "diamond hands") are those most assured about the long-term viability of bitcoin. Ergo, many of them—contrary to popular opinion—trade a few times per cycle to continually add to their bitcoin wealth over time, as well as generate a decent chunk of fiat money for spending through shrewd cycle trading. This is the very definition of having one's cake and eating it, too.

Fork Wars

Reflecting on Mark Twain's quote at the beginning of this chapter, the simplest of narratives about the second halving did indeed take place: new supply is cut, demand stays constant or slowly rises, and the prices must eventually go up. Indeed, this dynamic repeated in two successive cycles, but with exponentially diminishing bull market returns (100x for 2012–2013, 30x for 2016–2017) and linear diminishing losses during the bear market part of the cycle (85 percent in 2013–2016, 83 percent in 2017–2019).

This third cycle also supported one of the key observations of my thesis, which I call Terpin's News Relativity Paradigm (NRP):

In a bitcoin bull market, which is driven by scarcity and panic-buying, the impact of good news gets exaggerated, while bad news gets minimized or ignored.

The reverse is also true: in a bitcoin bear market, good news is ignored, whereas bad news is magnified, adding fuel to the short seller fires.

Point in case: the first bitcoin fork. Vinny Lingham, who first predicted $1,000 bitcoin in 2013, then correctly foretold the bear market starting in 2014 using the metric of merchants accepting bitcoin for payments, then immediately selling it for fiat (which makes it a net sell on the system that is independent of value). In early 2017, Lingham predicted that bitcoin's price, still under $1,000 at the time, would triple by year's end and reach $3,000.[lxxv]

In a viral blog post on Medium called "A Fork in the Road" that was published on March 15, 2017[lxxvi] (perhaps intentionally on the Ides of March), Vinny rang the alarm that if a proposed fork of bitcoin went through, it would set the entire Bitcoin ecosystem back immeasurably. The fork in question was initially called Bitcoin Unlimited (BTU) and later rebranded as Bitcoin Cash (BCH). He noted that Bitcoin had already received billions of dollars in free publicity on its way up, and that a fork would dilute the brand and make people question which was the real Bitcoin. He quoted Metcalfe's Law and tweeted, "Danger on the horizon. If Bitcoin forks, all bets are off and we can kiss $3k BTC in 2017 goodbye."[lxxvii] My former wife begged me after I read her the post to sell my bitcoin at $1,100 before it cratered. Fortunately, I didn't sell, and bitcoin not only didn't crash after the August 1 fork, it exploded to the upside.

What exactly was Bitcoin Cash, and how does a fork work in the Bitcoin protocol? The Bitcoin white paper discussed how miners would only work with the longest chain, which would prevent attacks from destroying the network. However, if some miners decided to fork the blockchain and create a second chain from the same proof of work, it would have its own coins (i.e., digital signatures). Upon the Bitcoin Cash fork, a parallel bitcoin blockchain was created, with its own miners but mainly relying on the same rules as Bitcoin, other than the lower fees. Ergo, everyone with a bitcoin wallet automatically received an identical amount of bitcoin cash on that parallel blockchain. If one had 125 bitcoins, they now also had 125 bitcoin cash.

Why did this initial fork increase the price instead of decreasing it, as Vinny Lingham suggested? Part of it was the wealth effect. Suddenly, everyone who had bitcoin now also had bitcoin cash through an algorithmic airdrop. On the exchanges, Bitcoin Cash was priced at $767.77 on opening listing, although it quickly dropped to $208.84 just three days later, as many bitcoiners quickly dumped their BCH for what they saw as the only real bitcoin, BTC. Heated struggles ensued over which exchanges would even list it and whether they would use the word "Bitcoin" to describe it or simply BCH. Bitcoin Cash cofounder Roger Ver and his supporters countered by selling bitcoin to buy up the less expensive Bitcoin Cash when the price dropped and helped support the price, which rocketed up to its all-time high of $3,099.99 on December 22, 2017, a day when bitcoin lost one-quarter of its value, sliding as low as $11,500 after starting the week on the verge of $20,000. This prompted *The Guardian* to remark that bitcoin investors were finally being introduced to "the law of financial gravity," and that its investors were "risking a rerun of the 17th-century tulip bubble."[lxxviii]

Since then, the price of BCH has substantially decoupled from the bitcoin narrative and now trades at less than 10 percent of the price of bitcoin. Given that we are currently entering the fifth cycle of boom and bust, the comparisons to the tulip bubble, which had a single stratospheric run, continue to be misinformed.

The ICO Era and its Effect on Bitcoin

Initial Coin Offerings, known as ICOs, created a series of firestorms in the early days of crypto, the echoes of which continue to this day. The first ICO was Mastercoin, which in the prior cycle raised a total of only $600,000—entirely in bitcoin at a value barely over $100 per bitcoin—with a fully diluted value of $1 million, with each bitcoin being exchanged for 100 Mastercoins (now rebranded Omni). The lead developer, J. R. Willett, wrote a thoughtful proposal he called "The Second Bitcoin Whitepaper,"[lxxix] where he explained his plan to build new assets on top of Bitcoin, rather than competing with Bitcoin. Paying homage to the Genesis Block, he conducted his crowdsale at a treasury wallet he called "The Exodus Address" (as in exiting Bitcoin and joining Mastercoin). The paper provided a humorous disclosure to dissuade most would-be investors not completely aligned with the cause:

Investing in experimental currencies is really, absurdly risky. . . . Please consult your financial adviser before investing in ANY wild scheme such as this (hint: they will probably tell you to RUN and not look back. . . . Anyone who puts their rent money or life savings into an experiment of this type is a fool and deserves the financial ruin they will inevitably reap from this).

Fair warnings were now issued, and the project increased in value 200x in four months. Most of the funding came through the nascent BitAngels network of bitcoin angels I started with David A. Johnston a few months earlier. David went on to become chairman of Mastercoin, then my cofounder in the Dapps Fund on his way to an illustrious career in crypto. He is currently one of the leaders in the nascent decentralized AI movement as a core contributor to the Morpheus protocol.

The best-known ICO prior to the Third Bitcoin Cycle was Ethereum, which raised $18 million in 2014, issuing 60 million ETH at prices starting at 30 cents apiece. It took cofounders Vitalik Buterin, Anthony Di Iorio, Gavin Woods, Joe Lubin, Charles Hoskinson (who left early on to start Cardano), and others nearly a full year to release the Ethereum token on July 31, 2015, where it initially listed at 74 cents before dropping to 42 cents. It would take until the next cycle for the price to climb over $15, which was quite a slow start for a cryptocurrency that peaked just six years after its 74 cent debut to reach $4,800 per token!

There were two major Bitcoin forks during this cycle. The 2017 bull market fork added value, and the 2019 bear market fork caused the cycle's eventual capitulation (more on this later in the chapter). Other than these forks, the new ICO bull market of 2016–2018 was the story of the cycle.

In late May 2016, on the cusp of the second bitcoin halving, the DAO raised an extraordinary $150 million in $10–15

Ethereum. The DAO was a token built on the ERC20 standard of Ethereum, which is a geek-speak for the twentieth proposal for new smart contract variants submitted to the Ethereum Foundation. ERC20 rapidly became the gold standard for issuing new tokens on Ethereum, including virtually all ICOs. Most early token sales raised a few hundred thousand to a few million dollars to build out a team and decentralized application (or, as David A. Johnston called it, a "dApp"). The DAO team had a bigger vision of raising a war chest of venture capital funds through a DAO (decentralized autonomous organization, which is effectively a leaderless system where governance happens by a vote of the token holders). The token holders would then invest in other ICOs and distribute the proceeds. This was problematic as a model to begin with since it triggered securities laws in any jurisdiction where tokens were purchased. But a more immediate issue occurred when a hacker stole $60 million of the funds through a code exploit, taunting the founders that if code is law, then the money is legally his by virtue of cracking the code. This resulted in the Ethereum Foundation creating a hard fork of its own (more than a year before the first significant bitcoin fork) in July 2016 to reverse the DAO hack. Those stolen funds represented 15 percent of the entire value of the Ethereum network at the time. This proved to be controversial, and some miners did not go along with the fork, creating Ethereum Classic (ETC) as a result.

The US Securities and Exchange Commission (SEC) saw things a bit differently and, for the first time, issued an investigative report just days after the ETC fork. The report concluded that the DAO was a security and that the offer should have been registered with the SEC if it were to be sold to any

Americans. No enforcement actions took place, as the SEC saw this as a learning moment. (This is one of the last times in memory that the SEC was so benign in judging matters concerning cryptocurrency.)

With each passing month, as 2016 rolled into 2017 and prices of both bitcoin and ethereum rose, more and more ICOs were taking place. The first Ethereum-based ICO, Augur, took place in August 2015. I worked with the Augur team on its media relations at the time, and I remember that one could invest with either bitcoin or ether, and there was a formula as to how much each token would be priced based on how much was invested. That ICO kicked off the new ICO cycle, coming out of the depths of Bitcoin Winter. Without Augur, there would never have been the DAO. Without the DAO, there most likely would not have been a 2017–2018 wave that raised $17.8 billion, according to TokenData,[lxxx]including $4 billion alone for one token, Eos, where I also had a front-row seat working on media relations with that team.

Late 2017 was a heady time, even more so than the first Bitcoin Summer in late 2013, as so many more people were involved this time. It was becoming clear to many of us that the four-year cycles really were predicting the bull markets, given the all-time highs for 2013 and for 2017, with four years in between, were only separated by 13 days in the calendar year (December 4, 2013, and December 17, 2017). It was also becoming apparent that altcoins, led by Ethereum and the voluminous amount of others that were created through the ICO process, were taking on a life of their own. They were also tied in great part to the bitcoin four-year cycle. "When bitcoin sneezes, altcoins catch pneumonia" is something I've been saying since at least 2018.

One would think the lessons would have been learned by now, that any new apparent peak all-time high can be quickly followed by a crash. This is then followed by a long bear market, since both parts of the equation have been repeating. Selling too soon can forfeit just as much money as holding on too long. Unfortunately, nobody wants to be reminded of the bear market in the middle of parabolic gains. Let the party roll on!

"Do you know why people act irrationally in a bubble?" asked economist Harry Dent, who was keynote for my 2018 CoinAgenda conference in San Juan, Puerto Rico, two months after the Third Bitcoin Cycle high. "Because they're drunk." Everyone in late 2017 and early 2018 was drunk with new success. Like the dotcoms of the late 1990s, the party would go on forever, changing society overnight. My lead developer on a few projects bought a Lamborghini for forty bitcoins, then proudly displayed 40 BTC as his license plate. My wife, who was worried about the cost of buying a fully loaded Mercedes SUV before the cycle started, bought a Rolls-Royce.

Jim Lowry, a friend and early bitcoin miner, is one of the best analysts for bitcoin I know. He looked at the CME excitement pushing up the price and sounded an alarm. "Everyone thinks that this opens the door to everyone going long on bitcoin, but it also means skilled short sellers will pop this bubble. They will borrow money and do it over and over again. If they CAN do this, they WILL do this." He sold all of his bitcoin on December 17th and did not buy any back until the next bottom in early 2019. He is one of the main inspirations for my model of buy once a cycle, sell once a cycle. One of my fund investments, Alphabit Fund, also sold all of its bitcoin that day, according to managing director Liam Robertson.

2018: Another Bitcoin Fall Leads to an Extended Winter

During the 2009–2012 cycle, there was pretty much only Bitcoin. It accounted for 95 percent of the market capitalization of crypto. By the end of the 2012–2016 cycle, that percentage (known as bitcoin dominance) dropped to 85 percent, as nascent tokens like Ethereum and Monero were picking up steam. It was the 2016–2020 cycle where cryptocurrencies other than bitcoin truly became part of the narrative. Bitcoin dominance dropped to an all-time low of 36.9 percent in January 2018, as jubilant Ethereum proponents talked about the inevitability of "the Flippening"—the day when the market capitalization of Ethereum surpassed that of Bitcoin.

The nearest this narrative ever came to reality was June 12, 2017, when Ethereum's market capitalization was 83.2 percent the size of Bitcoin's. This was the closest that Ethereum would ever come, dropping sharply to around 10 percent for much of 2019 before rebounding above 50 percent a handful of times in the Fourth Bitcoin Cycle bull market. As of the writing of this book, it stands at 31.3 percent of the value of the bitcoin market cap. In general, Ethereum tends to underperform bitcoin in a bear market and then outperform it when market conditions signal a change of seasons from bear to bull. We will examine cycle-based trading strategies in greater detail in Chapter 16.

When markets crash, the regulators come rushing in, looking for someone to blame (and to take the credit for being the top cop that busted them). While Bitcoin itself was related to very few enforcement actions (generally targeting exchanges like Kraken and Coinbase conducting staking or lending programs around Bitcoin), altcoins have been a major target for "regulation by enforcement" by the US SEC since at least 2016, when they issued their opinion on the DAO. Yet, unlike most markets where rules are actually made, the SEC has been adamant in saying there are no new rules that need to be made and that the ninety-year-old 1934 Act prevails. The SEC's actions are also guided by their interpretation of a 1946 Supreme Court case on orange futures, now known as the "Howey Test," after the Howey Fruit Company lawsuit by the SEC.

These enforcement actions had the effect of giving small startups a poor choice: plead guilty even if you disagree, or spend tens of millions of dollars defending yourself as your business dies, and in many cases, your assets are seized before the verdict is in. In our current cycle (2024–2028), deep-pocketed entities like Ripple and Coinbase have fought back, with ConsenSys even proactively suing the SEC before being sued themselves. The early results look good for the defendants, with the Ripple ruling essentially finding primarily in favor of the defendants.

This wave of crypto bankruptcies had a substantial negative effect on the entire altcoin market cap. So did exchanges not listing new tokens and even delisting any current tokens they thought might be subject to prosecution. Exchanges around the world blocked US investors and US projects, leading to a massive exodus of promising projects from historic tech and finance capitals like Silicon Valley and New York to the friendlier regulatory waters of jurisdictions like the British Virgin Islands, Cayman Islands, Malta, Singapore, Switzerland, and, increasingly, Dubai and Abu Dhabi.

This pattern had an escalating negative effect:

1) Once-promising projects were shuttered, and their market capitalization plummeted toward zero.

2) Projects that even looked like those targeted by the SEC lost their listings or were targets of short sellers.

3) As regulatory actions heated up, investors gradually exited their altcoin holdings entirely, driving down the price by 90 percent or more.

4) Remaining projects that had not converted their ICO money from ether (ETH) to cash before the market crashed started selling the ETH in their treasury to pay their salaries and to keep the lights on.

5) This also helped crater the price of ETH, collapsing it from a market high of $1,167.11 in January 2018 to a crushing low of $82 just eleven months later.

Bitcoin had a similar experience during this second Bitcoin Fall (remember, the first cycle was too early to have established seasons, given the first halving had not yet taken place).

Bitcoin Spring began on July 9, 2016, when the seed of the halving was planted. The price was $670, nearly four times the low mark of the prior Bitcoin Winter at $173.

Bitcoin Summer started when the prior all-time high of $1,236 was surpassed in early March, 2017. The price of both bitcoin and ether then went parabolic, with bitcoin reaching its all-time high of $19,800 in December.

Bitcoin Fall started immediately after the all-time high, with an initial sharp price drop five days later of 25 percent. The price would continue to drop until capitulation set in on December 16, 2018, with a cycle low price of $3,235.59. (Remember Jim Lowry, my miner/trader friend who sold all of his bitcoin on December 17, 2017, at $19,800? He bought back fourteen months later at less than one-fifth the price, enabling him to substantially increase both his bitcoin and his cash position.)

2019–2020: Searching for a New Narrative in the Depths of Winter

Bitcoin Fall hits you with wave after wave of bad news, which, according to my News Relativity Paradigm, causes much more panic selling than it would in a bull market. That means wave after wave of price drops, during which inexperienced traders seek to "buy the dip"—as mentioned earlier. This is a horrible mistake in bear markets before capitulation. The ultimate bad news of the cycle finally broke through the retested bottom price of $6,000, which was less than 30 percent of the prior all-time high less than a year earlier. This price point also had considerable support.

All that changed with Bitcoin SV.

Bitcoin SV (the SV stands for "Satoshi's Vision"), simply put, was a fork of the fork. On November 15, 2018, Craig Wright proclaimed himself to be Satoshi Nakamoto and stated he would kill off the current Bitcoin and Bitcoin Cash chains because they had evolved into coins that did not reflect his vision. Wright has been a controversial figure in the history of cryptography, long suspected of having early ties with the person or team that built Bitcoin, but never definitively outed by anyone other than himself as the true Satoshi.

The fork of the fork was far more contentious than the initial Bitcoin fork, with both Bitcoin Cash and Bitcoin SV miners vowing to sell the coins they would each get of their hated opposing currency from the fork to drive it into oblivion. Clearly, neither side could truly win this war, but when Wright promised to sell much of the bitcoin he mined as Satoshi to kill Bitcoin as well, panic set in. The floor of $6,000 evaporated, and the bitcoin price went into a free-fall. Personally, I stayed up all night looking at news, opinion, technical analysis, and the on-chain behavior of whales. I decided I needed to sell most of my bitcoin, even if it was just until the war was over. I gulped hard and started putting sell orders on two-thirds of my entire bitcoin holdings (both my exchanges and my bank wondered why so much money was moving at once). It was the right move. I sold my bitcoin at an average of $5,400 and then repurchased it all a month later at an average of $3,500, keeping all of my bitcoin and taking a sizable amount of cash off the table at the same time. I learned my lesson from the last cycle about having one's cake and eating it, too, but this time in a compressed time frame of a market panic.

Bitcoin slowly recovered in 2019. Many of you may be aware that I was hacked for $24.7 million of altcoins (the biggest hack ever of an individual) in January 2018. While my lawsuit against AT&T still continues for allowing the hackers to bribe an AT&T retail clerk to electronically transfer control of my phone number and SMS messages over to the hackers more than six years later, I did receive a payment of 562 bitcoin from the ringleader of the gang, Ellis Pinsky, who was fifteen years old at the time of the theft. As part of his deal with authorities to stay out of prison, he paid me in February 2019 at a cycle low price of less than $3,400 per bitcoin. Coconspirator Nicholas Truglia lost a $72 million civil RICO action in California and is now in prison in New York on contempt charges for not paying me $20.4 million in restitution as part of a plea bargain in his criminal case.[lxxxi]

The long Bitcoin Winter finally started to see new light from an unlikely source: the global COVID-19 pandemic. When the realization of its magnitude, following many dismissals of its seriousness by then-President Trump ("it will disappear . . . like a miracle"), finally kicked in, bitcoin witnessed a flash crash in March 2020, the same day a similar drop occurred in the stock markets. This quick drop ripped bitcoin back to its last leg of price support, the December 2018 bottom price in the low $3,000s. But this dump was very short-lived (and people with buy orders in that range were ecstatic). The realization set in that the US government would turn on the money printing machines like never before in history to cope with this pandemic, regardless of who won the election later that year. This led to a slow rise in prices up through the Third Bitcoin Halving, May 11, 2020, at $8,700. That's where the Third Bitcoin Cycle concludes, and a new chapter (both in this book and in the history of Bitcoin) begins.

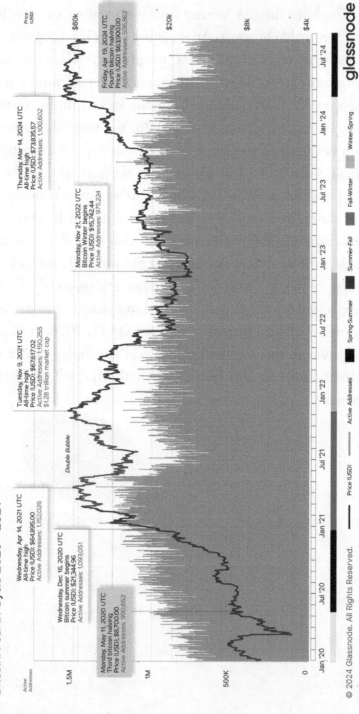

Bitcoin: Fourth Cycle 2020 - 2024

Monday, May 11, 2020 UTC
Third bitcoin halving
Price (USD): $8,700.00
Active Addresses: 990,652

Wednesday, Dec 16, 2020 UTC
Bitcoin summer begins
Price (USD): $21,344.96
Active Addresses: 1,093,051

Wednesday, Apr 14, 2021 UTC
All-time high
Price (USD): $64,895.00
Active Addresses: 1,152,026

Tuesday, Nov 9, 2021 UTC
All-time high
Price (USD): $67617.02
Active Addresses: 1,190,255
$1.28 trillion market cap

Double Bubble

Monday, Nov 21, 2022 UTC
Bitcoin Winter begins
Price (USD): $15,742.44
Active Addresses: 975,224

Thursday, Mar 14, 2024 UTC
All-time high
Price (USD): $73835.57
Active Addresses: 1,100,602

Friday, Apr 19, 2024 UTC
Fourth bitcoin halving
Price (USD): $63,900.00
Active Addresses: 506,862

Active Addresses

1.5M
1M
500K
0

Price (USD)
$60k
$20k
$8k
$4k

Jan '20   Jul '20   Jan '21   Jul '21   Jan '22   Jul '22   Jan '23   Jul '23   Jan '24   Jul '24

Active Addresses   Price (USD)

Spring-Summer   Summer-Fall   Fall-Winter   Winter-Spring

glassnode

Chapter Eight

Money Printing, Macroeconomics, and Memes

Don't fight the Fed.
  —Marty Zweig, legendary stock market investor[lxxxii]

The first panacea for a mismanaged nation is inflation of the currency; the second is war. Both bring a temporary prosperity; both bring a permanent ruin. But both are the refuge of political and economic opportunists.
          —Ernest Hemingway[lxxxiii]

Inflation is taxation without legislation.
          —Milton Friedman[lxxxiv]

One hundred years ago, a nation weary of war and a global pandemic embraced a magnificent new world of modern technology, as radio and the automobile transformed society. The economy boomed. The roaring twenties saw soaring stock market prices, home sales, conspicuous consumption, and a new class of financial elite becoming the envy of the world. Then Black Friday struck, the stock market plummeted, and the world spent a decade in despair. The Great Crash triggered both The Great Depression and the seizing of gold from ordinary citizens. This bleak landscape was only changed when the war drums began beating again in preparation for World War II.[lxxxv]

Our new millennium started its '20s with another worldwide pandemic, whose lockdowns dried up global economic activity and supply chains. Predictably, this stoked civil unrest and social division, followed by major, unpopular wars in the Ukraine and Gaza. Meanwhile, the stock markets hit all-time highs, fueled by Big Tech (seven companies outperforming the rest of the S&P 500) and the promise of rapid economic expansion through AI.

Powering all of this was the printing press—no, not Gutenberg, but the Federal Reserve, led by chairman and chief "inflation whisperer" Jay Clayton. It took the US economy two hundred years to accumulate its first trillion dollars of debt. It only took another thirty to top $10 trillion, shortly after the 2008 crisis that inspired the creation of Bitcoin. In the past fifteen years, the United States added another $25 trillion to its debts for a projected 2024 total of $35 trillion,[lxxxvi] with new debt accumulating at roughly $1 trillion every three months. A meme started in cartoon form, then went viral on YouTube, of Clayton using a money printer like a submachine gun. "Money printer go brrrr" was the message, and it spread.

How did the price of bitcoin react? Like other commodities, Bitcoin fared better and better as the pandemic rolled on. When the "transitory" inflation that resulted from all this free money turned out to be not that transitory after all, the Fed raised interest rates faster than at any time in half a century. Predictably, it slowed down inflation, but at the cost of a housing market slump and a crash in so-called "risk on" assets, such as tech stocks and bitcoin. These macroeconomic cycles once again played out in near-perfect lockstep to the Four Seasons of Bitcoin. Indeed, bad news was largely ignored in the bull market of 2020–2021 and then panicked over in the bear market of 2022–2023. Let's observe:

The Bitcoin Spring of 2020

Using my Four Seasons chart, Bitcoin Winter officially ends on the day of the next Bitcoin halving. Once again, the nadir price of Bitcoin Fall was reached in late December/early January of the year before the halving. The prior cycle's low price of $3,300–3,600 stayed low for more than three months before it began to inch up to the halving price of $8,700 on May 11, rewarding the contrarian buyers with an average return of more than double their money in a little over a year—and a return of twenty times their money in three years.

Similar to the prior two cycles, the road from Bitcoin Spring to Bitcoin Summer saw a slow rise in price, not passing $10,000 until the end of July and then $12,000 per bitcoin by the end of October. The fourth quarter once again was kind to bitcoin price, with the kickoff of Bitcoin Summer taking place in December, with it passing not only the prior all-time high of $19,800 from December 2017 but also the psychological barrier of $20,000 on December 16, 2000.

Bitcoin Summer and the Double Bubble of 2021

Once the fuse was lit at $20k, the price of a single bitcoin went off like a bomb during the holiday season of 2020. Nobody could travel during the first Christmas of the pandemic, so they stayed home, shopped, and gambled. In January 2021, a small army of stock market "degens" following the Reddit group called "Wall Street Bets" pumped GameStop and AMC stocks to astronomic levels. This coordinated online action was in part to punish short sellers (and to save their beloved GameStop), as well as to show the power of community investing. A simpatico asset class to these meme stocks, altcoins also began to soar, including the original meme coin, dogecoin (DOGE). This December 2013 creation, based on a joke and launched at the peak of the first 100x run-up of bitcoin by software engineers Billy Markus and Jackson Palmer, had one million visitors to its website the month it debuted. After a relatively quiet decade following its debut, meme mania helped DOGE run up more than 7,000 percent in the first fifteen weeks of 2021, creating a $50 billion market capitalization, making it the fifth-largest cryptocurrency. Much of this stratospheric gain was largely on the strength of first-time altcoin traders on Robinhood, the millennial-friendly stock market site that pivoted into crypto. Shockingly, Robinhood's Q2 earnings for 2001[lxxxvii] showed that 62 percent of its trades were in doge—more than bitcoin and ethereum combined.

Undistracted (or perhaps powered by) the altcoin frenzy, the price of bitcoin pushed up solidly in the typical parabolic form of Bitcoin Summer, hitting a new all-time high after an all-time high in early January through mid-April:

January 1, 2021	$29,370.85
January 2, 2021	$32,134.92
January 7, 2021	$39,398.68

February 14, 2021	$48,696.54
March 3, 2021	$50,538.24
March 13, 2021	$60,987.48
April 14, 2021	$64,895.00

Part of this was the scarcity effect kicking in again, as it has every single Bitcoin Summer. Once again, the good news was getting accelerated while the unfavorable news was ignored—or positively reinterpreted. The day after the unprecedented January 6th attack on the US Capitol by an angry mob seeking to overturn the presidential election by force, bitcoin prices rose nearly 10 percent. Is COVID-19 getting worse? That's good news for bitcoin if it means more money printing to further debase the dollar and add more speculative cash into the money supply.

The day of the first all-time high in this "double bubble" year (similar to 2013) was April 14th. This was also the perfectly timed debut of Coinbase as a public company, listing on NASDAQ using the stock ticker COIN[lxxxviii] that same day at a $100 billion market capitalization.

Once again, my friend Jim Lowry correctly picked the market top and sold all of his bitcoin. Another piece of positive news giving wind beneath the wings of the bitcoin rally was the number of corporations either stating they were buying bitcoin or even rumored to do so. Michael Saylor began the drumbeat in August 2020, buying 21,454 bitcoin at an average price of approximately $11,500. Widely decried for being irresponsible with his corporate treasury, notably when prices dipped in the bear market of 2022, Saylor has been proven correct in his conviction so far, as his initial investment has gone up sixfold in less than four years and his stock has outperformed tech stock superstar Nvidia and even bitcoin itself during that period.

Saylor also became a vocal proponent of other corporations putting bitcoin on their balance sheets, even going so far as to conduct seminars for them on how to do it in a compliant manner as a public company. When Elon Musk announced that Tesla would accept bitcoin for payment of its cars and that it had acquired bitcoin for its balance sheet in February 2021, it helped move the bitcoin price up toward the giant milestone of $50,000 per bitcoin, which was more than triple where it was just four months earlier.

Yet, as I said at the time, "Elon giveth and Elon taketh away." On May 13, Musk announced that he would stop taking bitcoin until it became "more sustainable" in environmental terms. "We are concerned about rapidly increasing use of fossil fuels for Bitcoin mining and transactions, especially coal, which has the worst emissions of any fuel," Musk wrote. "Cryptocurrency is a good idea but this cannot come at great cost to the environment." The price of bitcoin fell 10 percent after that tweet and dropped as low as $33,500 before the end of the month.[lxxxix] The Bitcoin Fear and Greed Index, based on the stock market Fear and Greed Index created by CNN Money[xc], went from a 95 percent ranking of nearly pure greed into the fear side of the equation in less than a month. By early July, bitcoin was on the verge of breaking below $30k, which would have been a clear signal of a bear market beginning.

Yet, the price stayed above that mark for the rest of the summer; in fact, it began to climb back up. It regained $40k in late July, partially on the news that El Salvador would make bitcoin legal tender. Bitcoin continued to move up steadily in October, just as surely as it had done in the first quarter, ultimately inching past the cycle's prior all-time high from April 14th:

October 1	$43,859.33
October 7	$55,415.01
October 16	$61,809.02
October 20	$64,517.65
October 21	$66,237.52
November 9	$67,617.02

(source: CoinGecko)

Multiple narratives competed to explain the rebound. Was it a double bubble like 2013? Or was it part of an *extended cycle* that wouldn't peak until early 2022? There were almost equal numbers of crypto analysts preaching the extended cycle theory at the time. After all, the first post-halving cycle took only twelve months to reach its all-time high, and the second post-halving cycle took eighteen months. Therefore, it would stand to reason that this third post-halving cycle could take twenty-four months. It was an interesting theory, with a fair amount of data to stand behind it. But it was dead wrong. The traditional cycle ending in the fourth quarter of Bitcoin Summer would prevail once again. "Always remember to sell in December," I warned Jim Cramer at a Street.com debate that focused on digital assets vs. TradFi, or traditional finance. "It's the Bitcoin equivalent of 'sell in May and go away.'"

Amid the excitement were three new narratives for this bull market cycle, each of which had its own unique aspects:

1) decentralized finance, which became known for its abbreviated nickname, DeFi;

2) non-fungible tokens, best known by its acronym, NFTs; and

3) the Metaverse, which took on extra meaning when Big Tech giant Facebook rebranded itself as Meta on October 28, 2021, just days before the Fourth Bitcoin Cycle's all-time high.

These three "change the world" narratives helped power the overall cryptocurrency bull market in 2020–2021. At its peak, non-bitcoin digital assets (Ethereum plus altcoins) exceeded the market capitalization of bitcoin by more than 1.5 to 1. Bitcoin peaked at a $1.28 trillion market cap on November 9th out of a total peak market cap for all cryptocurrency of $3.05 trillion, according to CoinGecko. This did not include NFTs, which in 2021 accounted for $41 billion in primary sales, but statistics on its market capitalization are harder to find, as well as less relevant given the substantially lower liquidity for NFTs, which are one-of-a-kind assets.

Briefly, these three assets helped power the 2020–2021 bull market for all crypto, with bitcoin being the largest beneficiary, at least by market cap (many smaller coins had higher returns, but often lost value more quickly in the bear market).

DeFi Summer

In many ways, the bull market of 2020 was kicked off by the rise of a class of altcoins designed to create yield, a concept that was foreign to bitcoin, gold, and other traditional hard assets. By programming altcoin protocols to let users borrow and lend on-chain (and eventually through a hybrid of on-chain and off-chain models), a new class of crypto was created. At its November 9th peak, DeFi, or decentralized finance as a category of altcoins, was valued at more than $172 billion, up from just $3.7 billion in June 2020, an unbelievable return for a new category of a new asset class.

A token called Compound kicked off the wave, followed by LEND (later rebranded as AAVE), followed by other rocketship tokens like Yearn Finance (YFI), which grew from its initial price of $800 to more than $82,000 per token in less than ten months. Powering these parabolic growth numbers was the new phenomenon of "yield farming," wherein users could move in between protocols (or combine them) looking for the best return on capital. Some protocols automated this or automatically compounded the returns; in some cases, their governance tokens were used to let users vote on the best yield farming methods to deploy the treasury of the token.

It was a fast-moving business model innovation, and the on-chain protocols could avoid the scrutiny of regulators as there was no central entity holding the money; it was simply a protocol where users interacted with one another. While it could be exponentially profitable, it could also be extremely complex to move between these competing protocols to maximize value. One hedge fund manager I've known for twenty years told me he deployed $4 million in 2020 and turned it into $40 million in a year, but it was among the most stressful things he ever invested in. "Every morning, I'd wake up seeming like I made the best returns of my life, then there would be a panic moment where I thought I'd lost everything," he said. Of course, some investors made money by just buying the tokens and not even staking or yield farming them, which was still highly profitable for those top tokens during the parabolic run-up of the category.

Soon, CeFi (centralized finance) companies like Celsius were able to promise even better returns and began to gain market share. Celsius launched in the fall of 2017[xci] at my CoinAgenda Europe conference in Barcelona, as bitcoin prices began to soar. Four years later, they had grown massively, and the price of the Celsius token grew more than 100x between the end of 2018 and May 2021.

As we would later learn from the lessons of Bitcoin Fall, there was too much risk taken on by these centralized entities, leading to their implosions, one after another. Lost in the hair-on-fire witch hunts of 2022 that proclaimed all of DeFi to be an unscrupulous scam was the fact that nobody ever lost a penny from the truly decentralized platforms (other than through hacks of the protocol, which is a different type of risk). As such, Aave, Compound, and YFI are still alive and operating today, with AAVE still having twelve times its billion-dollar market capitalization locked into the protocol. For more on staking and lending, which is still a substantial opportunity for making ordinary income while one is waiting for the longer cycles to play out with asset appreciation, please see Chapter 18.

NFTs, Non-Fungible Tokens

More than anything, I credit the NFT frenzy of 2021 with being responsible for bringing the creative class in touch with crypto for the first time. Degen traders have been gambling on Dogecoin since 2013. However, rank-and-file authors, artists, and musicians were genuinely captivated by the potential for NFTs to bring their work to an entirely new audience using a new medium and at a substantially higher price point.

Suddenly, artists who might have sold a signed limited edition for $500 were pricing their NFT series in the hundreds of thousands of dollars or more. The rapid rise of collections like Crypto Punks and Bored Ape Yacht Club launched thousands of me-too projects. Of particular cultural impact, relatively unknown digital artist Beeple sold a single collection of five thousand photos in NFT form for a record $69 million on March 11, 2021. After Beeple, every artist with even modest ambition became an NFT creator.[xcii]

A few weeks earlier, business school dropout turned star DJ Justin Blau (performing as 3LAU) auctioned off a collection of thirty-three NFTs, which included exclusive rewards like involvement in the writing of a song, for a total of $11.7 million. Never mind that IndieGogo has done these types of rewards for years at much lower price points, the breathless mainstream media helped inflate the bubble, which crashed even harder than fungible tokens did in the coming bear market, with the average NFT down 95 percent at one point.

NFTs will survive as a category, though, given that they are more of a collectibles market, similar to antiques or cars, rather than a traditional investment asset class like gold or bitcoin. I will not address them as an investment category in this book beyond this brief mention.

Metaverse Mania

Facebook's rebranding, coupled with nearly $30 billion of venture capital deployed into trendy, speculative business models around NFT studios with celebrity tie-ins and virtual worlds, with or without headsets, powered a brief wave of short-lived equity investments that, for the most part, completely col-lapsed. A handful of tokens did well during 2020–2021, then fell with the bear market. Those that survived pivoted from a narrative of "metaverse" to one of "Web 3 gaming," as gaming is being seen as a key driver of the 2024–2025 bull market (more on this in Chapter 9).

Right on Cue, Bitcoin Fall Hits Hard in 2022

There has been some debate as to whether the actual all-time high for the Fourth Bitcoin Cycle of 2020–2024 was November 9th or if it was actually April 14th, which had the more typical parabolic run-up. Prominent crypto ana-lyst Benjamin Cowen of the daily YouTube podcast *Into the Cryptoverse* stated he believed the latter was the case, calling the final run-up in November "a dead cat bounce with a wick."[xciii]

Indeed, there would be no third act for this bubble, and the rapid pace of Fed rate increases between March 2021 and July 2022 (a record eleven rate hikes totaling 5 percent) sucked the liquidity out of the economy as quickly as "Quantitative Easing" had sloshed it in. Nonetheless, it usually takes a few more dances at the start of a bear market to recognize that the music has stopped. The price of bitcoin rose slightly from January 1 through March 31, posting a 1.6 percent gain for the quarter, albeit with several dips on its way to perhaps the true "dead cat bounce." It's interesting to see that every parabolic bull run after the first halving had a corresponding bounce within thirty to sixty days after the high, often followed by a last-chance rally before the actual bear market set in. Amateur traders see this as a sign that the rally is continuing and double down at the exact wrong time. Experienced traders should see this as the last chance to exit the cycle, having improperly predicted the actual all-time high. For more detailed information on this and other common characteristics between the cycles during Bitcoin Fall, please refer to Chapter 12.

Once it kicks into full gear, Bitcoin Fall always includes a rapid change of direction, from up to down, from hopeful to doubtful, and from Greed to Fear. With the change of seasons comes the shift in the interpretation of news and views. Let's revisit my News Relativity Paradigm. Instead of prices rising as each rumor of new bitcoin adoption takes place, prices begin to fall with news of regulatory action, price drops, and eventually bankruptcies.

It should not be surprising that so much bad news always happens during Bitcoin Fall of each cycle. First, the impact of bad news is greater in a falling market. But there's a factual basis as well. Fraudsters and those who just gambled a little too much can get completely wrecked in a bear market, whereas they could look like winners in a bull market since they were often richly rewarded for overspeculating. "You don't find out who's been swimming naked," said legendary investor Warren Buffett in his 1994 letter to Berkshire Hathaway stockholders, "until the tide goes out."[xciv]

Case in point: Three Arrows Capital. 3AC, as they were known, was a young, upstart hedge fund whose motto was "Only up." Other entrepreneurs who were lavishly rewarded with multibillion-dollar valuations and a sudden onset of extreme personal wealth included:

- Do Kwon, founder of the algorithmic stablecoin pair Terra and Luna;

- Alex Mashinsky, whose off-chain staking and lending programs included a rewards token as part of its unsustainably high interest rate, which in turn led to a 100x increase in the value of the Celsius token;
- Barry Silbert, whose vast crypto empire included what is today the largest bitcoin ETF and the top crypto media company at the time, CoinDesk, came unglued over the failure of its overleveraged lending company, Genesis; and
- Sam Bankman-Fried of FTX, the ultimate boy-wonder billionaire turned convicted felon.

I will provide more detail on these similar but different lessons in irresponsible leverage later in the chapter.

Regarding the News Relativity Paradigm, the tide had yet to turn by March 31st. There was still much bullishness to find in terms of new "Layer Two" protocols and the hope by some that a third market top (the first "triple bubble") would emerge due to the theory of expanding cycles. So far, this has not been the case. Diminishing returns have been proven each cycle, but having each cycle last longer was disproven during this cycle. Once again, the all-time high was achieved in November/December rather than the following April/May.

There were enough believers in the triple bubble theory (I was involved in a few debates about this at the time) that markets were still somewhat hopeful for the bulk of Q1 2022, despite the negative macro overtones coming from inflation, interest rate hikes, the war between Russia and Ukraine, and new tensions with China. Yet, the cycle had turned, and very few sophisticated investors were dollar-cost averaging into bitcoin or other cryptos.

That said, as long as Bitcoin's price was over $40,000, there was no need to panic; after all, it had only first reached $20,000 in late 2020. However, the Four Seasons cycle theory dictates there should have been apprehension that panic could be right around the corner.

The first shoe to drop was Terra Luna. Brash, young Korean entrepreneur Do Kwon believed he had just built the best new digital asset since Tether, perhaps since Bitcoin. It was an algorithmic stablecoin whose ability to trade at a stable price (e.g., one US dollar) was programmed instead of being traditionally backed by assets. The first innovation in this manner was MakerDAO, which partially backed a stablecoin called DAI with Ethereum, then over-collaterized it for loans and yield. Terra Luna also had a two-token system, but the collateralization was one of its own tokens, LUNA, which had a fluctuating price based on demand. Its market capitalization supported the fixed-price Terra (UST) stablecoin, which heightened the risk should there be a run on the bank based on a collapse in the value of Terra.

The rise of LUNA was impressive. In the year between April 1, 2020, and April 3, 2021, the price of LUNA rose from 17 cents to $118, more than 600x. Legendary crypto VC and hedge fund manager Mike Novogratz was so bullish on LUNA that he tattooed it on his bicep. It was one of the great darlings of the "only up" bull market, reaching an eventual market cap of over $40 billion and top-ten ranking among all coins. As it increased, LUNA's market cap became additional collateral to support UST staying at one dollar. The problem with purely algorithmic coins is when there's a bank run. I helped one of the earliest algorithmic stablecoins, Corion, go to market in 2016. It had an algorithm that minted more tokens as the price got too high and burned them as the price dropped. The problem I saw was that in a market panic, one couldn't burn past zero, and I advised the team accordingly. They felt they had it in control (as did Do Kwon and Luna). However, Corion depegged and went to essentially zero. And so, after rapidly reaching great heights, Luna, like the Greek mythological figure Icarus, quickly crashed back to earth.

The mechanics of the Luna meltdown are still a little hazy. There are tales of traditional Wall Street short sellers too tempted by its overvaluation, knowing that shorting the UST token had a limited downside, as it could only go as high as a dollar. Still, if it genuinely depegged, the profits would be tremendous as it dropped toward zero. The other side of the trade had to cover the difference. That is precisely what unfolded in May 2022, quickly wiping out $45 billion in market capitalization between the two assets. In addition, there was a contagion of funds borrowed or staked on the related Anchor protocol, which paid a hefty 19.45 percent interest rate, issued mainly from Luna's excess reserves. This double-dipping led others to refer to Luna as a "ginormous Ponzi scheme."[xcv]

This quick destabilization of the crypto market, even though it had almost nothing to do with bitcoin itself, quickly dropped the price of bitcoin from above $40,000 to below $30,000 in less than a week. Suddenly, the bear market was here, with a vengeance. The price stabilized slightly above $30,000 for much of the following month until the next shock came.

On June 12, Celsius, which had $12 billion of assets under management and an $8 billion valuation for its Celsius token, "temporarily" paused withdrawals in an after-hours message that I recall reading in real-time. My first thought was to sell most of my remaining bitcoin and repurchase it later when the market recovered, as I did in late 2018. It was the right move, although unlike 2018, I did not act quickly enough and instead waited out the bear market with the bitcoin I hadn't already sold at bull market prices. The Celsius pause of withdrawals rapidly led to its July bankruptcy and a shell-shocked crypto market dumped below $20,000. It then stayed in the deep bear market territory for the next nine months before it climbed back to $25,000 in mid-March 2023. Yet, the worst was yet to come.[xcvi]

Sam Bankman-Fried[xcvii] was an unlikely poster child for the bitcoin bull market. Son of prominent Stanford Law School professors, the well-educated former Wall Street short seller became an overnight billionaire despite his disheveled appearance, cult-like organization, and well-publicized intention to give all of his billions to social causes through a form of aggressive "the end justifies the means" philosophy called effective altruism. He even became a darling of the regulators, perhaps in no small part due to his personal contributions of $9 million to Joe Biden and other well-connected Democratic politicians.

Almost magically, he built the world's second-largest crypto exchange in the Bahamas, backed by leading American VCs like Sequoia Capital and Andreesen-Horowitz. Shockingly, these top VCs did not take board seats for their multimillion-dollar investments and seemed to know very little about the inner workings of the company's now highly questionable finances.

The end came quickly when SBF, as he was known, tried to bite the hand that put him in business. Changpeng Zhao, known universally as CZ, is the most successful entrepreneur in the history of crypto, building the Binance crypto exchange through a 2017 ICO into a behemoth that grosses $10 billion a year. He also owned the majority of its network token, BNB, a $90 billion digital asset that also became one of the first Layer One competitors[xcviii] (i.e., clones) of Ethereum. Binance provided seed funding for FTX, but by 2022, SBF had begun a campaign to create a regulatory capture moat between FTX and the rest of the industry, painting Binance in a bad light. CZ, already suspicious of the way FTX used its own network token, FTT, as collateral on highly leveraged deals through its sister company, Alameda Research, issued a tweet that led to the unwinding of the company's unsustainable high-wire act:

> As part of Binance's exit from FTX equity last year, Binance received roughly $2.1 billion USD equivalent in cash (BUSD and FTT). Due to recent revelations that have came to light, we have decided to liquidate any remaining FTT on our books.
> —@cz_binance, November 6, 2022[xcix]

Within four days, FTX was on life support, and the price of bitcoin dropped sharply again, this time to a cycle low of $15,742.44, a stunning drop of more than two-thirds since the end of March and more than 77 percent off the all-time high of almost exactly a year prior.[c] It was half the price of the day Celsius tweeted about its "temporary" withdrawal ban at the start of the summer. This was the "blood in the streets" moment of capitulation, but very few buyers, including whales, were brave enough to step in just yet. In retrospect, investing that day would have led to a 5x return in fifteen months, but it wasn't clear yet that there wasn't more blood to come first.

Contrarian Bitcoin Winter Buyers Stop the Bleeding in 2023

Short sellers began the year speculating that Bitcoin could drop below $10,000, possibly even reaching as low as $5,000, bringing it back to its 2019 price levels. Dropping below the 300-week simple moving average (SMA) never happened in the history of crypto—and when it dropped below the 200-week SMA, it was always the best time to buy.

For now, the regulators and lawmakers who had gladly taken donations from SBF were running away from the association as fast as they could (albeit not returning the campaign donations). Stoking the fire, CNBC pundit and *Mad Money* host Jim Cramer added to the negative sentiment: "The truth is, it's never too late to sell an awful position, and that's what you have if you own these so-called digital assets," he advised at the very bottom of the market.[ci]

Many in crypto saw that as the time to start buying. I did, although my bigger signal was the collapse of Genesis. When it filed for bankruptcy protection on January 19, 2023, with more than 100,000 creditors and total debt of up to $11 billion, one would have expected a further drop in the bitcoin price. Instead, the price, which had already risen 25 percent from the bottom a few weeks earlier, rose slightly to $21,081.67. Why? It's because there were no sellers left. If you didn't sell after Terra Luna, after Celsius, after FTX, you were in bitcoin for the long haul. About a week earlier, when the price rebounded to $18,000 after spending nearly two months below that mark, I observed old whale wallets opening up to buy. I had whale friends tell me they had just made their largest-ever purchase of bitcoin. The coast was clear if you knew the signals. We will discuss this on-chain analysis throughout the following few chapters.

The remainder of 2023 played out much like prior winters, despite the mainstream media narrative that the asset class was dead or being outlawed. The Biden administration, led by Senator Elizabeth Warren and her "anti-crypto" army, seemed to be united in an attempt to score political points as protectors of the little guy, when it was clear to most crypto advocates they were mainly protecting the banks. Laws were proposed (and fought by the Republicans) to make self-custody of one's own digital assets regulated under traditional banking laws, effectively making everyone responsible for being a money services business, even if they are just buying a cup of coffee with bitcoin. Laws were passed in various states and proposed to shut down or highly tax bitcoin mining federally.

One of the most misguided attempts to cripple the crypto industry was Operation Chokepoint 2.0, a variation of prior government efforts to strip the right to use a bank for industries that were completely legal but unpopular with the party in power, without passing any new laws. This multiagency effort had been used in prior years to attack the online gaming, pornography, and gun industries. Now, Elizabeth Warren's "Potemkin army" (as Erik Voorhees cleverly dubbed it in his keynote at the Coin Center gala during Consensus 2024) had descended upon crypto with a similar plan.

In March 2023, only a handful of regional banks focused on serving the needs of the blockchain industry. Silicon Valley Bank (SVB) was the leading bank for tech startups in the Bay Area for decades, given its history as a venture bank that extended the runway of funded startups with a small amount of debt as a cushion. Signal Bank had a strong balance sheet, mainly operating with real estate and traditional loans. Signature Bank was a West Coast bank that, at one point, banked a majority of cryptocurrency firms. These banks were targeted as crypto-friendly and shut down by regulators because of alleged risk.

But instead of killing off crypto, it showed the inherent instability in the banking system itself. When SVB was shuttered, Treasury Secretary Janet Yellen initially said that all insured deposits would be safe. However, SVB had billions of dollars in high-tech company accounts, well above the FDIC level of $250,000. Public company Roku alone had $487 million on account. After a panicked weekend, when there was a run on the bank at other regional banks, Yellen said that the Fed would back all of these deposits. Given the fact that there were nearly $20 trillion of deposits in US banks at the time but less than $120 billion in FDIC insurance (less than 1 percent), it sounded to many like "FDIC Infinity," as the total deposits equaled 80 percent of the nation's entire GDP.

For its part, bitcoin went up nearly 40 percent within a week of the SVB collapse, moving up from $20,521.56 on March 12 to $28,262.24 on March 19. It would never look back from there, with $25,000 supporting the rest of Bitcoin Winter, which ended in a historical form in March 2024 with a new all-time high. The bitcoin price first exceeded $68,000 on March 4th and then posted another new all-time high of

$73,835.57 on March 14th. These events marked the end of Bitcoin Winter uniquely to date, as it achieved a new all-time high more than a month before the halving. Did this mean that Bitcoin Summer preceded Bitcoin Spring? I say no, because March 14, 2024, was still part of the fourth Bitcoin Cycle as the halving had not yet occurred. Bitcoin Summer will now happen when this new all-time-high price is surpassed after the halving.

I will explain these dynamics in the next chapter, Chapter 9, starting with the vital role of the Bitcoin ETF, which is mostly (albeit not entirely) responsible for this dynamic.

Chapter Nine

Bitcoin Becomes Scarcer than Gold (2024-2028)

In the absence of the gold standard, there is no way to protect savings from confiscation through inflation. There is no safe store of value.
—Alan Greenspan, *Gold and Economic Freedom*
(1966)[cii]

We have gold because we cannot trust governments.
—Herbert Hoover[ciii]

The Internet allows any two individuals to transfer data without permission from any central authority. Bitcoin does the same for value.
—Naval Ravikant[civ]

As detailed in Chapter 2, the early history of cryptocurrency included a parade of ideas, philosophies, experiments, and white papers about how to mathematically create digital gold. Unlike the alchemists of ancient times, the cypherpunks used math and code as their crucible. Nick Szabo even called his system, which was theorized but never built, Bit Gold. In his own white paper, which is entirely reprinted with my annotations in Chapter 4, Satoshi Nakamoto explained the parallels involved in mining scarce gold and using proof of work to "mine" programmatically scarce bitcoin.

We are now more than fifteen years beyond the Genesis Block, and nearly 94 percent of all the bitcoin that will ever exist has been mined. The remaining 6 percent will take more than one hundred years to complete the supply of 21 million bitcoins, each divisible into 100,000,000 parts, called "satoshis."

Gold, which for more than six thousand years has taken on the role of being the only universally agreed-upon asset to back or be readily exchanged for other currencies, has an estimated total current supply of 212,582 metric tons. Unlike bitcoin, this is an estimate, and there may be tens of thousands of tons of gold statues, coins, and jewelry from antiquity buried under the sands of time or secretly stored in private hands. Gold may exist on other planets or asteroids, lending the possibility of dilution if a large supply came to market. Thus far, there have been no successful attempts to artificially engineer gold out of baser elements, despite centuries of attempts, although diamonds and pearls have had their markets radically disrupted in recent years when technology replicated natural diamonds and pearls with physically identical creations at a much lower cost.

For now, gold is not only scarce, it is undeniably valuable. This is despite a campaign of more than fifty years to remove it as backing from every national currency on earth, marking the first time in history that the entire world is run by governments backed only by the "full faith" in the intrinsic value of their government's ability to pay its debts.

Of the current global gold supply, according to the World Gold Council estimates in February, 2024, 45 percent is in the form of jewelry, 22 percent is privately held as an investment in gold bars or coins, and 17 percent is held by the world's central banks, with the remaining 15 percent allocated to industrial and other uses. This supply grows yearly through the gold mining industry, but at a fairly consistent rate. In 2018, a record 3,656 metric tons were mined. In 2023, total gold production approached that record, with 3,644 metric tons mined. The top nations mining are China, Russia, and Australia.[cv]

In *The Bitcoin Standard*, Saifedean Ammous[cvi] proposed the stock-to-flow ratio (amount of new issuance divided by the total supply, i.e., the asset's annual inflation rate) as a guide to relative scarcity in comparing assets considered for use as money. Copper is easy to mine, so it would rank low on this scale. Gold is increasingly challenging to mine profitably every year, and it is estimated that annual production will begin to decline by 2050 unless new technologies come about to make it more feasible to reach hard-to-find veins deep in the earth or in treacherous climates such as Antarctica.

Suffice it to say that Bitcoin has its stock-to-flow ratios locked in for 140 years with no new technologies possible to find new bitcoin, as they are embedded in immutable code. The decrease in new supply every four years was described by AngelList founder Naval Ravikant at CoinSummit in 2015 as "the perfect pyramid scheme—not Ponzi scheme, pyramid scheme" due to early adopters being the most enriched. Pseudonymous blogger PlanB, a Dutch investor and analyst, has made a career out of creating a variety of models based on Ammous' stock-to-flow model to predict the price of bitcoin since 2018, calling them S2F, S2F2, etc. They've had a mixed record of success but have been correct more than wrong. They all end with bitcoin priced in the millions of dollars apiece within the next few decades.

With bitcoin, its first-year inflation was 100 percent, as there was no prior bitcoin. By the first halving, its annual inflation rate would drop overnight from 25 percent to 12.5 percent and get into single digits by the next halving. Prior to the most recent halving in April 2024, the annual inflation rate of bitcoin had already dropped to the approximate level of gold (1.71 percent for gold in 2023 vs. 1.94 percent for bit-coin). On the day of the 2024 halving, the miner reward was reduced from 900 bitcoin per day to 450, making the annual inflation just 0.825 percent—less than half the current annual inflation of gold.

The price of gold has been on fire thus far in 2024 due to the same concerns that power bitcoin growth, at one point reaching its all-time high price of $2,420 per ounce. This may serve to accelerate production, although it is a slow industry to add capacity. Like Bitcoin, gold investors are concerned about countering fiat currency risks of inflation, money print-ing, out-of-control government spending, and the threat of economic and social instability.

This will be the first cycle that bitcoin is scarcer than gold in terms of new supply—more than double the scarcity. With each new halving, this disparity will become more pronounced, with the 2032 cycle beginning with bitcoin almost ten times as scarce as gold on an annual basis. Presuming demand in eight years is equal to or higher than today, basic economics dictates that the price will rise. It is my belief that in addition to the fixed dynamics of supply, summarized above, and the seasonal price fluctuations around investor psychology for each new four-year cycle, a new dynamic of accelerated adoption and therefore demand will kick in this cycle and play out over the coming three cycles. This Bitcoin Supercycle will be discussed in Chapter 14. Now let's return to the current cycle, which, as of the writing of this book, has just begun.

2024 and the Dawn of the Bitcoin ETF

Passage of an Exchange-Traded Fund (ETF) for bitcoin has been a long-awaited event since it was first proposed by Gemini exchange billionaire cofounders Tyler and Cameron Winklevoss, in July 2013, when the price of bitcoin was still under $100 per bitcoin. It would take another eleven years, and the political pressure put on by large traditional finance groups like Fidelity and BlackRock, to get it passed.[cvii]

The hope was always that the ETF would make bitcoin an established Wall Street asset class, taking it out of the gray area of assets that a registered investment advisor cannot even discuss with a client. On June 15, 2023, BlackRock filed for a bitcoin ETF. BlackRock, under the leadership of politically powerful Wall Street icon Larry Fink, is the largest asset manager on Wall Street by a sizable degree, with more than $10 trillion of assets under management. It is also the company that popularized the ETF, buying that division from Barclays with Peter Knez at the helm and making him the CIO for BlackRock. In subsequent years, BlackRock received approvals on more than six hundred ETF applications, with only one rejection. Things were finally looking good for a bitcoin ETF, despite a reticence by SEC chairman Gary Gensler to approve anything crypto-related within recent memory of FTX.

Bitcoin price responded well to the announcement, albeit slowly. It was $25,107.74 on the date it was announced, running up to $31,134.71 by July 4th. It would end the year 2023 at $42,220,[cviii] completing the Bitcoin Winter turnaround that surprises investors every cycle. Nine more firms with solid Wall Street credentials filed for bitcoin ETF approval, including Fidelity, Franklin Templeton, and ARK Shares. Greyscale, which has been turned down repeatedly in prior cycles, also kept up the pressure to convert its existing Bitcoin Trust into an ETF.

With the new halving in sight, hopes were high that at least one bitcoin ETF would be approved in either the January or March windows for such an approval. As it turned out, the rumor was a stronger driver than the news, and as the SEC approved all eleven bitcoin ETFs on January 10, 2024, the price of bitcoin slightly dropped to $46,105. Traditional Wall Street pundits claimed it was a "sell the news" event, while Pantera Capital managing director Dan Morehead, whose popular newsletters have been very accurate going back to 2013 at predicting future bitcoin trends, countered with his own message: "Buy the rumor, buy the news," he wrote just prior to the approval.[cix]

Once trading started, it seems an industry was formed to analyze the daily buying by the ten Wall Street ETF firms, then subtracting the outflows of Greyscale's converted bitcoin trust ETF called GBTC. The reason for the outflows is generally believed to relate to the high fees of GBTC, six times the amount of its competitors. There is a legacy reason for this, as the publicly traded bitcoin trust was one of its kind in the market prior to the ETF approvals, and for a period of time, it was priced below the price of bitcoin. This didn't stop bears from opining that the outflows were because bitcoin was overvalued and investors were panic selling. One day, when BlackRock did not register any sales, the price of bitcoin dropped as though one day made a trend.

As the date of the fourth halving drew closer, various analysts pointed out the basic math that ETF inflows on most days substantially exceeded new bitcoins mined by more than five to one. After the halving, that could become ten to one. The bullish presentations finally had an impact on investors, and the prices started moving from a brief stay under $40,000 in January to new all-time highs in March:

January 23, 2024	$39,504.73
February 13, 2024	$50,500.14
February 28, 2024	$57,003.53
February 29, 2024	$62,558.58
March 5, 2024	$66,186.65 (new high)
March 14, 2024	$73,835.57 (new high)

That March rally introduced a never-before-seen phenomenon in the history of Bitcoin: a new all-time high for an upcoming cycle prior to the Bitcoin halving. Does this invalidate my Four Season model? Or, as I will suggest, does it leave room for a Supercycle variance when demand exceeds new supply by a level that disrupts price beyond the normal diminishing returns?

Let me explain:

In the first cycle, supply was gigantic (ten million of the twenty-one million bitcoins that would ever exist were mined by the end of the first cycle), but demand was small. For the first year, there were no sales other than a single transaction of

5,050 bitcoin for $5. By the end of 2010, with nearly one-quarter of the potential bitcoin already mined, there were still no true exchanges, and the first fiat transaction was for a pizza that cost the buyer ten thousand bitcoins, through an intermediary. It wasn't until 2011 that entrepreneurs and evangelists got involved in helping build out the system.

According to Glassnode,[cx] there were only seven active bitcoin wallets by February 2010, increasing to 29,187 by the time bitcoin had its first parabolic run-up to $30 in June 2011. From there, it grew to 182,763 by December 3, 2013. With the advent of centralized exchanges in every nation, unique addresses are no longer the most reliable indicator of growth. Crypto.com, for example, claims to have one hundred million customers by itself and estimates the number of global cryptocurrency users to be 580 million, an increase of 34 percent since 2023.

When familiarity and involvement reach the hundreds of millions of users, each of whom will eventually strive to own more bitcoin, then a different paradigm begins to take shape. The fact remains that if each of the 23.4 million households in the United States has a net worth of more than $1 million wanted to own just one bitcoin apiece, there would not be enough supply. In addition, there are another thirty-two million millionaires in the rest of the world.

For this and other reasons, I am not a proponent of the "end-of-cycles" philosophy that was widely discussed during the most recent halving.

> *The narrative for this cycle is "this is the last cycle."*
> —@naval on X, March 13, 2024[cxi]

This new narrative most often states that the introduction of traditional finance into the world of crypto means an end to the influence of early adopters who care about keeping their own custody. Why bother with all of those annoying devices if a trusted entity like BlackRock or Fidelity can do all the work for you? While I agree that the bitcoin ETF, newly approved Ethereum ETF, and other crypto ETFs to come will become popular investment products for mainstream Americans with registered investment advisors, 401(k)s, and IRAs due to regulatory clarity and transactional simplicity (you can buy it through your Schwab account), it defeats the purpose of Satoshi's innovation. Bitcoin was not created so that fifteen years later, it could be taken over by the very Wall Street investment banks that caused the Great Recession and other financial woes that Bitcoin was created to avoid.

This does not mean that ETFs won't be hugely successful. I do believe it is a key component in getting the 8 percent of a population typically required to switch behaviors (those magical moments when all of your neighbors were rushing out to buy their first color television, mobile phone, pocket calculator, desktop PC, iPhone, or Wi-Fi service). History shows that once early adopters have paved the way, the early mainstream feels safe to enter—generally when the new technology has been simplified and its barrier to entry, either financially or in ease of use, has been lowered.

However, the Four Seasons will survive for at least a few cycles because of the current holders of bitcoin. At present, less than 1 percent of all bitcoin is held by ETFs. For it to grow into double digits, it would require more than two million bitcoins to be sold. Those bitcoins are currently held largely by long-term holders. Long-term holders care about the amount of bitcoin they own, whereas the majority of new ETF buyers care about the amount of fiat currency as their yardstick for success. The fiat equivalent market cap for ETFs could go up ten times with only double the amount of new bitcoin if the price rises five times. I believe we can expect this narrative to play out over the next three cycles.

Projections for the 2024–2025 Bull Market

All models are wrong, but some are useful.
—George E. P. Box, world-renowned statistician[cxii]

I do not have a crystal ball, and I know I could be dead wrong on everything I predict here, no matter how many data points I have to back them up. But I would like to lay out my current best analysis for the direction I believe the Fifth Bitcoin Cycle may take.

It's Going to Be a Long Bitcoin Summer . . . Or Is It?

This will be the first binary question about the Fifth Bitcoin Cycle: Because a new all-time high occurred prior to the halving, will the new cycle end sooner? Crypto analyst and *Into the Cryptoverse* CEO Benjamin Cowan began to circulate the idea of a "left-translated cycle" that would finish early because it started early, later clarifying that it might return to a more normal cycle timing depending upon how quickly interest rate cuts occurred.

I believe that Bitcoin Summer will start only after the Fourth Bitcoin Cycle all-time high of $73,835.56 has been surpassed after the halving. Four years ago, it took seven months after the halving to push past the prior cycle's high. If the next Bitcoin Summer took place seven months after the halving, Bitcoin Summer would take place in mid-November 2024.

Once again, we have a halving take place during the US presidential elections. I believe this was programmed intentionally by Satoshi, knowing that election years are generally good for economic news (2008 being the exception), as the prevailing party looking to stay in power will push whatever positive interpretation of the data it can manipulate to get elected. Thus far, elections only had a significant impact on price once. That was in January 2021 when the January 6th revolt took place, determined to overturn the congressionally validated election of Joe Biden. It was a uniquely chaotic time in American politics, and bitcoin prices rose quickly as a safe haven within that instability.

This fall, we are facing the "rubber match" between Donald Trump and a Democratic contender, having won narrowly against Hillary Clinton to become president in 2016, then losing narrowly (and never admitting defeat) to Joe Biden in 2020. The presumed rematch against Biden was upended by a July switch of candidates to Kamala Harris after Biden announced he would not seek reelection, following a disastrous debate performance where his mental fitness to run a long campaign, much less the nation, came into question. This election also included the first viable third-party candidate in decades, Robert F. Kennedy Jr., who eventually suspended his campaign and now supports Donald Trump. Both Trump and

RKF Jr., have embraced cryptocurrency as an industry where America should be a leader. Should Biden replacement candidate Harris lose the election to Donald Trump, the price of bitcoin will likely go on a tear, with the kind of parabolic run-up it often sees during bull markets, especially when it is bolstered by good news.

The starting price is too high this cycle to have a 100x run like 2013, a 30x run like 2017, or probably even an 8x run like 2021. My long-standing projection was for it to go three times the halving price, which clocked in at $63,851. That would imply a terminal all-time high for the cycle of $191,553. Several psychological hurdles need to be met to reach that price, the first being $100,000, which is one-tenth of the way to the long-held hodler's dream of the million-dollar bitcoin. Prior 10x landmarks were met with both fanfare and quick price appreciation beyond that range, only to fall back again. In the first "double bubble" bull market of 2013, the price of bitcoin accelerated from $11 in January to $100 in March, then $1,000 in November, on its way to the cusp of $1,200 before the bear market settled in. In 2017, the price regained $1,000 in February and eclipsed $10,000 in October on its way to $19,800 in December.

The $100,000 narrative, complete with laser eyes on Twitter profiles (I had mine), fell short by a solid 30 percent in 2021 as there was just too much resistance. Macroeconomic factors prevented even the 10x halving scenario to $87k I projected.

This time around, it will be very bearish for the asset class if it does not surpass $100,000, given that would be only 1.5 times the halving price. I can see the price staying relatively flat during the summer months, bouncing around between

$50k and $79k before finally breaking the psychological barrier of $80,000 in October on its way to achieving $100,000 bitcoin in either December 2024 or January 2025.

From there, one scenario sees the price keep rising until it meets a final resistance it cannot break, e.g., $200,000. This run-up might be powered by a new administration that is friendly to bitcoin and a series of lowered interest rates.

From there, I see a double bubble as a strong possibility, with a long pause where prices drop back to the $100k resistance level (or lower), but start heading up again in October 2025 on positive news of more interest rate cuts, sovereign wealth funds buying bitcoin, ETFs hitting record levels and/or a variety of positive news that gets amplified during a bull market. This could finally push the November/December 2025 price past the $200k hurdle, but as it brings in fresh retail investors looking for million-dollar bitcoin, the whales begin to exit on new liquidity as the all-time high fizzles out around $220–240k.

A Gentler Bear Market?

Whenever I hear any pundit write about a new technology being so spectacular that it will end the need for market cycles, I run.

I recall a *Los Angeles Times* opinion piece in late 2000 refuting the popular opinion that the internet had solved the need for business cycles and that going forward, it would regulate economic value in a manner that was gently always moving up with no need for crashes.[cxiii] On cue, market forces did the exact opposite, destroying the internet-heavy NASDAQ index, which had just run up to an all-time high of 5,000 in March 2000. By the time the dot-com crash hit its bottom, the burnt embers of NASDAQ had simmered back to around 1,100, with highfliers like Amazon.com hanging on by a thread at under $5 a share.

In my opinion, technological advances and clever business model innovation will never fully offset human fear and greed, which are among our oldest, primary survival instincts. As long as that remains true, we will have business cycles. As bitcoin and the rest of the cryptocurrency markets become more mature, they will act more like gold or equities, with low double-digit annual gains or losses being the highest extremes. We have already seen a tremendous drop in returns per cycle on both a halving-to-high and "cycle low to next cycle high" basis. It's interesting that the drop in returns has been exponential, but the decrease in losses has only been linear:

Bitcoin Cycle	Gains (cycle low to next cycle high)	Gains (halving to high)	Losses (high to cycle low)
Cycle One: 2009–2012	300,000%	N/A (no halving)	96.7%
Cycle Two: 2012-2016	110,600%	9,080%	85.1%
Cycle Three: 2016–2020	14,237%	2,858%	83.4%
Cycle Four: 2020–2024	1,928%	663%	77.0%
Cycle Five: 2024–2028 (projected)	1,150%	200%	72%

Under this model, I see a classic bear market kicking in after the eventual all-time high, most likely at the end of 2025. In 2026, fear spreads that $200,000 bitcoin is overvalued. On cue, Peter Schiff and Dr. Doom will come out and say bitcoin has no value whatsoever. ETF outflows will begin, as nervous retail investors move into gold or AI stocks after reading something on X (perhaps from Elon himself) that convinces them that bitcoin is indeed crashing, which is generally a self-fulfilling prophecy during the bear market phase. The actual bad news that causes my predicted 72 percent capitulation event doesn't really matter. It could be a new centralized scam or bankruptcy that's utterly unrelated to the way bitcoin works, but it serves as contagion for the reputation of bitcoin and crypto. Jim Cramer will come on the air and tell everyone it's not too late to sell their bad investment in digital assets again. I see a floor in the $65,000 range, nearly retracing all the way back to the prior halving.

Once again, this will set up a great buying opportunity for Cycle Six, where I could see a halving price well over $125,000 and a new all-time high approaching $300k. We still have a few cycles to go before bitcoin eclipses the market capitalization of gold, which is currently $14.66 trillion, but it should get there well before the year 2140 when the final bitcoin is mined.

In the next chapters, I will review how to identify and act in each of the Four Seasons of Bitcoin, and then I will discuss more technical aspects of keeping on track with your investments throughout the coming Bitcoin Supercycle, which I see lasting at least twelve years before it begins to act like a mature, slower growth financial asset class.

I plan to regularly update my opinions on a blog I created specifically for this book, www.bitcoinsupercycle.org. You can also sign up for a free newsletter on the site for updates on the model and its performance. Visit the site to stay informed and receive your free updates.

Two observations from the first four cycles nearing completion have proved to be true (or at least true so far):

First is the law of diminishing returns. In general, the returns of any asset class will be lower as the so-called "law of large numbers" kicks in, e.g., it's much harder to double one's money when the market cap is $10 billion than when it's $10 million. This has been true for the first three cycles, and the consistency of the rate of those diminishing returns is at the heart of my Four Seasons cycle calculations.

Second is the consistency of seasonality. There has been a small window (less than 90 days) at the end of the year after the halving—and always in Q4—that the all-time high price of the cycle occurs. After that bubble pops, it has always been a similarly narrow window, 12–15 months later, where the market capitulates from its year of falling prices (always in the third year of the cycle).

We now have a fresh cycle to challenge both of these narratives—or to extend them. My principal advice is to be aware of these important trends and to make your buying and selling decisions around them. It will be clear as the time approaches whether they are continuing—or if a new paradigm has taken hold.

Book Three

The Four Seasons
of Bitcoin

Chapter Ten

Bitcoin Spring

No winter lasts forever; no spring skips its turn.
—Hal Borland[cxiv]

It is only the farmer who faithfully plants seeds in the Spring, who reaps a harvest in the Autumn.
—B. C. Forbes[cxv]

I trust in nature for the stable laws of beauty and utility. Spring shall plant and autumn garner to the end of time.
—Robert Browning[cxvi]

Simply put, Bitcoin Spring begins the day the "seed" of the next Bitcoin halving is planted, issuing in a new Bitcoin Cycle. While these cycles are intended to play out roughly every four years, they are based on a set number of 210,000 bitcoin blocks created in sequence.[cxvii] If each block issued one bitcoin, there would have been one hundred cycles spanning roughly four hundred years. But Satoshi designed the miner incentive system to reward the earliest supporters with a disproportionate reward for their early adoption and loyalty.

Miner rewards are given in each block to the miner who solves a mathematical equation. Over time, these equations have become increasingly difficult so that the computing power required to solve them is sufficient to protect the network from an attack. The larger the value of bitcoin grows, the higher the incentive to attack the network in order to steal or misdirect bitcoins. For most of 2009–2010, that difficulty was at level one, ramping up quickly after GPU mining became popular. As of the writing of this book, that level is now more than 90 trillion, making it 90 trillion times harder to "solve the block" (i.e., solve the mathematical equation required by the hash and add the now completed block to the blockchain). The miner who solves the block receives the entire reward, which, as we enter the Fifth Bitcoin Cycle, is one-16th the original reward (3.125 bitcoins per block vs. 50 bitcoins for blocks mined before the first halving). Due to this astronomical level of difficulty, there are no more "home miners" and the massively powered machines that now secure the network group into mining pools, where the miners in the pool that solves each block split the reward. Without pools, it could take a solo bitcoin miner many decades to solve a block and get the reward on their own.[cxviii]

Bitcoin miners also receive a second form of compensation in the form of fees. In the early years, these fees were fairly meaningless, at least in dollar value, representing pennies per transaction, which is spread across the entire network of miners who confirm a given transaction, and are then permanently sealed into a new block every ten minutes. The recent addition of Bitcoin Layer Two (a programmable layer on top of bitcoin, which does not use smart contracts), along with an NFT-like creation called Ordinals and an altcoin-like token structure called Runes, has added massive new fees available for Bitcoin miners, even making some of them profitable after the most recent halving, when mining rewards were cut in half.

Miner rewards (i.e., new bitcoin issued directly from the Bitcoin coinbase) are issued on a set schedule for distribution over 6,930,000 blocks across 33 bitcoin cycles. At an average of four years per cycle, it is expected to take 132 years to complete the distribution in the year 2140. The average cycle thus far has been forty-six months instead of exactly four years. If this continues at the same rate, the final bitcoin will be issued in late 2134. Either way, it is beyond the average life expectancy of anyone alive. Once the final miner reward is issued, Bitcoin is expected to be mature enough of an ecosystem to incentivize miners with miner fees alone. These fees now include revenue not anticipated by Satoshi with the creation of Ordinals and Runes (see Chapter 19).

Supply and Demand

The four-year cycle is a fundamental part of the Bitcoin white paper. In many ways, it's the most fascinating part of Satoshi's economic system: how does one create scarcity *and* demand in a new monetary system? There is plenty of precedent for creating artificial scarcity and FOMO-based demand in consumer products. Nearly every Christmas, some new hot toy for kids gets a whiff of viral excitement over it selling out in five minutes, with frantic mothers lining up around the block so their expectant tots can play with Tickle Me Elmo (or whatever the "scarce" good of the year might be). When they worked, these marketing campaigns created instant Veblen goods, even if just for the season. By the next summer, those toys were often in the discount bins as the true scarcity turned out to be a false flag, and the nation's children eagerly awaited the next virally marketed, overpriced toy.

With Bitcoin, the white paper laid out the plan clearly. Early miners or buyers could reap unheard-of capital gains if successful. If it didn't work, it would join other failed attempts at money alchemy in the dustbin of history. The first halving was on the road map nearly four years before it occurred. Just as surely as the difficulty to mine would rise as more participants joined the network, we knew that the mining rewards would be cut in half every 210,000 blocks. There was also the unproven assumption that reducing new bitcoin while increasing adoption would have to eventually create a price increase, perhaps explosively.

Fast-forward to November 2012: Satoshi had already left active guidance on the Bitcoin project, handing over the keys to maintaining and upgrading the code to Gavin Andresen, a soft-spoken cryptographer from Massachusetts who posted on BitcoinTalk in April 2011 that he had accepted an invitation to make a presentation about Bitcoin to the CIA at a conference, much to the distress of early crypto anarchists.[cxix]

The first four years of Bitcoin were alternatingly quiet and chaotic. As discussed in Chapter 5, there were many blocks in 2009 without a single transaction other than the miner reward. There were no true exchanges, and the first over-the-counter broker, New Liberty, had only one sale for the entire year—and it was just $5 for 5,050 bitcoins. By 2010, more miners fired up their laptops to earn fifty-bitcoin rewards, which continued twenty-four hours a day; by mid-year, some of them had hacked a way to use game processor units (GPUs) to overpower CPU miners in hashrate, earning most of the rewards. June 2011 saw the first parabolic price increase at prices of more than one dollar, with the *Gizmodo* blog post on Silk Road, resyndicated on Slashdot, resulting in a quick pump to thirty dollars, followed by a tremendous panic sell back to one dollar. Early bitcoin investor and evangelist Roger Ver bought a quarter million bitcoins for $1 each on Mt. Gox. By 2012, the first US exchanges were beginning to come online: first Tradehill, then Coinbase, and Kraken followed. New users heard about this "magic internet money" and bought or mined hundreds, even thousands, of bitcoin at a buck or two apiece. By November, the price had regained nearly half of its value, reaching the first halving block at a price on these early exchanges of $12.70.

The first halving was important in many aspects. First, it would prove that the code actually worked. Remember the Y2K scare of 2000, where a bug in mainframe computer code was to shut down critical infrastructure around the world? Well, that didn't happen, and the halving code worked like a charm, with the very first block of the Second Bitcoin Cycle issuing twenty-five bitcoins as a miner reward instead of the heretofore usual fifty bitcoins.

Beginning of a Trend

The first bitcoin cycle of 2009–2012 really didn't have a Spring, as there was no halving, just the Genesis Block. Its parabolic run-up did not occur until midway through the third year of the cycle—and it only lasted a few weeks, but it proved the explosive volatility of the asset to the upside. Naturally, it was met with a similarly seismic drop in value, but this pre-halving equivalent of Bitcoin Fall only took a few weeks to play out. The time between Cycle's all-time high and capitulation was under a month, whereas every cycle since has had periods of a year or more for Bitcoin Fall to drop its final leaf and become Bitcoin Winter.

By the time it was completed, the First Bitcoin Cycle had demonstrated the psychological effect of parabolic run-ups and drops on investors, setting up expectations for the first cycle with a halving. The first and only pre-halving cycle was a study in epic volatility, with prices shooting up 3,000 times from introductory price discovery at 0.1 cents in late 2009 to the cycle's all-time high of $30 in June 2011. Even after the rapid 97 percent crash to $1, which in a modern cycle with breathless media coverage might have wiped out the asset class, the price recovered nearly 1,200 percent by the first halving in late 2012. This is consistent with future Bitcoin Winters in both length and relative degree of recovery.

What buyer behavior led up to the first halving that began the Second Bitcoin Cycle? First, the price anticipated the halving and moved up by nearly 150 percent in the six months prior to November 2012. We would see this occur in every halving since, with the exception of 2020, whose pre-halving gains were suppressed by the early months of the global pandemic.

Comparing the Seasons of Each Cycle

How long does Bitcoin Spring last? Under my thesis, it lasts until the prior all-time high from the last cycle has been reached, thoroughly erasing any losses from Bitcoin Winter. While one would like to think that each cycle lasts about one year, that has never been the case, with Bitcoin Spring always being the shortest season. Conversely, Bitcoin Winter is always the longest season.

The table below measures each season from its first day to its last.

- Spring begins the day of the halving and ends the day the all-time high (ATH) of the prior season has been eclipsed.
- Summer begins that very day and ends with the ultimate all-time high for that cycle.
- Fall begins the day of the all-time high and ends with the post-Summer low, which is generally not the low for the cycle, as the prior Spring started at a much lower number.
- Bitcoin Winter begins with the capitulation event that took away most of the gains of Bitcoin Summer and only ends with either the halving or, as happened in 2024, a new all-time high prior to the halving.

Bitcoin Halving	Spring to Summer	Summer to Fall	Fall to Winter	Winter to Spring
1 2012–2016	Three months	Nine months	Fourteen months	Eighteen months
2 (2016–2020)	Seven months	Ten months	Thirteen months	Sixteen months
3 (2020–2024)	Seven months	Eleven months	Twelve months	Seventeen months
4 (2024–2028)	TBD	TBD	TBD	TBD

Cycle statistics give us plenty of interesting data, but most is inconclusive. The trend that seems to be strongest is the length of winter. Indeed, it has been incredibly consistent, taking about a year and a half for the market to trust the sector again. *Contrarian thinkers and students of cycle history know that the start of winter is absolutely the best time to buy, just like the end of summer is the best time to sell.*

As noted above, Bitcoin Spring is a surprisingly brief season, given the depth and intransigence of Bitcoin Winter. The longest it has ever taken to go from halving to a prior all-time high has been seven months. Bitcoin Spring took similar paths in Bitcoin Cycle Three (after the second halving) and in Bitcoin Cycle Four. In Cycle Three (2016–2020), it was a slow path to regaining the late-2013 high of $1,242, with rejection after rejection of $1,000 as 2016 ended. Similarly, the Bitcoin Cycle Four (2020–2024) was a slow path from the May halving price of $8,727 to $20,000 in the same calendar year, with multiple rejections in the historically bullish fourth quarter. Once it occurred, the fuse on Bitcoin Summer was lit, which we will further explore in the next chapter.

In Bitcoin Cycle Five, which just recently started following the fourth halving, Bitcoin Spring did not occur until a month after a new all-time high of $73k. Based on the data from the first three halvings, I presumed we might see eight months pass after the 2024 halving before we saw another all-time high. However, this cycle had the bitcoin ETFs, which had both a fundamental impact on supply and demand as well as a positive effect on the news cycle. Those were the key drivers for a new high before the halving.

What does this mean? Psychologically, this did two things for the model:

1) It eliminated forever the notion that a new all-time high *must* occur after the next halving. In many ways, this barrier got in the way of a Bitcoin Supercycle, and it has now been erased.

2) It opened the door to analytical discussions about whether the new cycle would be determined from the halving (e.g., the first day of Bitcoin Spring) or the new post-Winter all-time high.

We will analyze the implications of predicting future prices based on past behavior on a Bitcoin Spring model vs. a Bitcoin Summer model:

Bitcoin Halving	Halving to Cycle ATH (Bitcoin Spring Model)	First New ATH to Cycle ATH (Bitcoin Summer Model)
First Halving	10,057.50%	8.964.33%
Second Halving	2,852%	1,492.85%
Third Halving	690.44%	248.69%
Fourth Halving Prediction (low)	175% $111,825.00	142% $104,845.70
Fourth Halving Prediction (high)	345% $220,345	325% $239,963.75

My price predictions are from a combination of data, including the diminishing returns of each cycle. For my most conservative model, I take an extreme interpretation of this trend, which would lead to very little appreciation in the next three cycles. For my most aggressive interpretation, I look at my consistent predictions since 2022 that this cycle will top at roughly 3x the 2024 halving price basis and increase it based on the obliteration of Bitcoin Spring this cycle. None of this is financial advice, but it's the model that I am basing my own decisions on—with a willingness to input new, unexpected data when it occurs.

There will certainly be some positive and negative surprises, and I will do my best at my companion website to this book at www.bitcoinsupercycle.org to explain what has happened and how it impacts my model at every turn. Remember the George Box quote from an earlier chapter, "All models are wrong, but some are useful."

Chapter Eleven

Bitcoin Summer

Summer romances end for all kinds of reasons. But when all is said and done, they have one thing in common: They are shooting stars—a spectacular moment of light in the heavens, a fleeting glimpse of eternity. And in a flash, they're gone.

—Nicholas Sparks[cxx]

Summertime is always the best of what might be.

—Charles Bowden[cxxi]

Everything good, everything magical happens between the months of June and August.

—Jenny Han, *The Summer I Turned Pretty*[cxxii]

In a world of "magical internet money," Bitcoin Summer is where the magic truly happens. Every four-year cycle has had at least one instance of parabolic growth. Parabolic growth has occurred in other financial markets, but Bitcoin is perhaps the first where it was engineered to perform that way. The theory, clearly spelled out by Satoshi in the Bitcoin white paper, was based on each new cycle having lower inflation (i.e., new bitcoin compared to the existing total supply, also known as the stock-to-flow ratio). As long as the number of bitcoin users grows faster than inflation, the average price should keep appreciating each cycle. Similarly, the extremes between cycle high and cycle low, primarily driven by the human emotions of fear and greed within each cycle, should become less extreme as the user base grows more significant and cycle behavior has more data.

In his economic system, Satoshi also provided the earliest adopters (2009–2010) with a disproportionate amount of bitcoin to mine at a cost near zero, along with a model that encouraged holding and not spending those bitcoins. Each successive new wave of investors who bought into the framework ultimately saw the benefits of holding on to their bitcoin across several cycles (intracycle channel trading notwithstanding), even at higher prices, or ultimately regretted not doing so.

I have likened the Bitcoin halvings to OPEC cutting oil production. Reducing new supply almost immediately leads to higher prices. In the 1970s, an oil embargo by OPEC led to a quadrupling of oil prices and gasoline rationing. A similar dynamic plays out with each halving, except that the effect is not instantaneous. Any oil rig that shuts down saves on costs immediately with oil production. There are no immediate cost savings with bitcoin because the new supply of available bitcoins each day is decreased, but the mining costs stay the same. Therefore, any miner with a 25 percent profit margin when daily rewards were at 900 bitcoins is now losing 37.5 percent every day when the rewards dropped to 450 bitcoins in April 2024. This changes over time as the difficulty adjusts every two weeks. Without factoring in revenue from Ordinals and Runes, this process of regaining profitability can be slow. After the most recent halving, mining difficulty rose from 83 trillion to 88 trillion before finally adjusting downward to 79.5 trillion (meaning it was still 79.5 trillion times as challenging to mine one bitcoin in terms of the level of mathematical equation needing to be solved as it was during 2009–2010 when the reward was also 16 times higher).

Industrial-scale miners who stay online despite losses do so because they have fixed costs beyond variable electricity. However, they are more incentivized to sell bitcoin to offset those losses than when they are in profit. Most large miners have traditional financing to ensure that all of their expenses do not rely on bitcoin sales, as their ultimate enterprise value also depends on how much bitcoin they can retain on their balance sheet.

Bitcoin usage has been rising each cycle, from an insignificant number of users by the end of the first cycle to an estimated 2 to 5 percent of the world's population today, depending upon the source. The most bullish estimate of 580 million users by Crypto.com is that one-third of them held only altcoins. Historically, adoption speeds up when 8 percent of a population does anything, and I project that we will be at or near one billion bitcoin users by the end of the cycle in 2028. This is only slightly ahead of a Boston Consulting Group report that came out in July 2024, projecting one billion bitcoin holders by 2030.[cxxiii]

Adding 600 million new bitcoin holders during the 2024–2028 cycle, when only 450 bitcoins are mined daily, results in 656,250 bitcoins over four years (3.125 bitcoins per block times 210,000 blocks). Consequently, each new buyer can access an average of only 0.00109375 Bitcoin during this period (currently valued at $75).[cxxiv] This calculation does not consider that current bitcoin holders will also buy new bitcoin, and it assumes all mined bitcoin will be sold, both of which are unlikely.

We can speculate about the whereabouts of the early bitcoin pioneers who mined 10 million bitcoins, millions of which have never moved. We may never know how many are victims of lost keys, but roughly two million bitcoins have never moved, including 1.04 million linked to Satoshi Nakamoto's mining. Another two million have not moved in the past five years. This leaves about 16 million bitcoins in total by the end of the current four-year cycle, out of a world population of eight billion, 59 million of which are millionaires. *If every millionaire in the world wanted to own one bitcoin, there would not be anywhere near enough.* This will be as true when one bitcoin reaches $250,000 as when it was $2 or even two cents.

The First Cycle Was Parabolic, But It Wasn't a Classic Bitcoin Summer

Early volatility is not unusual in new asset classes. Petroleum went through wild fluctuations in its early years when there were doubts about ever succeeding whale oil as a viable fuel source. In the First Bitcoin Cycle of 2009–2012, before the first halving, there were so few users that parabolic increases had to happen for Bitcoin to appreciate into an asset class of any reasonable size. Since there was no halving (the closest thing would be the Genesis Block), this cycle does not yield easy comparisons, but it did have a parabolic run-up from near zero to $30 per bitcoin.

The 100x Summer

The first halving marked the dawn of what I call "the modern era" of Bitcoin. It started in November 2012 as the number of new bitcoins mined daily was cut in half. At that moment, nearly half the bitcoins that would ever exist had been mined. One could argue that solving one block during that era, where each block yielded a reward of 50 bitcoins, was sufficient to retire if one waited long enough. Indeed, in March 2024, that single block reward, mined at the cost of electricity for a laptop computer, was worth more than $3.5 million.

The first Bitcoin Spring only lasted four months, when the prior cycle's all-time high of $30 was reached in early March 2013 to begin the first true Bitcoin Summer. One of my model's contributions is to define Bitcoin Summer as the day the prior all-time high was reached rather than a set number of months post-halving. Data shows that the parabolic returns begin to accelerate on that day, as the tables and charts throughout this book will demonstrate. Just one month after Bitcoin Summer 2013 began, the Cyprus banking crisis helped power the price of bitcoin up to $240, which was a 20x gain for anyone who bought it the day of the halving just five months earlier. Other than the news-driven narrative of the *Gizmodo* article on Silk Road in 2011,[cxxv] it was the first example of my News Relativity Paradigm, which overemphasizes the importance of good news during a bull market and minimizes bad news.

There was more bullishness to come. The 2012–2016 cycle was not only the first after a halving; it was also the first "double bubble," as the price of bitcoin went parabolic in April, then crashed back nearly 80 percent in May and spent the subsequent four months trading in a channel between

$50 and $120. I called the mid-cycle bottom in July 2013 at $66 at a BitAngels gathering that month, concurrent to the Inside Bitcoins New York conference and my presentation on bitcoin to the New York Angels. As it turns out, nobody in the audience bought bitcoin following my New York Angels presentation. However, I was sternly warned by one of the audience members that the only things bitcoin was good for were drugs and prostitution and that I should run away from it as fast as I could. A few years later, that group voted bitcoin as one of their biggest missed opportunities of the decade, along with not investing in the pre-seed round of Pinterest.

The second leg of the bubble started in October, when the price shot up from $132.18 to $204, a 54 percent increase for the month. That was also the month that young serial entrepreneur Barry Silbert started selling bitcoin to accredited investors through his Bitcoin Investment Trust (BIT), which raised $65 million in its first few weeks and would go on to become the publicly traded stock Greyscale Bitcoin Trust (GBTC). In 2024, the SEC allowed GBTC to convert to an ETF and ten new entrants, making it the largest ETF until BlackRock overtook it in early May. By early June, BlackRock's IBIT bitcoin ETF had $21 billion AUM, and the entire bitcoin ETF market swelled to $64.7 billion. With its current momentum, it's only a matter of time before the bitcoin ETF market capitalization passes that of gold ETFs, which have $214 billion AUM as of January 2024, according to the World Gold Council.[cxxvi]

This fourth-quarter buying had its effect, and the bitcoin price went parabolic in November, ultimately reaching $1,242 on November 29, 2013. I remember a heady atmosphere with my wife, who was skeptical of buying any bitcoin when it was $120, breathlessly asking me how much I could buy at $400. I remember other early investors telling me that they had never seen the supply of bitcoin so tight, with some exchanges running out of bitcoins to sell.

As with most Bitcoin Summer seasons, we didn't know it was over until the cold chill of Bitcoin Fall arrived a few months later. I recall offering my employees a choice of bitcoin or Amazon gift cards for their holiday bonuses. All but one took the Amazon cards. I bought those Amazon cards with bitcoin, which was still hovering around $900 in mid-December, using the Gyft mobile gift cards started by Vinny Lingham. I recall spending about a dozen bitcoins on those holiday bonuses, and I thought it was cool that I could send the bitcoin from the back of a taxi in San Francisco as I crossed the Bay Bridge. That bitcoin I used to purchase a little more than $10,000 of Amazon gift cards is worth about $750,000 today.

The mood in January 2014 was bullish for a recovery, with many predicting that bitcoin would reach $2,000 or higher by the end of what turned out to be a very bearish year, the first Bitcoin Fall. Vinny Lingham, the biggest bull in 2013, was one of the few bears for 2014, saying the price could drop into the low hundreds. It did. But the insiders of this burgeoning industry were largely upbeat as the year began, flocking to the first North American Bitcoin Conference, where a young Dutch promoter renowned for his thick black glasses, Moe Levin, assembled more than 1,200 people in Miami Beach. The conference started with a spectacular rooftop party over-looking the shiny Atlantic Ocean, complete with scantily clad go-go dancers promoting a new bitcoin ATM. A day later, Vitalik Buterin read the Ethereum white paper to a packed crowd. He previewed it at my bitcoin media event at the Consumer Electronics Show earlier that month. The mood in Miami was upbeat; there was nothing stopping bitcoin now.

Those who sold at or near the top survived the long fall and winter, as did those who simply held their bitcoin and didn't need to sell. Many investors kept buying as BTC's price declined during the growth pains in 2014; those individuals were negatively impacted, economically speaking, in the short term. The most innovative money, including Ethereum, was bought into the early ICOs, at thirty cents per ether that summer (we will cover this in Chapter 16). But Bitcoin Fall officially started the day of the cycle's all-time high in late November 2013, even though few wanted to believe it. The first post-halving Bitcoin Summer was now in the books.

The 30x Bitcoin Summer

For the Third Bitcoin Cycle that followed the Second Bitcoin Halving, it took seven months for Bitcoin Summer to arrive. I remember a sense of anxiety as to how long it would take even to break $1,000 again. Was that a one-time fluke? Was it a shady manipulation of Mt. Gox? As 2016 turned to 2017, the price crept up slowly, moving back into the $800s after coming close to four figures a few times in January. Finally, on February 1, the price cracked $1,000; a month later, on March 1, it broke the old record of $1,242. Bitcoin Summer had officially returned.

Unlike in 2013, there was no double bubble, just a slow, steady climb for the next half year, mainly in two-month steps: March was flat, and April picked up a little steam, closing the month at over $1,400. May showed the promise of Summer, rocketing up to $2,412 and crossing $2,500 for the first time just two days later. June was flat, ending at just $2,424. July inched up to $2,745; then August gave a glimpse into the potential of the final quarter by passing $4,000 by August 12 and ending the month just a few dollars short of $5,000. September, which is historically a bearish month for bitcoin, dipped back under $4k briefly, ending the month at $4,400. However, similar to 2013, bitcoin's price was just warming up for its second fourth-quarter bravura performance.

In October, bitcoin finally hit the long-awaited $5,000 mark on October 11th—and didn't stop there, ending the day at $5,400. The bitcoin price then pushed past $6,000 on October 28th, followed by $7,000 merely four days later on November 1. Perhaps remembering the 2013 all-time highs took place in November, the bitcoin price accelerated its momentum, passing $8,000 on November 18th, followed by $9,000 a week later on November 25th, which was the Saturday of Thanksgiving weekend. Five days later, bitcoin passed the iconic price of $10,000.

This time, there was no Mt. Gox to crash. Rather, there were now centralized bitcoin exchanges around the world, including Coinbase, Bittrex, and Kraken in the United States; BTCC, OKex, Huobi, and newcomer Binance in China; Bithumb and Upbit in South Korea; ItBit and Kucoin in Singapore; BitStamp in London; Bitso in Mexico, and Arthur Hayes's giant crypto options exchange Bitmex, operating out of Hong Kong. Perhaps for that reason alone, the bull market continued into December, shattering records every few days. Let's look at the wild ten-week period after bitcoin cracked $5,000.

Day (2017)	Bitcoin Price
October 28	$6,147.52
November 1	$7,024.81
November 18	$8,042.64
November 25	$9,318.42
November 30	$10,861.47
December 3	$11,246.21
December 5	$13,749.57
December 6	$16,850.31
December 11	$17,083.90
December 15	$19,345.49
December 17	$19,783.06

At the end of 2017, there was once again joy, greed, and froth in the air. Not only had bitcoin cracked $10,000, but it was on the verge of passing $20,000. Whispers of $30,000 and even $50,000 bitcoin abounded. Besides the bitcoin bull run, the ICO phenomenon created a vast new class of altcoins, led by Ethereum. Bitcoin's dominance would drop from 86.85 percent of the crypto market at the start of 2017 to just 33.4 percent a year later, leading Ethereum maximalists to proclaim the day of "the Flippening" was near when the market cap of Ethereum would pass that of bitcoin.

The effect of the ICO craze extended the 2017 bull market, not just for bitcoin, which topped out in mid-December. Ethereum and altcoins would reach greater heights in January 2018. The all-time high for the crypto market was on January 7, 2018, at $786 billion, which I remember as a day when virtually all of the top one hundred coins were up double digits. The end of that bull market, while thrilling as I calculated every day what to sell and what to hold, was also a rough one for me personally. I lived in Puerto Rico, which had just gone through a Category 5 hurricane, Maria, which knocked out my power for months, forcing me to travel and stay in hotels when I was back in San Juan. Once again, the Bitcoin bull market ended in December, but few realized it was over until there were successive price drops in seven of the eight months from May through December 2018. The moment of reckoning for many was the Consensus conference in New York City in May, where many investors expected a bullish return from all the news that could come out of that packed show. Thousands jammed into the New York Hilton, and hundreds of ICOs were announced, but the price of bitcoin got hammered. It was clear that Bitcoin Fall had surprised the industry again.

The COVID-19 Bitcoin Summer

With the 2020 halving occurring at the beginning of the first global pandemic in one hundred years, would bitcoin respond differently than prior Bitcoin Summers? As a risk-on asset, would it crash back to under $1,000? Seemingly, this was plausible in March, when global stock markets, already in decline, experienced a one-day, double-digit crash known as "Black Monday." Bitcoin lost 25.05 percent of its value that month. This sharp decline was the primary reason there was no significant price appreciation in the six months leading up to this halving (see table below).

The rest of the 2020 Bitcoin Summer played out consistently with the prior two Summers, with a two-month

Percentage Gain	Six Months Prior through Halving	Six Months after Halving	Twelve Months after Halving	All-Time High for Cycle (and timing)
First Halving 2012–2016	147.57%	925.76%	8,033.47%	10,057.50% (366 days after halving)
Second Halving 2016–2020	45.03%	39.76%	262.2%	2,852% (18 months after halving)
Third Halving 2020–2024	0.07%	84.86%	533.7%	650.9%
Fourth Halving 2024–2028	133.6%	—	—	—

parabolic lead-up to the previous all-time high (28.17 percent in October 2020, followed by 42.42 percent in November). It had seven months of green months and four months of red months, with three of those four red months in the summer slump between the peaks of the double bubble, followed by the fourth red month in historically weak September.

This cycle had several firsts. It was the first cycle with tight monetary policy, which many believe hastened the onset of Bitcoin Fall. For a third time in a row, bullish attitudes lasted longer than the actual bull market, which ended in October 2021, the earliest month for an all-time high (prior ones were in November and December).

Perhaps the biggest lesson from studying the first three Bitcoin Summers is to realize they end before most investors recognize the music has stopped. We will examine the signs of recognizing the start of Bitcoin Fall in the next chapter.

What Will Bitcoin Summer 2024–2025 Bring?

I understand that some readers, including ones browsing at an airport bookstore, will skip directly to this section. After all, how does one get rich now by buying bitcoin, having missed the 100x, 30x, and 8x cycles?

As of the writing of this book, we are now about four months past the fourth halving. Yet, a new all-time high has already begun for the first time, taking place a month before the halving. As noted in Chapter 9, the Bitcoin ETF was the primary reason why a new cycle high for 2024–2028 took place early. Other factors were increased familiarity with the four-year cycle, particularly given that bitcoin and crypto survived one of its worst political shocks coming out of the FTX debacle during a time when the Biden administration was already looking to cripple the industry via Elizabeth Warren's "anti-crypto army" and other initiatives. Yet bitcoin survived and reached a new high of $69,000 on March 5, followed by another all-time high of $73,835.57 just nine days later, marking a remarkable rise of 380 percent since the fall of FTX just 17 months prior.

Leading up to the $73k all-time high there was a record of seven green months in a row prior to the bitcoin halving, with the final two months of that sequence up 43.63 percent in February and another 15.8 percent in March, which ended Bitcoin Winter by virtue of its new all-time high. The month of the halving, April, was down 14.36 percent, which mainstream media attributed to a "sell the news" effect. If this cycle is largely in line with past cycles but a little longer, we might expect eight green months and four red months if Bitcoin Summer ends in April/May 2025. Alternatively, if there was another Q4 high, the cycle could last seventeen to nineteen months past the halving, making a record for this Bitcoin Summer.

My best estimate for Bitcoin Summer of 2024–2025 is that we could have an eighteen-month cycle, probably with a double bubble. The quickest parabolic moves are likely to occur once bitcoin passes its current post-halving slump, as well as other important milestones like $100,000, $150,000, and potentially $200,000.

Here is the data from the past four cycles and my high and low estimates for the upcoming cycle. I will analyze the implications of predicting future price based on past behavior using a Bitcoin Spring model (halving price to cycle all-time high) and a Bitcoin Summer model (first new all-time high of the cycle to new cycle all-time high).

Bitcoin Halving	Halving to Cycle ATH (Bitcoin Spring Model)	First New ATH to Cycle ATH (Bitcoin Summer Model)
First Halving (2012–2016 cycle)	10,057.50%	8.964.33%
Second Halving (2016–2020 cycle)	2,852%	1,492.85%
Third Halving (2020–2024 cycle)	690.44%	248.69%
Fourth Halving (2024–2028 cycle) Low-end range prediction	125% $143,775	100% $147,671.80
Fourth Halving (2024–2028 cycle) Mid-range prediction	200% $191,700	150% $184,590
Fourth Halving (2024–2028 cycle) High-end range prediction	345% $284,345	225% $239,966.67

My price predictions are from a combination of data, including the diminishing returns of each cycle. For my mid-range model, I look at my consistent predictions since 2022 that this cycle will top at roughly 3x the 2024 halving price, while my Bitcoin Summer models are based on the double bubble acting more like 2021 than 2013. None of this is financial advice, but it's the model that I am basing my own financial decisions on—with a willingness to input new, unexpected data when it occurs. For other models and a guide to how fundamental technical analysis (TA) techniques borrowed from equities markets are used to predict short- and long-term price and volatility in the bitcoin and cryptocurrency markets, please read Chapter 15.

Now, we move on to the most tricky and treacherous season to navigate: Bitcoin Fall.

Chapter Twelve

Bitcoin Fall

Selling out at the bottom—and thus failing to partici-pate in the subsequent recovery—is the cardinal sin of investing.

—Howard Marks[cxxvii]

My dad used to say that every once in a while, the market has to shake out the grocery clerks.

—Bill Stewart[cxxviii]

The value of Bitcoin is astronomical, but the price goes all over the place as a million buyers and sellers try to figure out what that value is and how likely it is to manifest.

—Erik Voorhees[cxxix]

Bitcoin Fall is when the raucous party of Bitcoin Summer comes to an end. Like a great event that begins to thin out, most people don't recognize the end of the bull market until it's too late. This chapter will show you the telltale signs of the onset of Bitcoin Fall, backed by years of data and what I've identified as solid trends.

No asset class goes up forever, and Bitcoin has thus far fol-lowed several repetitive, and therefore somewhat predictable, patterns in its fifteen-year upward climb. Key among these patterns has been the timing of each new cycle's frothy top, which so far has happened precisely once per four-year cycle. Since 2012, each Bitcoin Summer has ended in the fourth quarter of the year following the halving, but it has generally taken several months for the obvious signs of the bear market to occur. Another clear trend has been somewhat decreasing volatility each cycle. While the future is impossible to predict with absolute accuracy, past performance has shown some unmistakable components that investors ignore at their peril.

My best advice to bitcoin investors is to follow one of the following strategies, depending on your willingness to actively monitor your investment and your appetite for risk:

1) Hold your bitcoin through the bear market, knowing that each new cycle high has always beaten the high of the previous cycle. This trend should continue as long as bitcoin adds more new users in percentage terms than new bitcoin. This growth should continue until 80 percent of the world has at least some exposure to the asset class, even if it's masked in structured products like an ETF or abstracted inside of a mobile phone designed for micropayments.

    The advantage of this strategy is its simplicity. There is no need to time the market, although you might want to buy more bitcoin when the market hits the depths of the bear market and ultimately capitulation. This so-called "dollar-cost averaging" (DCA) will let you acquire more bitcoin without risking any of your long-term holdings, so there is zero chance of missing out on rapid market moves by attempting to time the market. The ultimate HODL strategy is truly "set it and forget it." A meme was going around a few years ago with two comparative pictures: The "day trader's office" showed a wall of computer monitors; the "HODLers office" was a golf course.

2) My preferred strategy is channel trading within the cycle, buying as close to the bottom as possible (the end of Bitcoin Fall/start of Bitcoin Winter), then selling a majority of one's bitcoin holdings as close to the top as possible (the end of Bitcoin Summer/start of Bitcoin Fall). Statistically, these tops and bottoms have occurred in a very narrow range of weeks, which I will analyze later in this chapter. The most important part of this strategy is nailing the tops within 20–30 percent (one is highly unlikely to catch the exact day of the top or bottom, but there are many days you can be close enough to increase the returns of just holding substantially).

You will note that at the start of each chapter about a season, I have highlighted important events as well as the cycle highs and lows. Please note the circled areas where the cycle lows and highs cluster. Each cycle thus far (other than the primordial cycle of 2009–2012) has seen the same behavior:

Cycle highs concentrate at the end of Bitcoin Summer, which has been within the same narrow band of just thirty-eight days (just 2.67 percent of the average cycle length of 1,385 days).

Cycle lows concentrate at the end of Bitcoin Fall, within a similar narrow band of just sixty-five days (4.69 percent of the average cycle length of 1,385 days).

This means all highs and lows (and therefore the time when the utmost vigilance is required) take place in a total of less than 7.5 percent of the cycle.

A Deep Dive into Cycle Highs

Let's examine each cycle that began with a halving in terms of when one could have sold within 20 percent or even 30 percent of the top:

Halving Cycle	All-time high (price and date)	Time to sell within 20% of top	Time to sell within 30% of top
2012–2016	$1,242 on 11/29/13	11/27/13–12/09/13 (13 days to sell above 993.60)	11/27/13–1/11/14 (45 days to sell above $869.40)
2016–2020	$19,783.21 on 12/17/17	12/06/17–1/06/18 (31 days to sell above $15,826.57	12/27/13–1/11/14 (38 days to sell above $13,848.25)
2020–2024	$68,991.85 on 11/10/21	2/18/21–5/12/21, and from 10/12/21 to 12/03/21 (102 days to sell above $55,185.60)	2/15/21–5/15/21, and from 10/02/21 to 12/27/21 (177 days to sell above $48,287.40)

My principal observations of this data are as follows:

1) One needs to be very attentive to the heights of Bitcoin Summer, as it can turn rapidly to Bitcoin Fall. If history is a guide, one must be particularly attentive beginning in October of the year after the halving. October has been the second-best performing month across the past three cycles, second only to November (see historical monthly chart in Chapter 13). The all-time high prices for bitcoin in the first three post-halving cycles were reached on November 29, December 17, and November 10, always in the year following the halving (2013, 2017, 2021). *Put simply, of the 1,385 days of the average bitcoin halving cycle, the all-time highs of bitcoin have always occurred thus far in the same span of just 38 days.*

2) Even if investors miss the day of the all-time high in a cycle, they are not doomed to wait until the next cycle to exit at a substantial profit. Exiting in the top 20 or even 30 percent of the all-time high yields a substantially better result than either holding throughout the long bear market or panic selling at the bottom. One can then take these excess profits from selling near the top, wait out the rest of Bitcoin Fall, and then buy more bitcoin at or near the market bottom, which typically happens twelve to fourteen months after the market top of Bitcoin Summer. The market bottom is generally recognized after the fact as the point of capitulation, where all investors other than the most resolute have sold, no matter how much the loss, as they are convinced the price will go even lower. I will discuss the dynamics of capitulation later in this chapter.

3) Each post-halving cycle has been increasingly more generous with time to make up for missing the top. In the most recent 2020–2024 cycle, there was a stretch of 143 days to sell within 20 percent of the high (84 days during the February–May parabolic run-up and 54 days during the October–December rally), a remarkable span across the double bubble of 177 days (nearly half the year) where one could sell within 20–30 percent of the all-time high, with a 90-day stretch in February–May and 87 days in October–December. (Note: I am calculating the period when one could sell during this range, not the individual days, as there was some minor volatility within these months where the prices fell out of this band but later returned.)

4) The majority of days within 30 percent of the top were also within 20 percent of the top, so the day the price falls below the 20 percent range from the top is typically the time to sell everything you don't want to hold for the long term, as it's highly unlikely to come back that cycle, particularly if it's in the fourth quarter.

Similarly, the cycle lows stay within 20 percent of the bottom for a meaningful period. During the 2020–2024 cycle, Bitcoin Fall had its capitulation event on November 10, 2022, the day before onetime $32 billion crypto exchange FTX collapsed amid a sea of fraud accusations, but the price stayed low for months. **This also marked the second consecutive cycle where the capitulation event was almost exactly one year after the all-time high.**

Let's look at the total periods where one could buy within 20 percent or 30 percent of the post-halving cycle lows:

Halving Cycle	Cycle low	Time to buy within 20% of bottom	Time to buy within 30% of bottom
2012–2016	$170 on 1/14/15	11/27/13–12/09/13 (3 days to buy below $204)	11/27/13–1/11/14 (26 days to buy below $221)
2016–2020	$3,232.51 12/14/19	12/02/18–3/12/19 (31 days to buy below $3,879)	11/23/18–3/31/19 (38 days to buy below $4202.26)
2020–2024	$15,742.44 on 11/10/22	11/09/22–1/13/23 (45 days to buy below $18,890.93)	11/09/21–3/11/21 (124 days to buy below $20,465.17)

My principal observations of this data are as follows:

1) The best time to buy in any cycle is near the capitulation event. This always occurred in the fourth quarter of the year after the all-time high for that cycle or at the very beginning of the first quarter of the year before the next halving. For the past three cycles, this has occurred twelve to fourteen months after the all-time high. The dates of the cycle lows have also been in a very narrow range, always at the end of the year after Bitcoin Summer: 2014 (in this case a few days into 2015, but the year 2014 was brutal), 2018, 2022. Similarly *to the all-time highs, the all-time lows of each cycle have occurred within the same span of just 65 days out of the 1,385 days of the average bitcoin halving cycle.*

2) The time horizon to get in on low prices has always been longer than the time to get out. This is based on human psychology, where fear is a more rapid motivator than greed. And greed at the bottom of the cycle

is completely against the existing narrative of blood in the streets. Everyone wants to sell, far beyond the rationality of the historic cycle behavior, which is why it's the best time to buy. The simple fact is that all remaining short-term sellers sold at or before the capitulation point, so there are no sellers remaining. That's when it's safest to buy if you believe that bitcoin is not going to zero and will continue to have new cycles.

3) Each post-halving cycle has been increasingly more generous with time to make up for missing the bottom. In the most recent 2020–2024 cycle, there was a stretch of 45 days to buy within 20 percent of the cycle low, as well as 124 days to buy in at 30 percent above the cycle low. Both of these investments became wildly profitable within the short amount of time to the next all-time high, which was more than four times the cycle low.

4) Recognize the timing of the cycles and plan for them. I like to ask people in my speeches if they can tell me how many years in the history of bitcoin have been "red years" where the price at the end of the year was lower than at the start? The correct answer is three, and they are always the third year of the cycle: 2014, 2018, 2022. The odds are excellent that after making substantial gains in bitcoin for 2023, 2024, and 2025 that 2026 will be a substantially down year, i.e., the next Bitcoin Fall.

When Does Bitcoin Fall Turn to Winter?

Most media and pundits make the huge mistake of calling any downtrend "crypto winter" and begin to bury the category the longer the bear market lasts. One of the biggest mistakes one can make as an investor is to confuse the first phase of the bear market, Bitcoin Fall, with the second phase of the bear market, Bitcoin Winter.

Bitcoin Fall is where prices always drop until the moment of capitulation. It's the season of lower lows and descending triangles, and unless you are a day trader or options trader, it's a horrible time to "buy the dip" as the price is going to go lower as long as the market still has hope. That sounded strange to me for many years, but I now see it's true. The last possible short-term sellers must be swept away before the early buyers feel it's safe to buy back in for the next cycle.

As I will discuss in the next chapter, Bitcoin Winter is the lowest risk of any season. Having no sellers left means that bad news does not collapse a market that's already hopeless. This scenario has often played out, from the Great Depression to the dot-com collapse not collapsing further after 9/11. There were no sellers left. In general, the strategy for Bitcoin Fall is to sell as early in the season as it becomes clear that Bitcoin Summer is over, even if one does it slowly over a few weeks. The strategy for Bitcoin Winter is to buy when everyone else is panicked. There is a saying in real estate that one makes all their profits when they buy the home at the right price. I believe the same can be said about bitcoin. The highest profits are not realized by buying at the halving; they are achieved by buying heavily at or near the bottom.

The key to buying at the bottom is defining the moment of capitulation. There has been a tendency in each of the past three cycles to call the bottom too early:

In 2014, many thought the bottom was in when the price dipped to under $300 in early October. I remember this clearly, as the price was more than $900 in January and a whale friend of mine, early bitcoin investor and BitAngels Chicago city leader Matt Roszak, told me., "If it goes under $300, I'm selling the family silverware and backing up a truck to buy all the bitcoin I can." Indeed, on the opening day of my very first bitcoin investor conference, CoinAgenda, where Matt was a speaker and sponsor, the price dropped below $300 (and I was accepting bitcoin for conference tickets). The *Wall Street Journal* wrote about my conference, noting the irony of partying in the city's flashiest venues while the price of bitcoin was in freefall. I texted Matt and asked him if he had sold any silverware or rented a truck (he had not). He certainly has made savvy moves before and since, as he has been on the *Forbes* list of crypto billionaires for several years stemming from his bitcoin purchases going back to 2010, landing at number nine for 2024 at $3.1 billion.

In 2018, the initial crash signaling the full impact of Bitcoin Fall came on February 4, when the price dropped below $7,000, less than a month after it had a "dead cat bounce" to $17,172.30. Most of the year after the February 4 crash saw unsuccessful attempts to break above $12,000 in March, then to break above $10,000 in May, $9,000 in July, and $7,000 in September. This series of "lower lows" is a consistent trend among Bitcoin Fall years until capitulation occurs. Because there was such a long period of sideways movement between September 4 and November 12, when the price traded in a narrow range between $6,100 and $6,750, it was widely presumed that the resistance was heavy enough at $6,000 that a floor had been reached.

But that's not how Bitcoin Fall works. *Buyers demand capitulation to buy back in.* That's exactly what happened in November 2018, when Craig Wright proclaimed himself to be

Satoshi Nakamoto and planned to kill off Bitcoin in favor of his new fork, Bitcoin SV (see Chapter 7 for details). This was the panic moment required to cause capitulation. It simply would have stopped the bull market if it happened in Bitcoin Summer. At the depths of a fragile bear market, it looked to many like the end of bitcoin. Massive selling ensued, and the actual bottom occurred on December 17 at $3,232, causing huge paper losses for anyone buying in heavily at $6,000 in the belief that the floor resistance would stick. Narrow trading bands tend to break hard in one direction or the other. In Bitcoin Fall, they tend to break down.

For the 2020–2024 cycle, as detailed in Chapter 8, the full impact of Bitcoin Fall was not quite felt until Terra Luna pulled the rug out from under a blissfully unaware market price that was about to implode due to centralized frauds masquerading as bitcoin investments and overleveraged gambling. Many saw the Terra Luna collapse drop the bitcoin price out of its comfortable trading range of $40–48,000, where it had spent the first four months of the year with a painful drop from $40,000 to $29,126 in just eight days. The Celsius collapse added to the pain a month later, dropping the price of bitcoin from $30,000 to $19,042 in just nine days. We were almost at capitulation—indeed, buying under $20,000 was close enough to the bottom to have been an excellent investment. But true capitulation came with FTX, when the bitcoin price dropped below the historical support level of the prior cycle's high price of $19,783.21 for the very first time in Bitcoin history. Surely, bears reasoned, it was over for Bitcoin, and it would never return. Yet, it did with a vengeance, and a mere seventeen months later Bitcoin was sitting at nearly five times the Bitcoin Fall low with a $73,835.57 new all-time high.

Please note as well that every post-halving cycle has had one attempt at the beginning of the season to climb back to Bitcoin Summer all-time highs that was defeated. This is generally the last time to get out at anything near Bitcoin Summer prices. In 2014, it bounced from the December 17, 2013 crash to $532 (down from the $1,242 all-time high just a few weeks earlier) to a rebound price of $933.53 on January 5, 2014. It would be another two years until the price recovered to equal that amount again in December 2016. In 2017–2018, there was a bounce to $17,000 described above. In 2021, the dead cat bounced from the first of the "double bubbles" became the new all-time high later in the year. There would be no revisiting of that high after November 10, 2021, just a sideways market until the May and June 2022 events described above knocked the market down 50 percent on its way to capitulation.

I've now laid out a plan for how to sell at the start of Bitcoin Fall and how to buy back at the end of this hugely important season. I will now progress to examine the perils and opportunities of Bitcoin Winter.

Chapter Thirteen

Bitcoin Winter

In the depth of winter, I finally learned that there was in me an invincible summer.

—Albert Camus[cxxx]

Be fearful when others are greedy, and greedy when others are fearful.

—Warren Buffet[cxxxi]

Buy when there's blood in the streets, even if the blood is your own.

—Baron Nathan Rothschild[cxxxii]

Bitcoin Winter begins immediately after the dramatic capitulation event of Bitcoin Fall, marking the final change of seasons. The problem is that one only knows it was capitulation after the market regains its footing, weeks to months later. To paraphrase Ernest Hemingway, that's when buyers slowly, then suddenly, appear, beginning the long winter's journey into spring and the promise of new highs in the coming cycle, which thus far have always arrived.

It takes discipline to sell at the end of Bitcoin Summer when the rest of the world is eagerly buying up new highs. It takes courage to buy when the overwhelming narrative among the media, your friends, and even much of the community of experts is screaming at you to sell.

Even among experienced whales and dedicated bitcoiners who have been investing for several cycles, there is always trepidation in this violent opening segment of Bitcoin Winter. What if this moment which looks like capitulation is simply another leg down to yet another lower low on a descending chart that has been bleeding for more than a year? The smartest, most experienced bitcoin investors I know by and large did *not* invest the day after FTX collapsed, as there was still a reasonable possibility that the price could go even lower. I recall a fair amount of technical analysis making the rounds on Twitter and YouTube at the end of 2022 that showed a liquidity gap at $11,000 that needed to be filled. Therefore, many traders put buy orders in at $12,000, $10,000, and even $5,000 in the hopes of far greater carnage before the bottom was truly hit. All of those orders went unfulfilled.

What about those "smartest buyers" I knew and respected? After realizing that their lowball bids were just wishful thinking, they all bought in heavily at prices between $18,000 and $28,000, as they had time to see the recovery pattern begin. As I noted in an earlier chapter, it was clear to me that the worst was over about eight weeks after FTX when the bankruptcy of Genesis Global, the giant crypto lending division of Digital Currency Group, did not cause the price to drop. In fact, within a few days, the price of bitcoin went up, and one could track the buying behavior on-chain.

One of the key methods of determining whether capitulation has hit is the buying behavior of long-term bitcoin holders (defined as holding bitcoin for 155 days or more) and the selling of short-term holders (less than 155 days). Without fail, the majority of short-term holders, which include the least experienced retail buyers, buy and sell at the very worst times. They pull the trigger on large buys at the peak of the bubble, then the panic sell at a loss near the bottom. Not all short-term holders are retail investors, as the category also includes day traders and algorithmic traders. Therefore, short-term statistics can be misleading, as the average entry price tends to decrease as the bear market continues.

As of July 3, 2024, the average acquisition price of Bitcoin for holders in profit was $19,400. This figure may be skewed by lost coins. For holders in loss, who are primarily short-term investors, the average cost was $66,100. The average cost basis for all active holders stood at $50,300, according to Glassnode. These statistics help explain why long-term holders ("whales") remain unconcerned while short-term holders panic during typical market pullbacks from all-time highs.

Long-term holders, which include all Bitcoin "whales" and HODLers, are extremely good at selling at the top (the black areas of the chart below), with maximum drawdowns in mid-2011, late 2013, late 2017, early 2021, and, intrestingly, early 2024.

All of these flips from buying bitcoin to selling bitcoin (the grey areas of the chart) occurred right at the all-time-high prices for cycle, although the expectation is that the 2024–2028

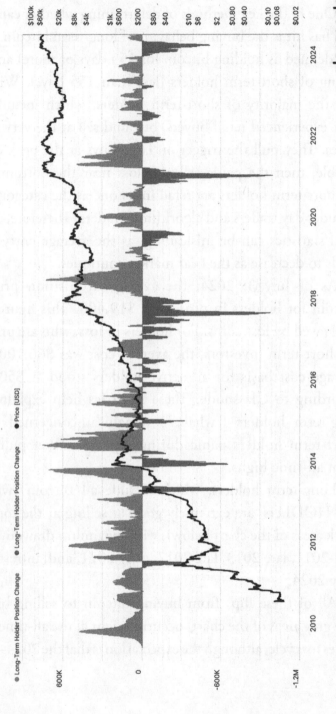

Bitcoin: Long-Term Holder Net Position Change

● Long-Term Holder Position Change   ● Price [USD]
● Long-Term Holder Position Change

glassnode

cycle will see much higher highs as Bitcoin Summer rolls on. For 2021, long-term holders sold at the top of the initial bubble, not at the later all-time high. This is most likely because they sold all or most of their bitcoin (or the amount allocated for trading instead of HODLing) during the first high in April 2021. This was logical given the exponential run-up in price the prior four months, where the price of bitcoin more than tripled.

Whales and other long-term holders bought the most bitcoin just after market bottoms, although the chart shows that many long-term holders made the mistake of buying back far before capitulation. Peak buying occurred several months prior to capitulation, with another wave thirty to sixty days after the bottoms were hit. This was particularly true during the double bubbles of both 2013 and 2021.

Stages of the Long Winter

Bitcoin Winter, the longest season by far, arrives in three distinct stages, microclimates if you will:

1) *Post-capitulation trauma and recovery.* This is equivalent to the Trough of Disillusionment in the famed Gartner Hype Cycle. With the four-year bitcoin cycle, I suggest there is a fresh hype cycle with every halving. Each new halving serves as the "technology trigger," leading to Bitcoin Summer's "peak of inflated expectations."

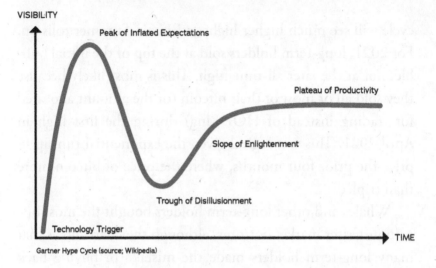

Gartner Hype Cycle (source; Wikipedia)

Like new stand-alone technologies, each new Bitcoin Cycle has not only continued and reinforced the historical promise of bitcoin, but it has also had its own new narrative for that cycle (e.g., new mining protocols in 2012–2016; forks and ICOs in 2016–2020; DeFi, NFTs and the metaverse for 2020–2024). Bitcoin Fall begins the drop into the trough of disillusionment that bottoms out the day of capitulation, with a prolonged climb out. As noted in the last chapter, it takes thirty to forty-five days to escape the trough enough to be 20–30 percent over the capitulation low price.

2) *Sell walls and retreats.* A substantial reason it takes so long for the bitcoin price to recover in winter is the number of sellers who want to get out at (or near) break-even from earlier, poorly timed investments. The number of bitcoin addresses in profit at every all-time high is 100 percent, of course. The number of bitcoin addresses in profit at the moment of capitulation has grown with each halving, due to the number

of HODLers who bought their early coins at a much lower price:

Cycle	Date and Price of Capitulation (closing price)	Bitcoin Addresses in Profit
2009–2012	11/15/11 at $2.05	13.146%
2012–2016	1/14/15 at $172.21	38.02%
2016–2020	12/16/18 at $3,237.06	44.516%
2020–2024	11/09/22 at $15,797.53	49.549%

This has historically led to a rolling sell wall effect: any lift in price during Bitcoin Winter is met with a wall of profit-taking (or taking a loss to exit the volatile asset class).

In the 2016–2020 cycle, you can see that despite an unusual bear market rally in the summer, the price on April 5, 2019, and March 12, 2020, were almost identical, around $5,000. That midsummer rally was caused by a unique episode in mid-2019 where more than 90 percent of all bitcoin addresses were in profit (see chart below), the only time this has happened during Bitcoin Winter. The cause was a token scam in China called Plus Token, which pumped the price of bitcoin with nearly $3 billion in cash acquired in a fraudulent multilevel marketing scheme that reached an incredible scale, selling worthless tokens for cash across the country. The price moved up very quickly, running from $3,963.78 on March 25, 2019, all the way up to $13,003.33 on June 26, with a chart for those three months that looked like an early bull market. The price even moved up from the high $8,000s to pass $13,000 in just ten days. I remember this well, as I was on my annual wine-tasting trip in France and

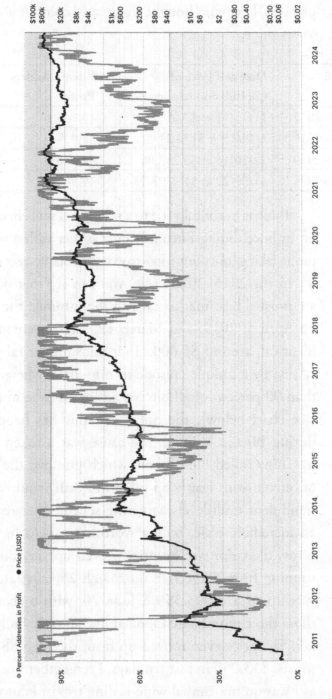

Bitcoin: Percent of Addresses in Profit

● Percent of Addresses in Profit   ● Price [USD]

ceremonially opened bottles of 2009, 2010, 2011, 2012, and 2013 when the corresponding price was passed. Alas, the price direction reversed itself once the gang behind Plus Token was arrested from its June 26 high of over $13k down to $6,611.51 by December 17, marking a drop of nearly 50 percent.

3) *Hope for the halving.* About six months prior to the halving, a whisper of hope enters the conversation, and the price slowly begins to climb. On July 10, 2012, the bitcoin price broke out of its flat trading pattern between $4 and $6, where it had been stuck since early January. It then moved to $9 one week later and spent most of the rest of 2012 trading over $10. For the six-month period before the halving (May 28–November 28), the price rose from $5.14 to $12.70 for a gain of 147.08 percent.

Four years later, the run-up six months preceding the halving moved the price from $449.70 on January 9, 2016, to the July 9, 2016, halving price of $670 for an increase of 49 percent. For the first four months, the bitcoin price was entirely bound in the $370–475 range, finally breaking to the upside in late May 2016, when it cracked $500 for the first time all year. It was one of the more boring times in the history of bitcoin price, but this quiet period ended just a few months later with 2017's explosion, growing the asset class 30x from the halving in eighteen months.

In the pandemic year of 2020, the price appreciation that began after the December 17 low for the second half of 2019 moved up to reclaim a five-digit price on February 14, 2020, at $10,300.05. This move upward was crushed less than a month later by the March 12 multi-asset pandemic crash, taking bitcoin all the way back to close at $4,860.35, with midday prices as low as $3,600, albeit just for a few minutes.

Even with that once-in-a-century black swan phenomenon, the price of bitcoin as it approached the halving proved to be remarkably resilient, moving back up to $8,727 by the May 11 halving, a rise of 142 percent in the sixty days since the pandemic crash. The halving was now here, and Bitcoin Winter was over. This was the only Bitcoin Winter that did not end with a six-month rally into spring, as the price was essentially flat from $8,756.32 on November 11, 2019, until the May 11, 2020, halving price of $8,727. The best explanation for this was a combination of the Plus Token lifting the average price for the second half of 2019 beyond where it would normally fall in the middle of Bitcoin Winter, plus the March 12 pandemic flash crash.

For the current cycle of 2024–2028, we saw the highest pre-halving gain of any cycle.

From October 19, 2023, to the April 19, 2024 halving, the price rose steadily from $28.706.16 to $63,900—passing the all-time high of $73,835.57 on its way. That is a gain of 122.6 percent to the halving, and 157.27 percent to the pre-halving high, which trumps the 147 percent gain in 2012, and with much larger dollar amounts. In the next chapter, we will discuss other bullish narratives about the 2024–2028 cycle that set it up perfectly for the start of a supercycle.

When Bitcoin Gets a Cold, Altcoins Catch Pneumonia

We are nearing the point in the book where we will discuss alternative cryptocurrencies, also known as altcoins. Many believe that Bitcoin is the only digital asset that matters. "Bitcoin is the only cryptocurrency," said Bitcoin Center founder Nick Spanos. "Everything else is just a project." These true believers call themselves Bitcoin Maximalists (Maxis for short). Michael Saylor, Max Keiser, Dan Held, and many others proudly proclaim that there is only one cryptocurrency. "There is no second best" is the Michael Saylor mantra.

More than half of the 580 million estimated cryptocurrency holders worldwide have assets other than bitcoin. In fact, nearly a third of them only hold altcoins. In the last cycle, Dogecoin created a new class of cryptocurrency enthusiasts. This cycle began with an explosion of fast-moving meme coins that went from a sideshow to an important $100 billion component of the altcoin market.

The reason I am previewing my guidance on altcoins in the Bitcoin Winter section is twofold:

1) Bitcoin Winter is where most altcoins go to die, as well as where new ones are born. If altcoins from the last cycle did not make sufficient traction to gather a significant treasury to weather the winter, then the wind has permanently gone out of their sails. The project collapses, and the failed founders can take their bull market Lambos and ride off into the sunset—or to their next project.

2) Bitcoin Winter is also where one still has the chance to make life-changing returns in under three years.

During the most recent winter of 2022–2023, three tokens launched with little fanfare or funding that have since grown an average of 230,866 percent. If you were lucky or connected enough to have bought into the fair launches of BitTensor, Kaspa, or Pepe, putting $10,000 into each, then you were able to have turned $30,000 into more than $69 million—and we are not even at the top of the bull market.

Token Name	Launch Price and Date	High Price and Date	Percentage Gain
BitTensor (TAO)	0.12 on 03/20/23	690.31 in 03/11/24	575,188%
Pepe (PEPE)	0.0000000658 on 05/18/23	0.00001718 on 5/27/24	26,009%
Kaspa (KASPA)	0.0002 on 5/24/22	0.183 on 2/19/24	91,400%

While these are extreme examples of incredible wealth creation in a short period of time, they are not unique. There are literally dozens of tokens with 100x returns in the past two years and hundreds of tokens with 10x returns in less than twenty-four months. All of these returns beat an investment in bitcoin, which is up a "mere" 369 percent in sixteen months from FTX to the new cycle's pre-halving all-time high of $73k.

Lessons to Remember During Bitcoin Winter

1) Start buying when it's clear that capitulation is in the rearview mirror. It would have been easy to think of Celsius as capitulation, but the system still had hope.

FTX drained the market of buyers, which made it safe for the price to rise without being beaten back by dormant sellers. When the price starts to rise after multiple drops, when more bad news does not affect price, it's finally safe to jump into the water again. *Historically, this happens twelve to fourteen months after the cycle's all-time high, so it's wise to not buy back in too early in Bitcoin Fall.*

2) Remember that investing in Bitcoin Winter is playing the long game. Expect to have zero significant returns for up to a year. The rich rewards of buying at the bottom will more than make up for your patience when the next cycle's Bitcoin Summer returns. *Historically, it has never taken more than three years to go from cycle bottom to next cycle top—and the rewards are far higher than waiting to buy in at the halving.*

3) It's also fine to add to your position at the end of Bitcoin Winter, when it's clear that the path to the next all-time high is more or less on schedule. You may have new income you wish to invest but are hesitant to add to your portfolio at higher prices. Don't fall into that trap: If bitcoin at the beginning of winter can generate 10x or more in three years, but paying three times as much at the end of winter might only reap 3x the gain, it's still a better investment than the S&P, gold, or treasury bills. In addition, it comes over a shorter period of time, so the IRR (internal rate of return) per year equalizes the impact of these investments. Making ten times one's investment in three years is roughly the same IRR as making 3x in one year. *Investing in the final pump before the halving can*

be as lucrative annually as investing at the absolute cycle bottom over a longer timeframe.

4) *Don't ignore altcoin opportunities.* Depending on your risk tolerance, willingness to do research, and ability to connect with other investors and founders, altcoins could create the most significant gains in your portfolio. We discuss these alternative strategies in Chapters 15–19.

Book Four

Mastering the Bitcoin Cycles

Chapter Fourteen
The Bitcoin Supercycle

Our intuition about the future is linear. But the reality of information technology is exponential, and that makes a profound difference. If I take 30 steps linearly, I get to 30. If I take 30 steps exponentially, I get to a billion.

—Ray Kurzweil

Technology advances at exponential rates, and human institutions and societies do not. They adapt at much slower rates. Those gaps get wider and wider.

—Mitch Kapor

The greatest shortcoming of the human race is our inability to understand the exponential function.

—Albert Allen Bartlett[cxxxiii]

What is the Bitcoin Supercycle, and why do I believe it may be happening now?

The term "supercycle" has most commonly been used to describe trigger-induced, extended bull markets in commodities. Typically, commodity prices move more slowly than equities—and they are glacial compared to crypto markets. Erik Norland, managing director and chief economist at CME Group, identifies two supercycles in commodities occurring in the past eighty years, with a third one brewing:

1) The first commodities supercycle ran from the mid-1960s through the entire 1970s. It was brought on by dollar depreciation and exacerbated by both the end of the gold standard in 1971 and the legalization of gold ownership for American citizens in 1975.

2) The second commodities supercycle started in the mid-1990s and lasted until 2008, when the Great Recession ended it. That supercycle was brought about by the rapid rise of China's industrialization, as bringing one billion people into the industrial age required an extensive amount of commodities, from oil to copper to lithium.

3) The current expansion cycle that is moving toward supercycle status began in 2021 and is still active. It was triggered by massive stimulus spending by the United States during and after the COVID-19 pandemic. That spending led to a wave of global inflation unseen since the 1970s. The latest contributing factor is the expiration and nonrenewal this year of the petrodollar agreement by Saudi Arabia after fifty years, wherein all global sales of Saudi oil needed to be in US dollars. Losing the petrodollar arrangement further weakens the dollar's hold on global reserve currency status.

Norland notes that all supercycles must have three things in common: (1) they must be broad-based across multiple commodities, (2) they must have a duration of five years or longer, and (3) prices must "supersize" over the term, often tripling in price or more. They also require an "outsized driver" to power the narrative, with dollar depreciation and China's industrialization driving the past two supercycles. Norland questions whether de-dollarization and inflation alone can cause a third commodities supercycle, but the significant increase in the prices of gold, silver, and copper since 2019 (66, 66, and 98 percent, respectively) would tend to promote the prospect of a new supercycle for commodities already being here.

Outsize Drivers for a Bitcoin Supercycle

What macroeconomic triggers would be strong enough to unleash a supercycle for Bitcoin? At least three are worthy contenders:

1) *Money printing.* During times of high inflation, gold and other commodities have been a flight to safety. As noted above, the early seeds of a gold and commodities supercycle are already underway. As Chapter 9 details, gold and bitcoin have similar characteristics and drivers. The bitcoin price has risen more than 20x from the March 12, 2020 flash crash bottom of $3,600 to the March 14, 2024 all-time high of $73,835.57. The US government, which took more than two hundred years to register its first trillion dollars of debt, is now stacking on new national debt at the rate of $1 trillion every one hundred days. Neither major candidate running for president in 2024 is committed to reducing this rate, and given the election is a rematch between

two administrations (counting Kamala Harris as an integral part of the Biden administration) that each added $8 trillion in their four-year tenures, it is highly unlikely to reverse anytime soon.

2) *Hyperinflation.* Inflation has destroyed 96 percent of wealth in the past hundred years. Anyone who had $10,000 in 1924 could buy a nice home and have enough money left over to furnish it. If they took that $10k and stuck it in a mattress, it would barely be able to pay for a few months of rent on a similar home in 2024. As Milton Friedman declared, "Inflation is taxation without legislation."[cxxxiv] However, hyper-inflation is far more insidious. While 4 percent inflation per year can ruin one's cash reserves over a lifetime, hyperinflation can destroy life savings in a much shorter period of time. The Hanke-Krus Hyperinflation Table, first published in 2013[cxxxv], ranks 47 episodes of hyperinflation that doubled prices in 45 days or less. The table included famous examples like postwar Hungary, where prices tripled daily, and 2007–2008 Zimbabwe, which doubled every twenty-four hours.

Hyperinflation continues to threaten many nations in 2024, particularly in Africa and Latin America. The IMF quarterly *World Economic Outlook* report in April 2024[cxxxvi] highlighted inflation rates of 249.8 per-cent for Argentina, 100 percent for Venezuela, 145.5 percent for Sudan, and 561 percent for Zimbabwe. Turkey had an inflation rate of 59.5 percent. These five nations have a combined population of more than 220 million.

Add in Nigeria (220 million) and Egypt (111 million), which are inflating at rates of 23.5 and 32.5 percent respectively, and you have more than half a billion people desperate to exchange their hyperinflating currencies for something that does not devalue rapidly. Most of these countries make it difficult to exchange their native currency for dollars, so these and other developing nations are among the fastest growing adopters of bitcoin, led by Nigeria, with 20 percent of the population using bitcoin daily for transactions, the highest rate in the world. As these numbers climb in Africa and Latin America, there will not be enough new bitcoin to serve millions of new users (see Chapter 20 for a detailed analysis). India also has an estimated 100 million bitcoin holders.

3) *Ease of use, lower regulatory barriers.* One reason why the impact of the Bitcoin ETF was so immediate and profound was its ability to quickly onboard anyone with an online brokerage into owning an instrument invested in bitcoin. Heretofore, new users had to sign up for a centralized crypto exchange, which in the early days was challenging to understand and navigate, and in recent years has been difficult to sign up for because of regulatory restrictions. Eight of the top ten crypto exchanges in the world do not allow Americans to be clients, including the largest one, Binance. Of the top twenty exchanges, only three (Coinbase, Kraken, and Gemini) onboard US residents. Even then, the amount of paperwork required to open an account vastly exceeds what is required to open a traditional bank account. This is in complete opposition to the

very purpose of bitcoin, which is to be accessible to anyone with a computer or mobile phone and access to the internet.

Times are changing, with two of the three leading candidates for US president promising to be crypto-friendly and lower entry barriers. Better interfaces and cold storage devices also make buying and selling bitcoin and other cryptocurrencies as easy as trading stocks. This will make onboarding the next billion users far easier than the first few million.

4) *Supply shock meets demand shock.* Simply put, demand for bitcoin is rising. As noted earlier, there is simply not enough new bitcoin to accommodate 600 million new users buying even $100 each at current prices. There is also insufficient bitcoin that will ever exist to accommodate every millionaire in the world buying one bitcoin each—at any price. Gold's market cap is nearly $16 trillion because of its widespread adoption, with the average American owning two ounces of gold and the global average closer to one ounce of gold per person on earth.

Similar to the rise of gold in 2024, bitcoin increases in value when more investors feel left out if they don't have any—or want more if they're already owners. Short sellers bet on the price going down; when they're wrong, there is a short squeeze sending prices even higher. This continues throughout each bull market until the bubble pops, but new demand coupled with low supply can accelerate the market top above the normal diminishing returns of the cycles.

In Chapter 9, I discussed the stock-to-flow model proposed by Dr. Saifedean Ammous in *The Bitcoin Standard* [cxxxvii] and the modeling work of PlanB, whose charting has been extremely close to predicting the market tops thus far. When he released the model in 2019, he predicted bitcoin's price through 2028, with looser guidance through 2040. At the start of 2024, he updated his model with even more bullish guidance.

His daily modeling predicted $68,343 bitcoin for June 22, 2024. The actual price was $64,240. His prediction for the price of bitcoin on the day of the Bitcoin halving, April 19, 2024, was $51,487. My prediction of the halving price from 2022 was $45,000. The actual price was $63,900. PlanB's model has bitcoin hitting the iconic all-time high mark of $100,000 in September 2024, then passing $150,000 in November 2024, and $200,000 in early January 2025. A word of caution about his models: he does not take into account market corrections, just 365-day averages over a straight line. His model ends up with bitcoin reaching a 365-day average of $471,739 by April 2028.

You can follow Plan B's updates for free on his X account @100trillionusd.[cxxxviii] His clever Twitter/X handle is both a reference to the 100 trillion Zimbabwe dollar note as an omen of where the US dollar may be headed, along with a potential market cap for bitcoin at $5 million per bitcoin. Here is his most recent chart, with price predictions through 2028:

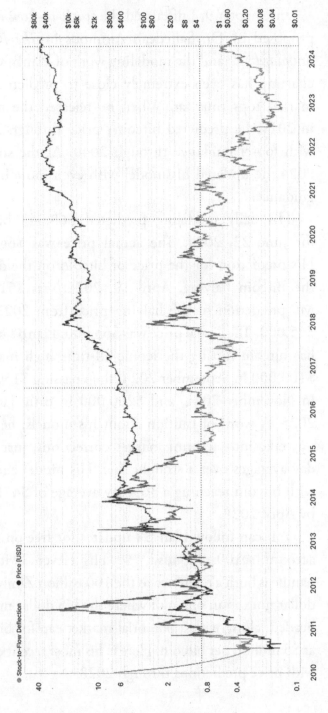

Bitcoin: Stock-to-Flow Deflection

● Stock-to-Flow Deflection   ● Price [USD]

glassnode

My modeling is not as bullish as PlanB's, and I present it in two ways:

1) The first chart takes the diminishing returns of the past four cycles (roughly 3,000x for the first pre-halving cycle, followed by 100x after the first halving, followed by 30x after the second halving, then roughly 8x for the third halving; from those trends, I project 3x the halving price for this cycle).

   I also note that in addition to the exponentially diminishing returns each cycle for the highs, there have been diminishing losses, but on more of a linear scale. In the first bitcoin cycle prior to any halving, there was a 97 percent crash from the cycle high of $30 to the low of $1. After the first halving in 2012, there was an 86 percent plummet from the peak of Bitcoin Summer in 2013 until capitulation in early 2014. For the second halving, there was an 84 percent drop from the 2017 top to the early 2019 bottom. Most recently, there was a 77 percent decline from the 2021 all-time high to the FTX capitulation in late 2022.

   Given that halving prices have always risen substantially in between cycles thus far *and* the cycle lows have always been higher than the halving price, either the halving prices will start being higher than the subsequent cycle capitulation or the rate of diminishing losses will be much less as the asset class becomes more mature. The latter proposition is the path I am taking in this chart.

2) My second chart accounts for a Supercycle effect, presuming higher than linear adoption and the beginning

of the "S Curve" that defines many other technology adoption lifecycles. I don't need to repeat the first four cycles above, so I will concentrate on my projections using a Supercycle approach over the next twenty years, at which point more than 99.9 percent of all bitcoin will have been mined, leaving less than 21,000 bitcoin to be mined over the final 96 years.

While I firmly believe that a Bitcoin Supercycle between now and 2044 could surpass these numbers, with adoption by four billion people (10x what it is today) powering $700,000 bitcoin by 2033 and $1,000,000 bitcoin by 2041, the conservative part of me wants to counteract these positives with the impact of futures trading and increasingly sophisticated financial vehicles. These instruments used by institutions, including ETFs, can mitigate the raw buying pressure by funneling it through futures contracts and derivatives to smooth out the price spikes, as has been done with gold and silver contracts for many years.

Wall Street investment research firm Bernstein boldly predicted in June 2024[cxxxix] that bitcoin could top $200,000 this cycle and break the $1 million barrier by 2033. ARK Invest CEO Cathie Wood had previously said she believed bitcoin could top $1 million by 2030. Whichever of the charts above comes closer to the factual performance in the next decade or two, even the most conservative of these models would most likely outperform traditional equities, bonds, and commodities by a significant margin.

In the next chapter, I will demonstrate techniques used by other crypto investment professionals and me to help maximize returns without being a day trader. It will include an

Bitcoin Cycle	Halving Price	Cycle High	Halving to High Percentage Gain	Cycle Low	Cycle High to Low Percentage Loss
2009–2012	$0.001*	$30	2,999,900%	$1*	-96.67%
2012–2016	$12.70	$1,242	9,679.53%	$172.21	-86.13%
2016–2020	$670	$19,783.21	2,582.72	$3,237.06	-83.64%
2020–2024	$8,727	$68,982	690.44%	$15,742.44	-77.18%
2024–2028 **	$63,900	$191,700	200%	$73,229.40	-61.8%
2028–2032 **	$148,887	$346,906	133%	$156,107	-45%

* There was no halving in the first Bitcoin cycle, so I use the first quoted sale price. I also use the lowest reported price of $1 during the 2011 crash, not the lowest daily close of $2.05.

** All numbers for the 2024 and 2028 cycles other than the actual halving price are estimates, based on my Four Seasons model, using diminishing returns and no supercycle accelerator.

Diminishing Returns Model (estimates using Four Seasons of Bitcoin, plus Supercycle)

Cycle / % Bitcoin Mined	Halving Price	Cycle High	Cycle Low
2024–2028 / 98.4375%	$63,900 (actual)	$284,345 in 2025	$93,834
2028–2032 / 99.21875%	$166,779	$435,293 in 2029	$217,646
2032–2036 / 99.609375%	$348,234	$557,175 in 2033	$367,736
2036–2040 / 99.8046875%	$478,056	$664,498 in 2037	$531,598
2040–2044 / 99.90234375%	$691,077	$898,401 in 2041	$763,461

introduction to some basic metrics and trading terms that help explain how to read a chart and how past performance can help predict future behavior more often than not. Of course, one can choose to manage one's bitcoin portfolio more aggressively, to diversify into other crypto assets like Ethereum and altcoins, or to stake part of one's crypto portfolio for additional yield. I discuss these alternatives in Chapters 16–19, then finish with two chapters about Bitcoin's long-term future as an asset class in Chapters 20 and 21.

Chapter Fifteen

Mastering the Cycles

Mastery is not a function of genius or talent. It is a function of time and intense focus applied to a particular field of knowledge.

—Robert Greene[cxl]

You must immerse yourself in your work. You have to fall in love with your work. You must dedicate your life to mastering your skill. That's the secret of success.

—Chef Jiro[cxli]

The big money is not in the buying or selling, but in the waiting.

—Charlie Munger[cxlii]

In the past, one did not have to master the cycles of Bitcoin to make a substantial, even crazy profit. Over the past decade, "buy and hold" was a solid way to beat the returns of every other asset class substantially. Those who bought and held bitcoin since the start of 2020 were up more than 10x by March 2024. Investors from 2016 made at least 100x their money invested at the halving. Earlier investors who stuck to the course since the first halving in 2012 made 5,000 times their initial investment. Pioneers who were fortunate enough to buy or mine during the first pre-halving cycle and held on through all the ups and downs are up an average of more than 50,000x their investment.

Given that half of all bitcoin were mined during that initial period, a fair amount of multimillionaires may become billionaires over the next few years by holding on to a few thousand dollars investments during this period. I remember the tale of a San Francisco bartender who put his life savings of $50,000 into bitcoin at $1. Do the math on what that price would be today. Roger Ver (aka Bitcoin Jesus) put $250,000 into bitcoin at $1, and he still retains enough to be a billionaire many times over.

It has been estimated that when the price of bitcoin exceeds $1,000,000, the majority of the world's billionaires will achieve that status from their investments in bitcoin and other cryptocurrencies. How so? According to *Forbes*, there are currently 2,781 billionaires, a list which in 2024 included a mere seventeen who made their wealth through digital assets. Only one of these, Binance founder Changpeng Zhao (CZ), was in the top 100. Yet, there are more than two thousand addresses with more than one thousand bitcoin, and 15,000 addresses with more than one hundred bitcoin, many of which are likely owned by people who in total have more than a thousand bitcoin. For every dollar of bitcoin wealth, there is at least one dollar of wealth in other cryptocurrencies, most of which are also unevenly distributed. The top 10 percent of Bitcoin addresses equate to more than 98 percent of the wealth.

What if you're starting now with a modest sum to invest? While one can still likely beat the stock market over the next decade with a buy-and-hold strategy, the bitcoin market is mature enough that it really behooves you to follow the Four Seasons of Bitcoin and trade at least twice per four-year cycle. As the previous chapters have explained, one can dramatically grow one's wealth over several cycles through the compounding effect of selling at or near the cycle top at the end of Bitcoin Summer, then waiting patiently (following the advice of Charlie Munger about the stock market) until the final capitulation at the end of Bitcoin Fall occurs. That is when you must buy back a larger amount of bitcoin at deeply discounted prices relative to your top-of-the-market sales.

Can one do even better buying and selling more often? Of course, but it has its risks. These are the techniques that I use and recommend to accumulate more bitcoin:

1) *Start early.* Bitcoin's diminishing returns have greatly rewarded those who invested early in its history. While nearly 94 percent of all bitcoin has been mined,[cxliii] we are still only five cycles into a total of thirty-three four-year cycles until the last fraction of a bitcoin is mined in 2140. If you're in your sixties and in good health, you'll likely see at least another four or five cycles. If you're in your twenties, and medical technology keeps improving, it's possible you might see another fifteen to twenty cycles.

If bitcoin is to reach $1 million, it will likely be in the next twenty years, perhaps as soon as two more cycles. The ultimate price of bitcoin could be as high as $10 million in fifty to one hundred years, given inflation growing the sum of all global wealth and bitcoin eating into it each year. That would be roughly 10x the price of the global market capitalization of gold; today, bitcoin is not even 10 percent of the size of the gold market. The fact that the bitcoin ETF market will likely exceed the ETF market for gold within a year shows the massive expansion potential for bitcoin against gold.

2) *Know when to buy, when to sell, when to wait.* The previous chapters in this book provide sufficient information to follow the Four Seasons of Bitcoin model and increase your returns by what has historically been 3–4x every four years over simply holding. Even if that ratio drops to 2–3x in the next few cycles, then less than 50 percent in a few more cycles, it will still provide better returns than the "set it and forget it" of HODLing.

If you wish to make more profit per cycle by trading more often, it will take more vigilance and more education. The rest of this book will provide an entry-level view into more sophisticated techniques and alternative asset classes. Done well, they can increase your returns above and beyond the Four Seasons approach. Done sloppily, you can get wrecked ("rekt" in bitcoin parlance). Most importantly, this will take studying and daily discipline. The basic Four Seasons approach only requires that you pay attention twice during each four-year cycle.

An in-between path, which I personally choose in lieu of riskier strategies like options trading, is adding to positions throughout the Winter, Spring, and early Summer on dips. One can also sell on rallies on the way down in Bitcoin Fall, presuming one didn't sell everything at the peak of Bitcoin Summer. Over the next four chapters, I will provide a summary of riskier trading strategies as well as investing in alternative digital asset classes.

One interesting trend to remember, beyond the four-year seasonality, is the monthly trends within each year. Bull market or bear, October and November have on average been solidly up, known as green months, while June through September have by and large been red months. This is true in particular for September, which has also been a month that stock market crashes have clustered around. On the other hand, historically, October has been another bad month for stocks, but in most years it has marked the beginning of a new or extended upward trend for bitcoin, earning it the nickname of "Uptober."

Like everything else in Bitcoin, this can be tracked and analyzed. My friend and presenting partner at CoinAgenda Dubai in 2023, Vineet Budki, managing director of Cypher Capital, has tracked monthly trends and made exceedingly accurate price predictions for the past few cycles. His X account @vineetbudki[cxliv] is worthwhile reading, as he is always on top of trends in both on-chain metrics, as well as venture capital heading up a $200 million digital asset fund. His most recent chart as of publication time is below:

3) *Start thinking in bitcoin, not dollars.* While I don't agree with Bitcoin Maximalists on everything, I agree with them on the ultimate value of bitcoin: "One bitcoin will always equal one bitcoin." Buying one hundred bitcoins for $100 in 2011 doesn't make it less valuable today. Everyone's minimum goal should be ownership of at least one full bitcoin (known as being a "wholecoiner"). If you can buy it today, please do so. If you can only afford to buy one-tenth of a bitcoin, you're

Bitcoin: Monthly Returns (%)

Time	January	February	March	April	May	June	July	August	September	October	November	December
2024	+0.62%	+43.55%	+16.81%	-14.76%	+5.01%							
2023	+39.63%	+0.03%	+22.96%	+2.81%	-6.98%	+11.98%	-4.02%	-11.29%	+3.91%	+28.52%	+8.81%	+12.18%
2022	-16.68%	+12.21%	+5.39%	-17.3%	-15.6%	-37.28%	+16.8%	-13.88%	-3.12%	+5.56%	-16.23%	-3.59%
2021	+14.51%	+36.78%	+29.84%	-1.98%	-35.31%	-5.95%	+18.19%	+13.8%	-7.03%	+39.93%	-7.11%	-18.9%
2020	+29.95%	-8.6%	-24.92%	+34.26%	+9.51%	-3.18%	+24.03%	+2.83%	-7.51%	+27.7%	+42.95%	+46.92%
2019	-8.58%	+11.14%	+7.05%	+34.36	+52.38%	+26.67%	-6.59%	-4.6%	-13.38%	+10.17%	-17.27%	-5.15%
2018	-25.41%	+0.47%	-32.85%	+33.43%	-18.99%	-14.62%	+20.96%	-9.27%	-5.58%	-3.83%	-36.57%	-5.15%
2017	-0.04%	+23.07%	-9.05%	+32.71%	+52.71%	+10.45%	+17.92%	+65.32%	-7.44%	+47.81%	+53.48%	+38.89%
2016	-14.83%	+20.08%	-5.35%	+7.27%	+18.78%	+27.14%	-7.67%	-7.49%	-6.04%	+14.71%	+5.42%	+30.8%
2015	-33.05%	+18.43%	-4.38%	-3.46%	-3.17%	+15.19%	+8.2%	-18.67%	+2.35%	+33.49%	+19.27%	+13.83%
2014	+10.03%	-31.03%	-17.25%	-1.6%	+39.46%	+2.2%	-9.69%	-17.55%	-19.01%	-12.95%	+12.82%	-15.11%
2013	+44.05%	+61.77%	+172.76%	+50.01%	-8.56%	-29.89%	+9.6%	+30.42%	-1.76%	+60.79%	+449.35%	-34.81%
Average	+3.35%	+15.66%	+13.42%	+12.98%	+7.44%	+0.25%	+7.98%	+2.69%	-4.78%	+22.90%	+46.81%	+5.45%
Median	+0.29%	+15.32%	+0.50%	+5.04%	+0.92%	+2.20%	+9.60%	-7.49%	-5.58%	+27.70%	+8.81%	-3.59%

one-tenth of your way to owning a full bitcoin. If my projections for the next three cycles come to pass, this may be one of the last times you'll be able to buy a whole bitcoin for less than $100,000.

This strategy was employed by more than 100,000 wallets during the last Bitcoin Winter, as the number of bitcoin wallets with one bitcoin or more grew from less than 900,000 at the beginning of 2022 to passing the one million wallet mark in May 2023. It has stayed over one million wallets for thirteen consecutive months.

To put this in perspective, of the 54.5 million bitcoin addresses with at least $1, less than 2 percent (about one million wallets) have at least one whole bitcoin. As more people get bitcoin addresses, this percentage will go down. For much of the time between 2013 and 2017, a reasonable goal was to be "one in a million" and own 21 bitcoin. At $1,000 a bitcoin, that was a little over $20,000. As of the recent March 2024 price, that same purchase was more than $1.5 million. For those with portfolios of more than $10 million, this is still a reasonable goal that I believe is likely to outperform the rest of your portfolio over time.

4) *Seek more bitcoin in Winter and more dollars in Summer.* This statement is not contrary to the point above. The best way to maximize one's bitcoin holdings over time is to sell bitcoin for cash at the peak of Bitcoin Summer. Patiently, keep that cash in yield-bearing stablecoins or liquidity pools (see Chapter 18) or in traditional investments like stocks, commodities, or real estate. Then you sell or encumber those stable

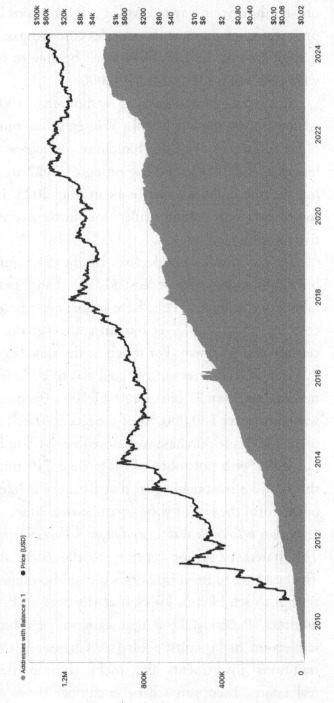

Bitcoin: Number of Addresses with Balance ≥ 1

● Addresses with Balance ≥ 1   ● Price [USD]

glassnode

investments about a year later to deploy cash into the bleeding market after the capitulation that has always happened at the end of Bitcoin Fall. Repeat this a few cycles, and you will have substantially more bitcoin than where you started.

Determining the Fair Value of Bitcoin

In the Bitcoin white paper, Satoshi described a cryptographically secure system of creating the digital equivalent of gold, which for thousands of years had backed most currencies. Bitcoin, if successful, could once again separate the creation, saving, and spending of money from being a function of the state to a right of the individual. Fifteen years later, bitcoin has grown from an experiment with no value into a trillion-dollar-plus asset class with the market capitalization of gold as a target in sight.

Technically, there was a baby Bitcoin supercycle during its first five years, with the price of one bitcoin running up from $0.001 in 2009 to more than $1,000 per bitcoin in late 2013, which is one million times the price in less than five years. One can see this early parabolic growth on the Bitcoin Cycle Master chart (a combination of on-chain metrics that help determine the fair value of bitcoin, which in turn helps identify when it is undervalued or overvalued). Thus far, there has been a remarkable correlation between the on-chain data and the predictive model of my Four Seasons of Bitcoin, with bitcoin fairly priced at each halving, then overvalued at the all-time highs and drastically undervalued at the cycle lows:

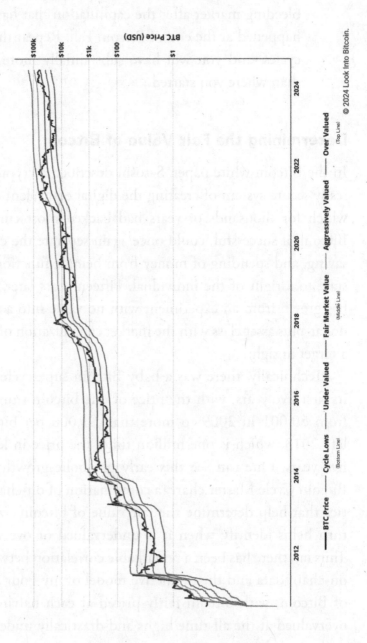

Look Into Bitcoin: Bitcoin Cycle Master

BTC Price (USD)

$100k
$10k
$1k
$100
$1

2012 2014 2016 2018 2020 2022 2024

— BTC Price — Cycle Lows — Under Valued — Fair Market Value — Aggressively Valued — Over Valued
(Bottom Line) (Middle Line) (Top Line)

© 2024 Look Into Bitcoin.

The five lines tracking the historic performance of bitcoin from its inception have bands ranging from cycle lows (highly undervalued) to cycle highs (highly overvalued), with the middle band indicating fairly valued. There are only four times in the history of Bitcoin that the price touched the bottom line of highly undervalued—late 2011, early 2015, early 2019, and late 2022. Each of these touchpoints corresponded almost exactly to the lowest price of each cycle. These low bands generally correspond to the 300-week moving average, which the price of bitcoin has never fallen below. *While nothing in modeling or life is guaranteed, this on-chain low-water mark every four years is the best signal to buy, as it has never been wrong.*

From those lows, the price climbs toward the halving price, which has always been significantly higher than the cycle low. Four out of four halvings have now registered at or slightly higher than the fair market value of bitcoin on the date of halving, which I find to be one of my most interesting statistics of all. It proves the importance of the halving as the fundamental driver of each cycle.

Following each halving date, there is a period of sideways trading as the least efficient bitcoin miners retool or capitulate. Once the mining difficulty adjusts and the historical profitability of miners is restored, the prices begin to rise based on supply and demand. As described in earlier chapters, Bitcoin Summer takes place when the prior all-time high is breached, kicking off a parabolic rally.

In the current 2024–2028 cycle, Bitcoin Summer actually preceded Bitcoin Spring for the first time. In this case, the prices dropped from March 14, 2024, an all-time high of nearly 15 percent, to the halving, then stayed relatively flat for the next three months, making it act more like a typical Bitcoin Spring than Bitcoin Summer. I believe this temporary retreat in price occurred for two reasons:

1) Many miners became unprofitable because of the halving and were unable to secure more financing because of the interest rate environment and lower bitcoin prices. They were forced to sell most of the bitcoins they mined to keep the lights on. This occurred at the start of May. Bitcoin prices rebounded above $70k by the start of June, then dropped as low as $50k by the end of the summer. None of this invalidates the bull market ahead.

2) There is a trifecta of sellers at the start of this cycle that is not normal in most cycles:

   a. Japanese bankruptcy trustees will finally distribute upward of $9 billion of bitcoin to holders who are creditors of Mt. Gox from a decade ago when the exchange failed. There is a fear that the majority of recipients will immediately dump the bitcoin on the open market, although this is not consistent with the behavior of early bitcoin investors from 2012 to 2014.

   b. The trustees for FTX's more recent bankruptcy have been selling bitcoin to pay back creditors on a cash basis. However, the value of their bitcoin has risen almost fivefold since that 2022 insolvency. Payouts are estimated to be more than $11 billion, although not all of that is from bitcoin sales. FTX also had cash and real estate, appreciated.

c. Unlike every other approved bitcoin exchange-traded fund, the GBTC ETF continues to have more outflows than inflows. This is due to its high fees, which are six times the rate of competitors, as well as many of its investors who bought GBTC public stock when it was priced at a significant discount to bitcoin and are cashing out their profits.

Mastering the Cycles

Each new cycle brings new information, as well as fresh challenges, including the following:

Conflicting data. Every halving has at least one instance where two trends that were once reliable are now in conflict. The first two cycles (one without a halving) contained overwhelmingly fresh data with little to compare it against. The second halving identified a repeating trend of Q4 all-time highs, which end Bitcoin Summer with an exclamation point, as well as the timing of capitulation at the end of Bitcoin Fall, which once again landed twelve to fourteen months after the all-time high.

After the third halving, there was a conflict in determining which of two trends would continue: the lengthening of the time between halving and the all-time high (twelve months in 2013, eighteen months in 2016–2017) or the high always occurring in the fourth quarter the year following the halving. As noted in an earlier chapter, there was data backing both of these trends, but only one could win. When the lengthening cycle theory did not prevail, it strengthened the Q4 all-time high predictability. This does not guarantee that it will repeat again, but it has had a powerful hold on expectations thus far.

Breaking precedents. It was a given that all-time highs must occur after the halving, until in 2024, the new all-time high came first. Investors and chart theorists are still trying to figure out the meaning of this. Will the cycle end early? Will the cycle break all-time highs beyond expectations, creating the start of a supercycle? These are the questions investors must study carefully as new data arrives.

Diminishing returns. Each cycle has had less of a parabolic rally on a percentage basis from beginning to cycle high, which has always occurred in the third year of the cycle. This is even true for the pre-halving cycle of 2009–2012. These epic spikes have decreased in magnitude every four years on more of a logarithmic scale, whereas the diminishing losses after the bubble pops decreased in a linear fashion. Without a Bitcoin Supercycle, the asset class could be as flat as the gold and silver markets, where a 20 percent annual gain is considered a bull market. Under that scenario, the bitcoin price could take another few decades to break $1,000,000.

While it's best to plan for diminishing returns and losses using my most conservative model in the last chapter, one must always be prepared for the prospects of a supercycle to begin at any time going forward. Given how technologies break out quickly, from automobiles to color televisions to the internet, we must be careful students of the charts to see when the S Curve of technology adoption is in play. There are other theories around growth cycles to be aware of and consider, including Elliott Waves and Wyckoff distribution.

Ralph Nelson Elliott (1871–1948) first wrote about his Wave Principle during the Great Depression of the 1930s, properly identifying that a collective trader sentiment is a form of crowd psychology, fluctuating between optimism and pessimism in repeating sequences of intensity and duration. Both Elliott and his followers wrote about a Grand Supercycle lasting a century or more, each containing Supercycles of forty to seventy years. Within each Supercycle, cycles run for a few years each. While I don't believe bitcoin fits the Elliott cycle model per se, the "cycles" part of it has elements that are similar to my Four Seasons model.

Richard Wyckoff (1873–1934) was a contemporary of Elliott's who is considered to be one of the fathers of technical analysis of stocks, alongside Charles Dow, founder of Dow Jones. His Wyckoff distribution model shows trends in the stock market where one should sell (distribute) at the highs, then buy (accumulate) at the lows,[cxlv] with prediction models based on volume analysis and price action. The method has many variations, but it is consistent with the basics of the Four Seasons of Bitcoin model.

Advanced technical analysis developed over the past century for the stock market has been used to predict movements in the bitcoin and cryptocurrency markets. These include Fibonacci retracement, head-and-shoulders pattern formation, ascending and descending triangles, bull and bear traps, and the dead cat bounce.

You only need to be concerned about these if you plan on being a day trader or options trader. Excellent YouTube and X/Twitter programs have developed in the past five years, with aggregate audiences in the millions. Despite my not being a day trader, I keep up with the best programs, including *Into the Cryptoverse, Carl the Moon, Crypto Banter, Ellio Trades, Ivan on Tech*, and *CryptosRUs* on a near-daily basis.

Chapter Sixteen
The World Computer

Bitcoin is great as a form of digital money, but its script-ing language is too weak for any kind of serious advanced applications to be built on top.

—Vitalik Buterin[cxlvi]

If Bitcoin is the promise, then Ethereum is the delivery: Fair computing built atop fair settlement, for anyone, at any time, forever. Ethereum is the World Computer.

— Inevitable Ethereum (compilation)[cxlvii]

Innovation distinguishes between a leader and a follower.

—Steve Jobs[cxlviii]

Continuing to refer to ethereum as an "alt" is as outdated as referring to a lambo as a "horseless carriage.

—Vitalik Buterin[cxlix]

Why am I discussing Ethereum in a book named *Bitcoin Supercycle*? First, I believe in innovation and have witnessed first-hand the growth of Ethereum from its earliest days. In just a few short years, the project progressed from a frantically paced, at times chaotic, founder-led startup to the world's leading smart contract blockchain ecosystem with a market cap in the hundreds of billions of dollars that impacts millions of people daily.

Second, this is a book about understanding and investing in cryptocurrency, so I believe it would be irresponsible not to point out that Ethereum and its subsequent clones, known as EVM-compatible blockchains, have created life-changing wealth for many investors. EVM stands for Ethereum Virtual Machine, and it's the programming engine that makes self-executing smart contracts interact with a consensus-driven blockchain initially modeled after Bitcoin. If you are a Bitcoin maximalist or feel that you need to stay focused on your goal of maximizing your bitcoin wealth with no detours into the world of Ethereum or other alternative cryptocurrencies, then you can skip the next four chapters and resume reading at Chapter 20.

Congratulations to those of you still reading! You are now open to the possibilities of a multichain future, as am I. The Ethereum white paper, *A Next-Generation Smart Contract and Decentralized Application Platform* is nearly six times as long as Satoshi's Bitcoin white paper.[d] Ethereum is the protocol, and ether is its native token. For its first seven years, ether was mined like bitcoin but using a different mining ecosystem and language designed to not advance the difficulty as fast, saving on energy while protecting the network from attack. Ethereum mining fees are called gas. With its 2022 migration from proof-of-work to proof-of-stake, billions of dollars in gas fees now go to users staking ether instead of miners. In Chapter 18, we explain how investors can earn yields on Ethereum and other digital assets.

While many early bitcoin holders believe that Ethereum and other "altcoins" detract from the value of bitcoin, I believe the opposite is true. If only bitcoin existed, there would be no other place to diversify within the cryptocurrency asset class. In addition, the very properties that make Bitcoin the best system for a decentralized store of value, including its hard-to-change rules, make it ill-suited for future innovation in other areas. Decentralized finance (DeFi), token sales, smart contracts, NFTs, Web3 gaming, and decentralized AI got their start or major expansion on Ethereum or an EVM-based chain.

Once you've mastered your understanding of the investment opportunities within Bitcoin, you are ready to see what other protocols have to offer and how they fluctuate along the same general cycles. The best place to start is Ethereum. Because I advise and invest in many new projects, my personal ratio is skewed, but I generally favor a portfolio that's 60 percent bitcoin, 20 percent ether, and 20 percent altcoins. I believe the 80 percent in bitcoin and ether, properly managed, have dramatically outperformed traditional equities and should continue to outperform them for the next twenty years. The 20 percent devoted to altcoins can outperform or underperform, depending on how skillfully one buys, holds, and sells, and there is a chance that the entire altcoin portfolio could be decimated. That said, picking a single altcoin that increases by 100x can dramatically affect the entire portfolio. I will discuss proposed allotment strategies in the next chapter.

Ethereum's World Computer

I first met Vitalik Buterin when he was a student at the University of Waterloo, just before he dropped out to write the Ethereum white paper, which changed his life and the direction of the cryptocurrency markets forever. Like most altcoin builders, Vitalik's first love was bitcoin. He cofounded *Bitcoin Magazine* when he was just sixteen years of age. The occasion of our meeting was him interviewing me on a trip to Toronto about where bitcoin was headed (we also met in Waterloo, where I presented to a startup incubator at the university). I then met up with him again just two months later with his Ethereum cofounder Anthony Di Iorio to help plan the launch of their promising ICO, which planned to raise $18 million, which was by far the most significant token sale to date.

Satoshi's key breakthrough with Bitcoin was using proof-of-work cryptography to prevent double-spending and verify transactions between any willing parties on earth, improving upon Wei Dai, David Chaum, and other cypherpunks whose systems lacked that critical component. Vitalik's breakthrough was creating a "Turing complete" blockchain, wherein smart contracts could execute on the blockchain; hence its description as a "world computer" and a "virtual machine,"[cli] improving Nick Szabo's theoretical work on smart contracts. Bitcoin was a phenomenal peer-to-peer system for electronic cash, but it was a ledger, not a computer. Vitalik's vision was to create the world computer.

The fund I started with my BitAngels cofounder David A. Johnston, the Dapps Fund, invested $1 million in bitcoin into the Ethereum ICO, yielding 333,333 tokens. Our fund took our carry and distributed the tokens to the LPs when it started trading. Those who held until the 2021 all-time high of $4,815 earned a return of 160,000 percent. Had we as a fund distributed the tokens when they reached that price, the tokens we purchased would have appreciated to $16 billion.

While no token has outperformed bitcoin from its start, the Ethereum ICO wildly outperformed the 100x that bitcoin had grown since July 2014 when the Ethereum ICO took place. Since then, it has been as wild a ride for Ethereum as it has for bitcoin, reaching a high of $30 during the second Bitcoin cycle, then dropping to $5 before rocketing up to $1,100 during the third Bitcoin cycle. The price of ether then cratered to $80, and there were whispers that the Ethereum Foundation would not be able to pay its bills for very long. This nadir was followed by the 2021 all-time high of $4,815 in the fourth Bitcoin cycle. In addition, Ethereum now lets one earn interest on one's cryptocurrency, paid out in ether, generated by the gas fees being redistributed to stakers. Staking for interest (or "yield" as it's more commonly called) makes ether an asset that compounds, whereas bitcoin does not. The current yield on ether is 3.2 percent, resulting from running nodes to support the network's proof-of-stake consensus. One can also do this through a third-party provider or token, as outlined in Chapter 18.

How Much to Diversify

How much of one's crypto portfolio should one put into Ethereum? Michael Saylor says it should be zero. "Diversification is exchanging a superior asset for an inferior one," he stated in a recent interview on YouTube. "You don't want to have the Amazon of Singapore. You want Amazon." True to his word, his corporate treasury holds more than 200,000 bitcoin and zero other cryptocurrencies. In the less than four years since he first bought bitcoin, Microstrategy stock has grown by 1,460 percent through March 2024.

Some believe Ethereum's best days are behind it and that it will be overtaken in gains this wave by newcomer

Solana, which launched in 2017. I remember being offered the Solana ICO at 20 cents and turning it down. Four years later, it reached $240, dramatically outperforming ether and bitcoin. During the Bitcoin Fall of 2022,[clii] Solana dropped in value by 95 percent to $8, and many were calling for its demise. It was too centralized; it broke down too much, and it was the protocol that the failed FTT token was created on. Sam Bankman Fried and FTX were among the top holders of Solana, so its appreciation helped pay back FTX creditors once the complicated web of Alameda Research was unwound.[cliii]

Alternately, some of the best returns in each cycle have been finding "hidden gems" either at the token sale or even on the open market when they are priced well outside of the top 100 tokens and riding them to top 50 status. These tend to be tokens in a hot category, which we will discuss in the next chapter on altcoins.

Here are some metrics to help decide on the extent of diversification into ether:

1) *Bitcoin is less risky and less volatile than Ethereum,* which one can clearly see comparing their four-year charts. Ethereum tends to outperform bitcoin in the bull market and underperform it during the bear (see chart). One winning strategy in the past three cycles has been to hold bitcoin until it surpasses its prior all-time high, then diversify into ether until it reaches its presumed all-time high for the cycle, using similar calculations described in the Four Seasons of Bitcoin chapters. At that point, you can either move back into bitcoin and/or sell both bitcoin and ether, waiting out

Bitcoin Fall, when the price of bitcoin, ether, and altcoins fall in tandem.

2) *Ether has higher highs and lower lows.* Each cycle thus
far has had a larger percentage gain on the way up
and a more sizable drop on the way down, which is
consistent with the volatility noted above. It has been
reported that ether has followed a similar pattern of
diminishing returns to bitcoin, but one cycle behind.
Let's look at how this theory plays out:

You will notice that ether's first complete Bitcoin cycle (2016–
2020), from a 2015 pre-halving low of $0.42 to a 2018 cycle
high of $1,119.37, made for a gain of 266,417 percent. This
is roughly double the prior cycle's gain for bitcoin of 124,100
percent. One cycle later (2020–2024), ether rose from a
pre-halving cycle low in late 2018 of $82.83 to a 2021 cycle
high of $4,815, a gain of 5,713.11 percent. In this case, the
gain was more than double that of bitcoin for the same period
but roughly half the price gain for the prior cycle.

What does this mean for the current halving cycle? It's
hard to tell because the data was not consistent. If ether hits
a 2025 cycle high that is one-half the 2021 cycle high for
bitcoin, the top price would be $9,990, which is in line with
many predictions as to where ether might top out this cycle.
Assuming my prediction for a bitcoin price nearing $200,000
this cycle, which would be more than twelve times the capitulation price in 2022 of $15,742.44. For the moment that
my projected price occurs, ether would need to outperform
bitcoin this cycle—it would have to pass $11,000 per ether,
which is not out of the question by any means. The current
race is neck and neck, with bitcoin gaining 368 percent from

Bitcoin Cycle	Bitcoin Gain (prior cycle capitulation to cycle high)	Bitcoin Loss (cycle high to capitulation)	Ether Gain (prior capitulation to cycle high)	Ether Loss (cycle high to capitulation)
2009–2012	2,999,900%	–96.67%	n/a	n/a
2012–2016	124,100%	-86.13%	$0.42 to $21.25 (June 15, 2016) 4,959.52%	$21.25 to $6.00 –71.76%
2016–2020	11,387.5%	–83.64%	$6.00 to $1,375 22,816.7%	$1,375 to $82.83 93.98%
2020–2024	2,031%	–77.18%	$82.83 to $4,815 5713.11%	$4,815 to $896 –81.39%
2024–2028 (partial, as of highest price in March 2024)	$15,742.44 to $73,737.94 368.4 % (3/14/24)		$896 to $4,098.69 (as of 3/12/24) 357.44%	n/a (cycle not complete)

its low-water mark in late 2022 to its current, most recent all-time high as of March 2024. Ether lagged this performance slightly, just up 357.44 percent from its 2022 capitulation until its recent high. Unlike bitcoin, the price of ether has not yet beaten its 2021 all-time high.

Under what circumstances would ether outperform bitcoin this cycle? First, the Ethereum ETF has been approved and just started trading as of the final edits on this book. Thus far, no Ether ETFs include a return from staking, making them an inferior investment than simply buying staked Ethereum on LIDO or other protocols. If the SEC lets ETFs stake ether on behalf of the ETF, it would provide good reason for traditional investors to choose it over a bitcoin ETF: native yield.

If ether does not beat its prior all-time high this cycle, it is a bad sign for the future of Ethereum. Of the top twenty-five cryptocurrencies by market cap, only bitcoin and BNB, the Binance network token, have existed for more than two complete cycles and set new all-time highs each cycle. Others, including Ethereum, are likely to set new all-time highs this cycle but have not yet done so. As I show in the next chapter, most altcoins—even ones in the top 100—are essentially "one-hit wonders" and do not grow every cycle. Only time will tell if Ethereum continues to keep pace, even exceed, the ongoing performance of bitcoin.

Chapter Seventeen

Altcoin Season and the Memecoin Casino

I am not a product of my circumstances. I am a product of my decisions.

—Stephen R. Covey[cliv]

You miss 100% of the shots you don't take.

—Wayne Gretzky[clv]

I'm a great believer in luck, and I find the harder I work, the more I have of it.

—Thomas Jefferson[clvi]

By this point in the book, you should have a solid understanding of Bitcoin and the opportunity it still presents to investors, even if the era of 100x returns in a year is behind us. You should also have a basic understanding of Ethereum, the second-largest cryptocurrency. As of March 11, 2024, the total market capitalization for all cryptocurrencies was $2.8 trillion, with a daily volume of $194 billion traded. This compares to the all-time high on November 8, 2021, when the total market briefly reached $3.05 trillion with $179 billion in trading. For comparison with bear markets, the total market cap for all crypto precisely one year later, on November 8, 2022, was just $828 billion, with just $25 billion in volume.[clvii]

At the height of bull markets, alternative cryptocurrencies—known as altcoins or "alts"—are the sizzle, outperforming bitcoin on average. The top altcoins radically outperform bitcoin, with several dozen having 100x returns in under a year. This happens every cycle. In the bear market, altcoins bleed as investors either lock in their gains or flee in fear of further losses, turning their alts into bitcoin or stablecoins (which I will explain in the next chapter).

During bull markets, bitcoin dominance (the percentage of the market cap that is bitcoin) often drops as a wave of new altcoins go parabolic. Before the first ICO in August 2013, bitcoin dominance was always more than 93 percent. Even the early wave of ICOs, including Ethereum, did little to change the dominance of bitcoin's market cap until February 2017, when a massive wave of popular new tokens hit the market, including Bancor, BNB, Chainlink, Cosmos, and Qtum. Bitcoin dominance dropped from 85 percent in February 2017 to just 39.1 percent four months later in June, hitting its all-time low in January 2018 at just 33.82 percent, with roughly two-thirds of the market capitalization being altcoins, led by massive gains by Ethereum. About a year after the bear market bottomed, bitcoin dominance returned, reaching 68.8 percent in December 2019. The bitcoin dominance following bear markets is even more pronounced when one removes stablecoins from the equation, reaching 74 percent at the end of 2020, just prior to that cycle's Bitcoin Summer. With the addition of so many new altcoins each cycle, the peaks for bitcoin dominance are lower each cycle, with a 97 percent peak in October 2016, 74 percent in December 2020, and 58 percent in April 2024 The delta between highs and lows has also smoothed out, with the range of bitcoin dominance only varying between 45 and 58 percent dominance since May 2021.[clviii]

Evaluating Altcoins and Timing "Altcoin Season"

If you decide to invest in altcoins as an investor, there are a few rules to remember. Making money in altcoins is much harder than consistently profiting in bitcoin, as you have to pick the right coins—or at least the right category.

Here are some guidelines:

1) *Buy the right coins.* Like bitcoin, you want to buy alts when there is "blood in the streets," but you must purchase the right ones. There is nothing to be gained from buying a coin that dropped 90 percent in the bear market only to see it drop another 90 percent or lose all of its volume, so it's effectively unsellable on the open market at any price. This is where homework comes in.

   For example, I look at the top 100 coins on CoinMarkeCap and CoinGecko daily. If I see a new coin I've never heard of break into the top 100 with a 30 percent gain, I want to learn more about it. Occasionally, I will also look at the top 500 coins to see if anything is moving up quickly with significant volume. I read the white paper, see what the token seeks to accomplish, and examine the team to see if they have the experience and vision to pull off their road map.

If it passes my basic tests, I will also ask around on my team and within my network to see if anyone else has heard of this token or has any observations about it, either from a technical, business or marketing perspective. If I'm satisfied it could be a winner, I may make a small buy and see if it goes up again the next day. Dollar-cost averaging in to a hot new token is a safer path than making a considerable conviction buy too early, even if the former might be more profitable if my intuition turns out to be correct.

2) *Buy the right narrative.* A friend who runs a digital asset hedge fund has done exceptionally well buying the correct narrative.

When Ethereum gas fees and slow transaction times had developers and users alike looking for alternatives, layer-1 protocols were the answer. Layer One refers to a primary blockchain, like Bitcoin, Ethereum, or Solana, that everything else is built upon. Technically, the blockchain protocol serves as the network's foundation, a distributed ledger technology (DLT) designed to securely record transactions on a public, immutable, and trustless ledger.[clix] New layer-1 block-chains, both EVM-compatibles like BNB, Avalanche, and Fantom, and non-EVM-compatible protocols like Solana or Cardano, built on their own new consensus network, went on to dominate the top gainers and top market caps of that era, 2017–2018. These new EVM-compatible blockchains did everything Ethereum did. They even used the same randomly generated Ethereum addresses, so that one wallet address could be used to receive several different layer-1 tokens, as long as you're running the right software in your wallet.

Layer-2 protocols were the biggest winners when Ethereum allowed new scaling solutions, including Polygon (MATIC), which grew from $0.015 in November 2020 to its all-time high of $2.92 on December 26, 2021, for an astonishing thirteen-month gain of 19,333 percent (almost 200 times money invested). Fantom (FTM) had a similar parabolic growth leading up to that cycle top. We will examine below what some of the top narratives for this cycle have been to date.

In the DeFi Summer of 2020, DeFi and yield farming tokens provided massive gains in a matter of months. I discuss much of this narrative-based bull market in Chapter 18.

3) *Buy and sell during the right season.* Altcoin seasons do not fall exactly within the Four Seasons. During Bitcoin Winter, altcoins generally continue to drop, whereas bitcoin has already begun to rebound. In Bitcoin Summer, alts tend to peak after bitcoin. This is largely because sophisticated "whale" investors who actively trade—or at least trade my seasonal approach—sell a lot of bitcoin at the peak of Bitcoin Summer. This does not mean they are out of the market. Many of them use the stablecoins they received for bitcoin at or near all-time highs to buy their favorite altcoins, running the price up even further. This happened in the Fourth Bitcoin Cycle, when after bitcoin hit $60,000 for the first time on April 17, 2021, then altcoins continued to advance, led by dogecoin hitting an all-time high

of 66 cents the day Elon Musk appeared on *Saturday Night Live*, May 8, 2021. There are typically a few altcoin rallies within each cycle, so it pays to keep and observe a watchlist of the coins you have and the coins you seek, checking it at least daily. I can't stress enough how altcoins move in exceedingly faster waves than the relatively stodgy, predictable bitcoin and ether four-year cycles.

4) *Information is key.* Read the white papers, watch YouTube, and follow "Crypto Twitter." Often, I will see an altcoin rise 40 percent overnight. When I look online to see why it moved so quickly, I generally find a piece of information that explains it well, e.g., an airdrop, a new business partnership, a mainnet (the final public version of the blockchain after testnets are completed) going live. Most of these events are discussed openly on Twitter and in the Telegram or Discord channels supporting each coin, so many people following these threads bought in before the price rise. These internal channels also give a great view into the sentiment around any particular alt, as well as the size of its community.

5) *Don't put all of your eggs in one basket.* As noted earlier, Robinhood reported that 62 percent of its crypto trades in the bullish second quarter of 2021 were in dogecoin, which dropped faster and further than bitcoin after its peak. Bitcoin has since recovered enough to make a new all-time high, whereas doge is still trading at one-sixth its 2021 high. Suppose you're going to put 20 percent of your crypto portfolio in alts. In that case, you should make it a mix of large caps (top

100 tokens) and hand-selected, carefully researched new coins, fitting a narrative similar to successful large caps, but preferably with circulating supply of less than $20 million.

6) *Look for families of coins sharing the same narrative.* Instead of investing in a single memecoin or AI token, diversify by selecting multiple options within the same category—such as five memecoins or three AI tokens. A particularly effective strategy in the past cycle was investing in tokens built on rapidly growing layer-1 protocols. For instance, if Coinbase launches and airdrops a BASE token around its Base, layer 1 EVM, you should also investigate which decentralized applications (dApps) are being developed on this new protocol. This approach is crucial because the growth of new large-cap protocols is often driven by the number of successful applications built on top of them. Every successful protocol typically needs its own lending protocol, decentralized exchange (DEX), and memecoins to sustain its growth. This strategy proved successful for tokens built on Binance (BNB) and Fantom in the last cycle. Even without a token, the Base chain has already seen the emergence of promising projects, such as the memecoin Brett (BRETT). You can benefit from their potential success by identifying and investing in these growing ecosystems early.

Choosing a Narrative

For the 2009–2012 cycle, there was pretty much only Bitcoin and Litecoin.

For the 2012–2016 cycle, a few new privacy protocols were developed, including Darkcoin (now called Dash) and Monero, as well as the earliest ICOs, which included Ethereum and Waves.

For the 2016–2020 cycle, there was an explosion not only of ICOs but of altcoin narratives: oracles (Chainlink was the big winner, but there were other competitors, such as Aeternity); exchange network tokens, like Binance's BNB; and DeFi, with started with the launch of EthLEND (now AAVE) in late 2017 and Compound Finance in late 2018, as well as Uniswap, incubated by a grant from the Ethereum Foundation in late 2018.

With the recent 2020–2024 cycle, three narratives dominated:

1) First up is the expansion of DeFi, with the explosive debut of Yearn Finance (YFI) and "DeFi Summer" in the summer of 2020, when decentralized finance protocols grew from a few million dollars to one billion dollars of total value locked (TVL) in these staking, lending, and liquidity providing protocols (which I will explain in further detail in Chapter 18). As of April 2024, there was more than $100 billion of value locked, a 100x increase, despite the destruction of centralized finance ecosystems using crypto during Bitcoin Fall of 2022.

2) A second narrative was the growth of non-fungible tokens (NFTs), perhaps buoyed by the increased value in all luxury collectibles during the pandemic, from fine wine to Patek Philippe wristwatches. This powered several tokens designed to support the NFT

ecosystem, including Blur, Rarible (RARI), and Super Rare (RARE). On Christmas Day, 2021, OpenDao (SOS) conducted a "vampire drop" to the Ethereum wallet of everyone using the NFT platform OpenSea to create an open-source alternative. It failed partially because the NFT market crashed.

3) A third trend, which continues to be a promising area for the current cycle, is Web3 gaming, which also includes metaverse tokens. Web3 is a phrase popularized during this cycle to describe cryptocurrency, including NFTs, as the third iteration of the Worldwide Web. Web 1.0 introduced the "read" function, allowing content published worldwide to be viewed and downloaded anywhere, any time, with one click. Web 2.0 upgraded the Web to "read/write" through the viral growth of blogging and interactive social media. Web3 brings an ownership layer to the Web, in which digital files, freely shared and duplicated with no loss of quality, are joined by digital assets, scarce and valuable like money or gold, which transfer ownership in a trustless manner globally. Gala Games, Illuvium, MetaverseX, along with metaverses Decentraland and Sandbox, all grew quickly into multibillion-dollar market caps at their 2021 market peaks.

Altcoins in the Fifth Bitcoin Cycle

What can we expect of the new 2024–2028 cycle? Judging by what grew most quickly at the end of the last cycle, decentralized AI is off to a great start to being a dominant narrative in this cycle. Alpha Sigma Capital, where I am a general partner of its parent group, Alpha Transform Holdings, created an index of decentralized AI tokens that grew more than 500 percent between January 2023 and March 2024.

Another strong narrative for the current cycle with its roots in the prior cycle is memecoins. While memecoins go back to the late 2013 creation of dogecoin (if not before), the new wave kicked off in August 2020 with the release of Shiba Inu (SHIB), one of the most successful memecoins of all time, launching at under $100,000 market cap—and donating half its tokens to Vitalik Buterin (who, when the value of those tokens went up to $1 billion, donated them to a COVID-19 nonprofit in India). By October 27, 2021, the market capitalization reached more than $45 billion. As importantly, it created the narrative of the Shib Army, fearlessly on to their Shib, looking for places that accept SHIB, and awaiting the day that each SHIB is worth one penny (roughly the equivalent mission of laser-eyed bitcoiners eyeing the $100,000 bitcoin). Shiba Inu has since spawned three other tokens (Bone, Leash, and the upcoming Treat), as well as a layer-2 protocol, Shibarium, NFTs, and an upcoming stablecoin.

March 2023 saw the dawn of the largest, broadest memecoin cycle yet, with the release of Pepe (PEPE), the chill green frog from *Boy's Club* comics by Matt Furie that went viral on 4Chan in 2015 and led to the Rare Pepe NFTs on the Counterparty protocol shortly thereafter. This was the first significant memecoin launch on Ethereum since Shiba Inu, and after a long accumulation period, took off like a rocket in February 2024, shooting up 15x to a market cap of more than $5 billion by May. Brett, also a character from *Boy's Club*, took off on its own parabolic tear with a different team launching it on Base, clearing $1 billion in three months and topping out during its first run at $1.8 billion.

Memecoins have been the main narrative thus far in the cycle, with 500,000 new memecoins launched on Solana alone. While most are failures and many are "rug pulls" (where the team literally sells coins and then runs away with the funds), more and more retail investors have been drawn into the "memecoin casino" by chance to pick a DogWifHat, which grew from $100,000 market cap to eclipse $3 billion in four months. All of these memecoins have no utility other than attention. As the website says, it's just a dog with a hat. It now has huge volume and liquidity and the memecoin vertical eclipsed a $100 billion market cap.

Other promising narratives for the new cycle include real-world assets (RWA); multichain DEXs; decentralized physical infrastructure (DePIN), which was incubated in 2020 with Helium, a token that controls decentralized telephony; and decentralized science (DeSci), which is still in its infancy but includes OriginTrail (TRAC) and VitaDAO (VITA). One should look at these categories, which are tracked on CoinMarketCap or CoinGecko, and look up the "Categories" tab by ranking. While the layouts are slightly different, they both show seven-day, one-day, and one-hour percentage changes. For example, the category for Decentralized Identifier was up 31.9 percent for the most recent 24-hour period and 63.9 percent for the week. Yet, the individual tokens in the category varied quite a bit, with the best-known and largest one in the category, Worldcoin, up 41.5 percent for the week but down 13.7 percent for the day. The second largest token, Galxe, was up 49.8 percent for the week, as well as 40.4 percent for the day. One can look at the charts and fundamentals to see if one of these looks to be the better token to consider for your portfolio, as well as going down the list to much smaller tokens with a lot of room to grow in the category, such as Everest ID, up 10 percent for the week, but with a market cap of $8 million, compared with $737 million for Worldcoin and $438 million for Galxe.

Launchpads and IDOs

Launchpads have been around as long as crypto, but they typically referred to a venture studio. In the 2016–2020 cycle, crypto exchanges began to incubate or accelerate tokens it wanted to list by offering them for initial sale on their exchanges. This was known as an Initial Exchange Offering (IEO) and it was meant to replace the ICO that had fallen in disfavor as the US SEC pursued hundreds of projects as unregistered securities, even though it was uncertain as to how they could comply with that agency's vague requirements. The IEO era, which started in 2016, did not last long as many exchanges double-dipped, taking the majority of funds raised as a listing fee and then dumping the coins they also required, often killing the project or disabling it for a long time.

The IDO era began in late 2020 with a UK-based team called Polkastarter. IDOs are Initial DEX Offerings, which start trading directly onto a decentralized exchange (DEX) like Uniswap. An IDO launchpad (Polkastarter soon had dozens of competitors, including Seedify, DAOMaker, Starter and Launchpool) chose projects it thought would succeed on the DEX and let thousands of users it had whitelisted bid for the initial DEX offering (IDO). This pre-listing price was determined by the marketplace and generally fell in between the price that private investors bought months earlier and the price retail would pay on Uniswap, typically listing the day the IDO ends. In early 2021, I had six projects I advised and/or invested in launch on Polkastarter in a period of three months. Each one of these offerings grew substantially after the IDO, which kept investors coming back for more and more . . . until the music stopped in 2022 with Bitcoin Fall, which also decimated the already crowded market for IDOs.

For this cycle, IDOs are back, stronger than ever, with new entrants like ApeTerminal. Generally, retail investors can only get very small allocations on these platform ($500 to $5,000), but since the best performers have gone up 20x in a few days, it has become a high-value proposition, provided you read the white papers, investigate the teams, early advisors, and investors, and allocate carefully.

One psychological factor in these early, unproved projects doing so well is perceived scarcity (IDO rounds are small), demand (they are often quickly oversubscribed) and FOMO. Another factor is that private rounds and IDOs are bought on the basis of fully diluted value (FDV), which is the value of the entire project, regardless of how long it takes to distribute the tokens or how long the lockups might be. When a project lists, it is usually ranked by circulating supply, which is the amount of tokens actively in circulation and available to trade. Ergo, one might buy into a project at one cent per token with 100 million tokens in FDV. When it launches, it is common for only 10 percent of the tokens to be released at the token generation event (TGE), so the circulating supply is only one-tenth the amount of the FDV. In the hypothetical case of the token above, it would have an FDV of $100 million, but a circulating supply of only $10 million, which sounds cheap to retail investors and they might bid it up to $50 million, which means its FDV is now $500 million.

Typically, all levels of investors and especially team members have unlock schedules of nine months to four years, depending on many factors. This is designed to prevent the token price from collapsing if the early investors all sell, but it can also be destructive if the lockup is too long by forcing the team to sell their tokens in the midst of a bear market. I advise teams I work with to look at the Four Seasons schedule when they choose their unlocking timetable.

IDOs are higher risk on paper, but if you know what you're doing they can be very rewarding. Most crypto VCs focus on investing in these early-stage new narratives each cycle, hoping to have a substantial amount invested in one or two that turn into a 100x market leader of that cycle.

Chapter Eighteen

DeFi for Income

It is better to have a permanent income than to be fascinating.

—Oscar Wilde[clx]

The question isn't at what age I want to retire, it's at what income.

—George Foreman[clxi]

My problem lies in reconciling my gross habits with my net income.

—Errol Flynn[clxii]

Investing in bitcoin when there is "blood in the streets" and selling it at the height of a market frenzy is the most profitable way of taking advantage of cyclical volatility. While riskier, investing a portion of your portfolio in Ethereum and/or alt-coins has thus far created even greater gains. If you are skilled and fortunate enough to invest at the beginning of a new narrative, the gains for that part of your portfolio can double or triple your entire net worth in one four-year cycle.

But what about income? Presuming that you didn't start with a trust fund paying all of your basic expenses and/or a great job that lets you both save and enjoy a comfortable life, you will need income during the bear markets so you don't have to sell any of your digital assets while the prices are low. A traditional way of earning income from assets is through treasury bills or passbook savings accounts. For much of the past decade, interest rates were near zero, which made those options less attractive. Real estate investing and the stock market are good options, but selling real estate when you want to redeploy back into bitcoin at the start of Bitcoin Winter can be challenging, as it takes time, and commissions plus fees can eat up much of whatever gains you could make on a one-year investment.

This is where DeFi comes in. Decentralized finance, or "DeFi," has only existed in any meaningful form for the past six years and is one of the most revolutionary concepts to come out of cryptocurrency. Bitcoin allows anyone in the world to send a payment to anyone else in the world in a trustless fashion with no intermediaries. DeFi allows anyone in the world to perform more sophisticated financial transactions, including lending and borrowing, earning compound interest, prediction markets, and insurance pools in a similar, decentralized manner with no third-party gatekeepers. Much of this involves using stablecoins, which have existed for less than a decade.

The Rise and Rise of Stablecoins

Stablecoins are cryptocurrencies with a stable value, usually of one US dollar. Tether, which I helped bring to market in its infancy, was the first stablecoin, and it has become one of the most profitable companies in history, turning bitcoin and other cryptocurrencies into dollar credits backed by cash and cash equivalents, such as US treasury bills. Originally called RealCoin, Tether was founded in Santa Monica, CA, in 2014 by Brock Pierce, Reeve Collins, and Mastercoin CTO Craig Sellars. It was rebranded Tether later that year. The original Tether was issued on the Omni (Mastercoin) blockchain. [clxiii] Today, Tether is issued on Ethereum, Solana, Tron, and several other leading blockchains. It also bridges to most EVM-compatible blockchains, including Arbitrum and Base, which are popular for their lower fees. Interestingly, Tether on Tron has become a popular form of currency worldwide due to the lower fees.

Tether, now based in Lugano, Switzerland, has become an extremely profitable business. It charges a fee to redeem to US dollars; it mints new coins when cash or cash equivalents come in, and it burns the tokens when cash is redeemed. Besides fees, the company keeps the interest and dividends from those interest-bearing accounts and bonds, which has now grown to handle $33 billion daily in volume, with $112 billion under management. Tether has a remarkable amount of throughput, with more than one-quarter of its total market cap trading daily. Other fully backed-stablecoins include USDC, which was created by Circle. Algorithmic stablecoins are riskier, as the Terra Luna meltdown showed. However, MakerDAO and its partially backed stablecoin DAI have survived, and new algorithmic altcoins based on perpetual swaps like Ethena and NUSD, have been introduced in the past year and have seen a great deal of early adoption and success.

Most of DeFi remains on Ethereum, so if you want to participate in staking and lending, you will generally have to keep your proceeds in an Ethereum-based stablecoin. However, the

Bitcoin Layer 2 movement has been advancing quickly, which I cover in the next chapter.

Let's examine some of the specific options for earning income on DeFi (or borrowing against the value of your cryptocurrency):

Compound is a protocol designed by Robert Leshner in 2017, earning him the well-deserved title "Father of DeFi." Leshner comes from a traditional financial upbringing, graduating with a degree in economics from the prestigious University of Pennsylvania and earning a CFA. His parents work in investment banking. Compound was the beginning of a trend that, when fully developed, can both disrupt and transform the entire legacy financial system.

The cryptocurrency exchange Kraken explains Compound's utility clearly:

> Put simply, Compound allows users to deposit cryptocurrency into lending pools for access by borrowers. Lenders then earn interest on the assets they deposit. Once a deposit is made, Compound awards a new cryptocurrency called a cToken (which represents the deposit) to the lender.
>
> Each cToken can be transferred or traded without restriction, handled by the Compound code, meaning lenders can withdraw deposits anytime. To incentivize this activity, Compound uses another cryptocurrency native to its service, called COMP. Every time users interact with a Compound market (by borrowing, withdrawing, or repaying the asset), they are rewarded with additional COMP tokens."[clxiv]

As of July 14, 2024, Compound protocol has more than $2.1 billion in cryptocurrency collateral staked, supporting $837 million in loans. The protocol has integrated with centralized custodians, including Coinbase Custody, as well as hardware wallets, such as Ledger. It is now not even in the top ten of the market it created, according to DeFi Llama, which tracks all staking and lending protocols, ranking them by Total Value Locked (TVL), which is the rough crypto equivalent of Assets Under Management (AUM).[clxv] The current TVL market capitalization is $91.4 billion as of July 14, 2024; it was over $100 billion earlier in the year.

Lending and borrowing work to achieve two important goals for the sophisticated crypto investor:

1) After cashing out profits at the top of Bitcoin Summer, one can convert those profits into stablecoins. Those stablecoins can then generate yield through lending, staking, or liquidity provision.
2) At the start of Bitcoin Winter, it may be wise to consider switching sides of the lender/borrower pair and use one's stablecoin collateral to buy more bitcoin when it's clearly near the bottom of the cycle, then pay the loan back when cashing out after the following Bitcoin Summer.

More recently, Leshner started Superstate Funds, which offer tokenized funds for qualified purchasers in supported jurisdictions, beginning with a $100 million fund tokenizing US treasury bills, paying out 5.35 percent interest with fifteen basis points as a management fee. Unlike most funds, subscriptions and redemptions can be exercised daily, using a token USTB, which is then redeemed for the widely accepted stablecoin, USDC. This is certainly an interesting, low-risk option for nontechnical investors who are accredited or in jurisdictions supported by the tokenized fund. More recently, traditional finance titan BlackRock partnered with Securitize to launch a half-billion-dollar fund to essentially do the same thing: tokenize Treasury bills.

Let's look at the four major categories of participating in DeFi for income:

1) *Lending:* AAVE has become the main marketplace for lending, with $7.5 billion in decentralized loans outstanding. Lenders put their USDC into a pool, which they can withdraw at any time, earning interest that is compounding daily, 24/7. In the summer of 2024, the current rate to borrow is 8.15 percent APY, which then pays lenders in the pool of 5.8 percent for USDC stablecoins. Rates for Tether are 8 percent to borrow and 5.6 percent to lend. The platform currently has $20 billion of collateral supporting these loans. Other than a protocol error or smart contract hack, the money lent is safe, as the collateral is liquidated when it falls below 80 percent of the loaned amount. Borrowers can avoid liquidation by simply adding more collateral.[clxvi] Aave uses its token (AAVE) for governance, and it uses the profits between the lend and borrow spreads to buy back AAVE tokens from the market and then burn them, forever lowering supply. This is a tokenomics model referred to as a "reverse dividend," as AAVE holders are rewarded with an ever-diminishing supply of tokens in a growing ecosystem.

2) *Staking:* Proof-of-stake[clxvii] is an alternative consensus mechanism to proof-of-work, dating back to its invention by legendary anonymous developer Sunny King in a protocol called Peercoin (PPC). Peercoin was a top-ten coin in 2012–2013 but barely in the top 1,000 tokens. Peercoin may have faded from the scene, but proof-of-stake has not only succeeded, but it's now the dominant consensus mechanism. Even Ethereum ported to a proof-of-stake mechanism after seven years of operating with a proof-of-work protocol powered by ether miners.

Proof-of-stake is generally considered less secure and more centralized, as the person with the most tokens has the most votes (which most often is the project founder(s). One way proof-of-stake blockchains have become popular is by incorporating staking rewards. There are typically two types of staking rewards: first, the gas fees to secure transactions are paid back to those who stake coins to secure the network, as is the case with Ethereum; second, many protocols encourage usage by offering a high yield, paid entirely in tokens from the project's coinbase. Just as bitcoin is ushered into existence by rewards to miners, a certain percentage of a proof-of-stake blockchain is distributed to those who stake their tokens for various periods of time. Like bitcoin's lowering of miner rewards, many proof-of-stake blockchains will start with a very high yield—often more than 100 percent—that drops over time. A more common range of healthy staking rewards is in the 15–30 percent annual yield range. One must analyze the benefit of securing extra tokens against trading those tokens. It behooves you to stake your tokens, as not doing so is literally leaving money on the table.

Until recently, Bitcoin investors didn't have any staking option, as it is a proof-of-work asset and not a proof-of-stake. In early 2024, Core DAO launched a system that allowed bitcoin holders to stake their bitcoin in a decentralized manner using a delegated proof-of-work by appending extra metadata to the op-return field in bitcoin blocks. This keeps the bitcoin in the holder's own custody while rewarding them with CORE tokens. The system has been received well, with more than $300 million of bitcoin staked as of July 2024, paying 9 percent staking rewards.

3) *Liquidity Providing.* One of the most popular use cases of decentralized finance has been the decentralized exchange—DEX for short. Governments have fought decentralized exchanges under the notion that they were violating know-your-customer (KYC) regulations. The reality is that peer-to-peer commerce with no intermediary is effectively the same as cash transactions, so DEX leaders like Uniswap have been able to fight off regulatory challenges and grow into multibillion-dollar ecosystems.

Uniswap launched in late 2019 with $21 million in monthly volume, solely on Ethereum. Less than five years later, monthly volume across seventeen blockchains now exceeds $60 billion. In the near future, Uniswap and other decentralized exchanges will make centralized exchanges like Binance look obsolete. This is most likely one reason that Coinbase developed its own layer 1 EVM, Base.

DEX's work through Automated Market Making (AMM), a technology first developed by Bancor, which conducted the largest ICO of its time when it debuted at my conference, CoinAgenda Caribbean, in early March 2017. Uniswap was not first to market, but it was smoothest with execution and interface and is the top DEX in the world today, although Raydium, the leading Solana DEX, is catching up fast in terms of volume.[clxviii] AMMs work by having a liquidity pool balancing equal amounts of ether (or another platform protocol token) with any other token in the same protocol one wants to swap. Those putting up the liquidity for the transactions of others share in those transaction fees. This complex process includes the risk of "impermanent loss," in which you end up with an involuntary swap to the asset you're balancing. Much of this can be automated further with tools like Acryptos to earn double-digit annual returns, but it does take active management to maximize the process.

4) *Yield farming.* Simply put, yield farming uses the above three mechanisms, often layered on top of one another. One might deposit collateral at Compound, then borrow at Aave and use those borrowed tokens to buy and stake a high-yield cryptocurrency. This works well when the markets are going up, but it can be disastrous when markets correct. One token that attempts to automate yield farming through its governance token is Yearn Finance, which launched at the

start of 2020's DeFi Summer at around $8 and shot up to more than $93,000 by early May 2021. It still trades in mid-2024 at $5,000 per token.

Final Words on Generating Income from DeFi

Which path you choose is entirely up to you. Remember that you can still beat "buy and hold" by simply selling once a cycle after the end of Bitcoin Summer, then buying back in about a year later when there is blood in the streets at a much lower price. But if you do want to make your crypto work for you, my main advice is to stake all the crypto you own that is stakeable. Additionally, if you don't want to put your Bitcoin Summer "winnings" into traditional investments like the stock market before you redeploy them at the start of Bitcoin Winter, then you should consider lending and borrowing, as described above. Liquidity-providing and advanced yield farming are far riskier and require diligence and monitoring (they are definitely not "set it and forget it" investments). If you wish to study them more, you may find one or both might be a fit for a portion of your portfolio.

Chapter Nineteen
Alternative Strategies

Risk comes from not knowing what you're doing.
                              —Warren Buffett[clxix]

The biggest risk is not taking a risk. In a world that's changing really quickly, the only strategy that is guaranteed to fail is not taking risks.
                              —Mark Zuckerberg[clxx]

Yesterday's home runs don't win today's games.
                              —Babe Ruth[clxxi]

I wanted to finish this last chapter of Book Four with a potpourri of strategies that didn't fit neatly into any prior chapters. They include options and futures trading; NFTs and their bitcoin equivalent, Ordinals; equity investments in Web3 companies, with or without token airdrops; and digital asset hedge funds and venture capital.

Options, Futures, Perpetual Futures, Covered Calls

Options and futures can be a fantastic driver of accelerated profits, but it can also lead to huge losses. Options are typically safer, as mistakes or misjudgments only lose the money one puts up for the option, which can expire without being exercised. Futures contracts are contracts, so if you're on the wrong end of a trade, you must come up with the difference. Every month, there are tens of millions of dollars of liquidations where collateral for these trades is sold to cover the positions. I am not an options trader, but I have many friends who are and make money doing so. It's a job, and your positions must be monitored at least daily.

Depending upon your risk level, you can take extremely high leveraged risks. Some crypto exchanges have allowed ratios as high as one hundred times leverage. More responsible traders take more measured bets. A longtime crypto trader friend recently executed this trade: he looked at the all-time low of an altcoin whose future he believed in. He saw the price had never fallen below 17 cents, and the price was just above that. He also knew they had just announced a new upgrade he thought would lift the price, and he saw the macro environment for crypto improving. He bought options on 100,000 tokens with 3x leverage, then sold the tokens on a spot market a few weeks later for 39 cents. Without leverage, he would have made a profit of $22,000 minus fees on a $17,000 investment. With this responsible leverage based on research and conviction, he made $66,000 in profit. The token went up to $1.12 a few months later, and today it trades at 29 cents, but his trade was very profitable, and he was able to move in and out of the same token a few times when the data said the risk/reward was at compelling levels.

There are several good books, courses, and daily podcasts about crypto trading. My friend Tone Vays, a former Wall Street trader turned crypto derivatives specialist, runs annual trading retreats and conferences and can be followed at @tonevays on X. Several of the crypto YouTube stars focus on bitcoin derivatives trading instead of altcoin picks, including Carl "The Moon" Runefelt, who used options trading in crypto and the success of his social media following and YouTube content to advance from a bag boy in a Stockholm supermarket to driving a Bugatti around his new home in Dubai. Dubai has become the new crypto capital; many of the leading YouTube stars either live there or spend a lot of time in the crypto-friendly UAE. MMCrypto is another popular crypto derivatives trading podcast on YouTube streaming from Dubai, starring the team of MM Chris (Chris Jaszczynski) and Davinci Jeremie, a former silver bug who started recommending bitcoin when it was under one dollar. Both daily podcasts are good barometers of where the crypto markets, particularly bitcoin, are headed. Chris generally posts his actual trades live on his channel.[clxxii]

Depending upon your jurisdiction, you can use traditional brokerages like CME or, if you are not American, crypto exchanges specializing in options and futures like Derabit and ByBit. If you wish to trade but not use options, there are many alternatives, although Americans have limited choices, with Coinbase, Gemini, Kraken, and Paxos/ItBit being the major players.

NFTs and Real-World Assets

At the other end of the spectrum from the fast-paced world of crypto derivatives trading is the less volatile category of non-fungible tokens, widely known by the acronym NFTs. As noted earlier in the book, this category exploded during the COVID-19 pandemic after so-called "blue chip" collections, including Bored Apes and Crypto Punks, increased in value by more than 500x from their mint price (in the case of Punks, they were initially given away). But the fad faded, and based on the scarcity of individual NFTs, the NFT narrative dropped dramatically as floor prices became the norm for all tokens. It is uncertain whether the category will ever regain its luster, although it went through a similar boom and collapse in 2017 with the innovation of breedable Crypto Kitty NFTs.

The narrative in this cycle around NFTs is real-world assets (RWAs). In the last chapter, I discussed RWAs as a narrative for fungible tokens, as several RWA platforms are in development. These will be powered in part by fungible governance or network tokens. But the real opportunity being discussed in both crypto and TradFi circles is tokenization. I have been saying for many years that tokenization is just as important as decentralization, if not more so, in most applications. In 2014, my BitAngels cofounder David A. Johnston proclaimed, "Anything that can be decentralized will be decentralized," terming the phrase "Johnston's Law" (he even made T-shirts). I responded with Terpin's Corollary: "Anything that can be tokenized will be tokenized." While I believe both statements are true, I also believe that far more items in the world can be tokenized than decentralized.

Indeed, we need decentralization for trustless payments and DeFi to work properly at scale. However, for real-world assets, which by their very nature are not decentralized, tokenization opens up the ability to make anything that is inherently analog, which includes most assets on the planet, into a digital asset. Real estate has long been the Holy Grail of tokenization, allowing properties worldwide to be sold, rented, and fractionalized without regard to borders. The complications around expanding that market are largely regulatory since many jurisdictions regulate real estate transactions in very much analog terms, as well as security laws that often regard fractionalization of an asset as equivalent to making it into a security, opening up the door to an array of regulations that must be addressed.

Regulatory demands for tokenizing real estate and, even more so, stocks and bonds make tokenization the logical area for traditional Wall Street to enter and dominate this category. JP Morgan's head of Onyx Digital Assets, Tyrone Lobban, stated he believes "trillions of dollars" could be issued in tokenized assets, including money market funds, "at the scale of institutional assets."[clxxiii]

If you work in institutional finance, this is an opportunity to apply your crypto skills to well-paid positions, integrating the best of DeFi into a highly regulated world of traditional finance. I have long been saying that it's only a matter of time until stocks are issued directly by the companies as tokens, letting them trade 24/7 globally and allowing Apple Computer or Walmart to know who their shareholders are for the first time. Today, they are hidden behind a wall of intermediaries. It will also allow Apple to sell shares globally instead of seeking alternative listings in other countries. It makes no sense to me that you can buy Dogecoin in any country, but to buy Samsung stock in the United States, you need to do it through an ADR format. The ultimate innovation would see these shares serve a dual purpose as a loyalty mechanism. Go into an Apple Store and get a discount on the new iPhone based on how many Apple shares you own. It's easy with tokenization, which can prove you own those shares. This is known as token-gating.

Ordinals, Runes, and Bitcoin Layer Two

Ordinals are the equivalent of NFTs on bitcoin. Bitcoin does not have smart contract capabilities (at least not yet). Still, Ordinals were able to inscribe images onto the tiniest unit of one bitcoin, a satoshi, kicking off the new digital asset collectible trend in 2023. It amuses me that bitcoin maximalists derided the Ethereum community for creating digital art on NFTs, but they are all excited about having similar functionality when it's built on bitcoin. A sense of permanence comes with having a piece of digital art inscribed on Bitcoin, as it can be viewed for as long as Bitcoin exists—potentially thousands of years or more. Unlike paint that fades or software programs written for CP/M machines in the 1970s that become obsolete, an inscription on Bitcoin endures.

While I don't have a massive selection of Ordinals, I am proud of one I own, also an RWA. It perfectly reproduces a large piece of physical art I purchased at Art Basel in 2023 from the artist Edsen, depicting Marlon Brando as the Godfather surrounded by paint splashes and a few splotches of bloodred ink as highlights. The four-by-five-foot acrylic hangs in my Miami penthouse, but the Ordinal will be on the blockchain for generations to come. You can view it on the Ordinals viewer by my inscription, which is Ordinal #47,254,695, at the Ordinals block explorer (https://ordiscan.com/inscription/47254695). Block explorers are what one uses to view digital assets on a blockchain.[clxxiv]

Ordinals are still relatively small compared to the NFT market, which has an overall value of $40 billion across one million listed NFTs, with daily trading of between $15 million and $30 million per day. Ordinals and Runes (a newer protocol to allow fungible tokens to be built on the bitcoin; Ordinals are inscribed, while Runes are "etched") passed $1 billion in market capitalization in June 2024. They are both still very much in their infancy, and while some new series may mimic the exponential gains of altcoins, the liquidity of any NFT is generally thin. Runes are fungible but so new that the jury is still out as to whether they will attract sizeable trading volume or become more of a collectible category, such as Ordinals. [clxxv]

Two fungible tokens that are not Runes made it into the top 100 of CoinMarketcap in early 2024. Ordi and Sats both topped $1 billion market capitalizations for much of the first quarter of 2024, supporting the narrative of Bitcoin Layer-2 as an innovation and investment opportunity. Keep an eye on this space as bitcoin maximalists have been talking about building on bitcoin for a long time, but the technology is finally catching up to enable it in 2024.

Equity Investments in Web3 Companies

I have been on panels since 2013 discussing whether crypto investors should invest in companies or coins. I have generally sided with coins as they have outperformed Web3 equities. Even the winners have not kept up with the price of bitcoin. Barry Silbert said his seed investment in CoinBase in 2012 did not outperform bitcoin until its IPO at $100 billion market cap! I have also seen that most of my equity investments underperformed bitcoin, largely due to execution risk (which is not a component of a bitcoin, but my token investments taken as a whole kept pace, averaging the ones that outperformed bitcoin for periods with the ones that cratered).

In recent years, there has been a trend to invest in companies and receive an airdrop or warrant of tokens. In theory, this is like having the best of both worlds, and it protects the investor from buying a token and then finding out all the value accrued in the company (or vice versa). As an industry participant, I try to find opportunities to invest in both the equity and token (ideally through an airdrop) at an early-stage valuation, as well as advise or serve in a marketing capacity, given my background of launching so many successful projects. I suggest that anyone who wants to build a portfolio and is willing to roll up their sleeves, especially if you have an entrepreneurial, marketing, legal, accounting, sales, or business development background, try to negotiate deals where you have the opportunity to earn as well as pay for equity and/or tokens. It makes a difference in your returns and keeps you close to the team to both help out—and to know if there's trouble brewing.

Funds and Syndicates

I've been a limited partner and a general partner at several digital currency funds, so I have experienced being on both sides of the equation. The advantage of being a limited partner with a fund is they do the work, make the decisions, take responsibility for trading, accounting, and protecting the assets, plus all other legal compliance work. The disadvantage is they generally charge "two and twenty" as a fee, meaning

2 percent of assets under management, plus 20 percent of the profits. Therefore, you need to find a team that cannot only beat bitcoin but also beat it after those fees are accounted for. Key to this will be managing the downside during bear markets. Check out the five-year performance of the team and pay particular attention to how they perform during the bear markets. If their track record beats bitcoin after fees, you have a rare find and should consider investing if you wish to have funds in your mix.

You should also be aware of the difference between digital asset hedge funds and digital asset venture capital funds. Hedge funds typically take their entire investment at once because they actively trade based on the entire amount. VC firms take the money as they need it, using what is known as "capital calls" at various times during the duration of the fund. Hedge funds are usually open-ended with no set redemption time to end the fund. VC firms generally have seven- to ten-year time horizons, paying out the proceeds on exits near the end of that period. Some funds are multi-strategy, meaning they do some liquid trading and some venture investing. The goal of hedge funds is generally for income and appreciation with less risk than a venture fund. Venture funds have higher risk but can often outperform hedge funds. The venture funds I've invested in have generally outperformed the hedge funds, but most across the industry do not.

Book Five
Million-Dollar Bitcoin

Chapter Twenty

The African Spring

The thing worse than rebellion is the thing that causes rebellion.

—Frederick Douglass[clxxvi]

You show me a highly unequal society, and I will show you a police state. Or an uprising. There are no counter-examples. None. It's not if, it's when.

—Nick Hanauer[clxxvii]

First they ignore you, then they laugh at you, then they fight you, then you win.

—Mahatma Gandhi (attributed)[clxxviii]

To fully understand Bitcoin's financial potential, which provides both funding and a launchpad for all other cryptocurrency projects, one must understand how quickly governments, societies, and the forms of money that power them can change.

In late 2010, a street vendor in Tunisia had his wares confiscated by the government. In anger and frustration, he set himself on fire in public. This desperate act led to escalating large-scale protests over the impoverishing policies of dictator Zine El Abidine Ben Ali, which led to the Jasmine Revolution. Streets filled nightly, and the autocratic regime was overthrown within a matter of weeks. Today, the martyr's picture is on a Tunisian government stamp.

This was literally the match that set off what is now called "the Arab Spring," a series of anti-government protests, uprisings, and armed rebellions that flamed up across much of the Arab world. The protests spread like wildfire across the region, aided by the new technology of Facebook, which helped organize responses in real time, just as the fax machine did during the fall of the Berlin Wall and much of Eastern Europe. Massive, organized protests led to social unrest and violence, forcing long-standing dictators Muammar Gaddafi out of Libya and Hosni Mubarak from Egypt. Yemen and Syria became engulfed in civil wars, while Morocco, Iraq, Algeria, Lebanon, Jordan, Kuwait, Oman, and Sudan all had sustained demonstrations, often met with armed resistance from pro-government forces. When the smoke cleared, much of the established Arab leadership had been toppled, and the social fabric of the region had dramatically changed.

Bitcoin Empowers Social Change and Economic Freedom

I began this chapter by using violent examples from the Middle East a decade ago to demonstrate how rapidly societies can transform when the population is repressed and sees a path to a better life. Western Africa and South America have many of the same issues today as the Arab world did in 2010, amplified by high inflation bordering on hyperinflation and a suppression of economic freedom.

Africans have become used to mobile money over the past twenty years, as the rapid expansion of mobile phones throughout the continent lifted many remote areas out of poverty by connecting them for the first time with employment prospects from the world's information economy. In Kenya, most of the population buys groceries with M-PESA, a form of mobile money issued by the leading national mobile carrier, Safaricom. This and similar efforts across the continent set the stage for what was about to happen next.

Nigeria is a young, industrious country of 220 million people, roughly the population of the United States in the 1970s. It has a rapidly inflating local currency, the naira, and a long history of corruption, crime, and poverty. Bitcoin has gained the largest foothold here of anywhere in the world, with more than 20 percent of the population using it daily, as noted earlier in the book. Stablecoins are also popular here, as well as throughout the Middle East. Whereas people once tried to exchange their troubled national currencies for US dollars in the streets, they now exchange bitcoin and tether on their phones.

The use of stablecoins instead of physical currency and bank-issued debit cards is a growing trend. Former president and leading presidential candidate Donald Trump noted in his pro-bitcoin keynote address during Bitcoin 2024 in Nashville that he supported the expansion of the stablecoin industry as a way to spread US dollar dominance throughout the world, strengthening its currently shaky position as the world's reserve currency.

Bitcoin Economy, Bubbling from the Bottom Up

One of the people facilitating this revolution is my friend Ray Youssef, a larger-than-life, soft-spoken man obsessed with making life better for Africans through Bitcoin. The son of Egyptian immigrants, Youssef started a series of small businesses in New York City, discovering Bitcoin through a friend who showed him how to trade bitcoin in exchange for gift cards. This led to him building Paxful, a US-based company selling bitcoin peer-to-peer in Africa and other parts of the Global South. He and a partner grew Paxful to $200 million a month in transactional volume. Later he found complying with US regulations to serve Africans too cumbersome, so he left Paxful and set up a new company, NoOnes, based in Africa, using a similar business model.

I first met Ray several years ago and recently spent time with him in Dubai and Riyadh right after the conferences I mentioned at the start of this book that coincided with the April 2024 Bitcoin halving. He told me that it was his mission to bring bitcoin to 600 million people in the Global South (Africa, Latin America, and Asia, excluding Japan) before the year 2030. His new company, NoOnes (serving all of the financial nobodies in the world), provides peer-to-peer transactions to buy bitcoin at scale, with $100 million in monthly volume for a company that's less than a year old.

Ray likes to refer to the status quo in Africa as "financial apartheid"—Africans have a hard time trading with their neighboring countries due to the lack of traditional banking services that cripple the ability of Africans to buy materials, sell outside of their local area, and diversify from a national currency that is rapidly losing value against the rest of the world.

"Bitcoin and NoOnes give those entrepreneurs the opportunity to show what they can do when markets are free and money is allowed to flow," he said in a March 2024 opinion piece for *Bitcoin Magazine*. "All they need to grow is a level playing field. They just need a shot, a path towards success, and when we open up any window of opportunity, they bust right through it. That's why NoOnes is not simply creating the best site to buy Bitcoin. We are going all out to give them life-changing opportunities."

El Salvador Starts a Trend

While Ray Youssef and others are helping impoverished Africans, Latin Americans, and other citizens of the Global South acquire bitcoin peer-to-peer so they can separate their money from their state. El Salvador president Nayib Bukele made history in June 2021 when he announced at the annual Bitcoin 2021 Conference in Miami that his nation would be the world's first to accept bitcoin as legal tender, along with the US dollar. He went on to buy two hundred bitcoins and, more recently, has been adding to the nation's strategic bitcoin reserve by purchasing one bitcoin every day. Bukele was widely derided by global economists for his decision to adopt bitcoin, yet by March 2024, it had turned a profit of more than 50 percent on its bitcoin purchases. The Bukele administration also developed a Bitcoin City and started a geothermal bitcoin mining project using volcanic energy. In February 2024, he was reelected president in a landslide victory, winning 85 percent of the vote.

The Bitcoin Presidential Election of 2024

Leaders of other countries have visited Bukele to explore adding bitcoin to their legal tender. Argentina may become the largest country in the near term to embrace bitcoin. Most recently, two of the three major US presidential candidates took pro-bitcoin policy positions, including former president Donald Trump, who said he would add bitcoin to the US strategic reserve, alongside its current reserves for gold and oil.

Trump delivered a well-received keynote address at Bitcoin 2024 in Nashville, the first time a former US president or leading candidate has spoken at a bitcoin conference. This is in direct contrast with the Biden administration, which sought to cripple bitcoin mining and limit access to banking services to the bitcoin industry through its "Operation Chokepoint 2.0" in early 2023.

In this historic July 27, 2024, address, Trump reiterated his pledge to create a strategic Bitcoin stockpile, starting with the more than 212,000 bitcoin currently in the government's possession from criminal forfeitures. I was in the private front rows section roped off for those who had attended a VIP meet-and-greet reception with the President earlier that day and was delighted to hear a former US president say "Never sell your bitcoin"—a position this book modifies through cycle trading, but with the same goal of having more bitcoin as time goes on. At the governmental level, it was groundbreaking. This has now become a significant campaign issue in the US presidential election, for the very first time, with two major candidates stridently pro-bitcoin and the incumbent party (now with a new leader after President Joe Biden decided very late to not seek reelection) aggressively anti-bitcoin and anti-crypto. Some pundits believe a Trump victory alone can shoot the price of bitcoin above $150,000 prior to his January 2025 inauguration.

The day prior, Michael Saylor presented a rare slide presentation where he laid out the Bitcoin maximalist way to grow wealth for individuals, corporations, institutions, and nations. He showed that his "triple Maxi" strategy, which has been in practice at Microstrategy for less than four years, where it has outperformed every other asset class over that period, including Bitcoin and NVIDIA stock.

Between the bottom-up push of the populace discovering a better way to store wealth and engage in free commerce and a few brave political leaders innovating against the historical narrative, the future for bitcoin crossing the billion-user threshold by 2030 looks on track. I personally believe we need a few more technological improvements to the onboarding and daily usage experience, but like the internet, these will come over time. None of us dial up from a second phone line to reach slow-loading pictures on the Web anymore. In the same way, the bitcoin and crypto experience of the future will be as easy as using Venmo or PayPal for it to go viral in the mainstream. This may take place through partnerships with major telcos, banks, and even consumer products companies, eager to be involved in the value chain of consumer-friendly digital assets.

In the next and final chapter of this book, I will explore how the growing demand for bitcoin as a payment system and store of value from the Global South, with its billions of young, financially repressed workers, creators, and entrepreneurs, coupled with the high-return investment demand from the older, wealthier Global North will be met with a severe demand shock, right when the supply shock is also being most strongly felt.

This "double squeeze" will be a major contributor to the beginning of the Bitcoin supercycle effect—an end to diminishing returns for a period of one to three cycles. My twenty-year projections, detailed in the past chapters, are wildly conservative compared to Michael Saylor's keynote at Bitcoin 2024, where he calculated an estimated price per bitcoin in 2045 of $13 million per bitcoin, with a "bear" scenario of $3 million and a bull scenario of $49 million. If a $50 million bitcoin ever takes place (a $1.05 quadrillion market cap, fully diluted), it would be a 1,000x return from the prices in early 2024 and a 1,000,000x return from early 2013. Even with inflation, it would be the world's largest asset class, eclipsing stocks, bonds, and even real estate. I will be very happy with $1,000,000 bitcoin by 2033 and $2,000,000 bitcoin by 2045, as I believe would most bitcoin holders today.

(Feel free to pause now and buy some Bitcoin while the prices are still well under $100,000.) I will now move on to the final chapter.

Chapter Twenty-One

The Path to Million-Dollar Bitcoin

Being rich is a good thing. Not just in the obvious sense of benefiting you and your family, but in the broader sense. Profits are not a zero-sum game. The more you make, the more of a financial impact you can have.

—Mark Cuban[clxxix]

How high can bitcoin go? The real question is how low can the dollar go?

—Patrick M. Byrne[clxxx]

When prosperity comes, do not use all of it.

—Confucius[clxxxi]

My crystal ball gets a little dusty on timelines beyond eight to twelve years. A lot can happen between 2024 and 2140 when the final fractions of a bitcoin are mined. Perhaps there will be a consensus among miners and developers to convert bitcoin to proof-of-stake when there are no more bitcoins left to distribute and the difficulty level is in the centillions. The only thing I can be sure of is that we won't find any more bitcoin when we land on Mars.

Global South and Global North Driving Different Trains to the Same Destination

There are eight billion people on Earth, and they pretty much all use money to survive. The basic forms of money have changed dramatically since the caveman's time. They have even changed quite a bit since the US Civil War. How we invest for our retirement and legacy has also changed.

The Global South has six billion people, with a median age of twenty-five and a current life expectancy of sixty-eight years. It is where the most rapid changes will occur regarding the adoption and daily use of bitcoin. The Global North has 1.6 billion people, with a median age of thirty-nine and a life expectancy of seventy-eight years. Its largest impact will not be on adoption per se, but on bitcoin price since the Global North increasingly looks to bitcoin as a key investable asset, and it can buy substantial amounts of it, relative to the global supply.

By the year 2030, I project there will be one billion people who hold at least some bitcoin. Given the typical S curves of technology adoption, this number of holders will likely increase to at least three billion by 2040 and close to eight billion by 2050, when the world population is expected to be 9.7 billion, according to the United Nations.

Let's recap how my analysis made me comfortable with a bitcoin price projection of nearly $200,000 by 2025. The same basic math of supply and demand that led me to predict $10,000 bitcoin by the year 2020 when it was less than $300 in 2015. Indeed, bitcoin crossed the $10,000 mark by the end of 2017, three years ahead of my schedule.

This is how we reach $1,000,000 bitcoin by the year 2045, probably sooner:

1) *There is an increasing number of people worldwide, and they all require money.* Many of these people will change behavior to enable their money with better utility, as the rapid growth of the credit card industry in the 1960s, ATMs in the 1970s, and more recently, PayPal and mobile payment apps in the 2000s and 2010s will attest. Currently, we are approaching eight billion living human beings on Earth, and that number will be at least eleven billion by the year 2140, when we run out of new bitcoin. Bitcoin provides better utility than other systems, more privacy, and it is a hedge against inflation that has historically outperformed gold.

2) *There is a limited amount of bitcoin.* We have mined more than 92 percent of the bitcoins that will ever exist. By 2035, 99 percent of all bitcoins will have been mined. By the time there are five billion people holding any bitcoin, the average of those holdings can only be about 0.004 BTC per person. At current prices as of July 2024, that would be $260 per person. At $1,000,000 per bitcoin and five million people holding it, the average would be $4,000 per person. Remember that the average person on earth owns one ounce of gold, which is currently valued at just under $2,500 per ounce.

3) *Demand is rising while new supply is evaporating.* Demand will come most rapidly from the Global South, where a few hundred dollars a month in bitcoin will change hands per person as a superior form of money to buy basic necessities, compared with local currencies. You can multiply this by six billion people. Meanwhile, the richer, older Global North will aspire to own at least one-tenth of a bitcoin per person but

will have to settle for an average of 1/100th of a bit-coin. Even that low amount per person will be nearly impossible, as multiplying this by the top one billion people holding bitcoin equals ten million bitcoin for this category alone.

4) *The rich want more bitcoin than everyone else, but they will have a hard time getting it.*

From the top down, if 20 percent of the world's 59 million millionaires owned an average of one bitcoin each, that would be 11.8 million bitcoins. This would be difficult to achieve, as there are only 21 million, and most of them are in the hands of long-term holders—or lost.

Get Rich Slowly

Patience is a virtue, and nowhere is this so dramatically true as with bitcoin. Patient buyers from 2015 were exponentially rewarded for holding on to just $1,000 of bitcoin (four of them at the time) through ups and downs, through bitcoin popping to unheard-of heights, then crashing down 80 percent or more and being pronounced dead by big media and big finance. But those who held on to those $250 bitcoins from just nine years ago have nearly *300 times as much money* as they had in 2015. As of July 2024, a $1,000 investment in 2015 is worth more than $280,000. Investing $10,000 in 2015 is now worth more than $2.8 million.

Even without using the Four Seasons of Bitcoin approach to nearly quadruple those gains across each cycle, the buy-and-hold returns were life-changing. I believe the cycle-to-cycle positive trend will continue, albeit at a slower pace but definitely beating gold and the S&P for the next twenty years.

For those of you who want faster returns but with more risk, I have explained those strategies in Chapters 16–19.

At one million dollars per bitcoin, the question is no longer "will bitcoin survive"—it's what parts of the global ecosystem it will replace or make more efficient. Michael Saylor said he believes the ultimate value of bitcoin can be $13 million per bitcoin or more, as it will ultimately compete with not only gold but the stock market and real estate for the best, multigenerational store of value to be handed down as a legacy asset. If you leave cash in your will, its value will likely decrease in spending power by another 90 percent or more in the next century, presuming the dollar doesn't need a reset after the national debt passes several times the GDP and/or the national debt interest payments alone exceed all tax revenues.

Here are my longer-term projections for bitcoin, with far less data about macro for the decades ahead. I am basing these projections purely on my assumptions of supply and demand. I'm adding the overall returns, including the annual internal rate of return (IRR) per year. My starting point is the thirty-day average from the time of writing this chapter, which is $60,000.

Cycle Peak	Projected High	Total Return	IRR	$1 mm bitcoin	$1 mm btc IRR*
2025	$191,700	219.5	219.5	1566.67	1566.67
2029	$346,906	478.18	42.04	1566.67	75.54
2033	$557,175	828.63	28.1	1566.67	36.7
2037	$664,498	1007.5	20.32	1566.67	24.16
2041	$898,401	1397.34	23.14	1566.67	18
2045	$1,140,000	1800	15.05	1566.67	14.34

*The last two columns are the overall returns and IRR if bitcoin topped $1 million in that year.

The numbers above are for "set it and forget it" mode. You can calculate these estimates on your own based on when you purchased bitcoin, using a simple IRR calculator. I used my projections from Chapter 14 through 2041, then added my new prediction for 2045 as the cycle we will pass $1,000,000, which I believe is conservative. If you are thirty-four years old and wish to retire by fifty-five, you should concentrate on buying one whole bitcoin (more if you can afford it). You can see by the charts what the returns could be over the next twenty-one years, especially if you use the Four Seasons multiplier.

Four Seasons Compounding Magic

The prospective returns for religiously using the Four Seasons approach to selling at the top and buying back at the bottom look even better than the "buy and hold" strategy. I have calculated prospective returns using two models. In the first "Conservative" model, I use numbers slightly below my conservative projections from Chapter 14. This model sees bitcoin passing the $1,000,000 mark twenty-one years from now, which is much longer than the market consensus among moderately bullish analysts, many of whom see it passing the million-dollar mark by the 2028–2032 cycle. I have also been highly conservative in the amount bitcoin drops in price during Bitcoin Fall, using variations between highs and lows that are more in line with gold and other commodities. This is my "worst case" model for bitcoin.

In the "aggressive" chart below, which I believe is the "best case" scenario, bitcoin price passes $1 million by 2033 and the pullback continues on a linear path of diminishing losses, starting with a 66 percent drop from the Bitcoin Summer in 2025 to the low in 2026–2027, and never diminishes beyond a 40 percent drop in 2046–2047. Key to the outsized gains in this model is constantly buying the lows. A "set it and forget it" model would start with a $60,000 investment in one bitcoin and end with $3,650,000 for a sizeable return of 5,983.33 percent, enough for most people to retire on—at least using today's dollars with little room for annual inflation at even 3–4 percent per year.

By selling everything at the top and repurchasing it all at the bottom (note: I am sure most of you won't sell 100 percent, nor should you, just in case there is a wild parabolic spike beyond anyone's expectations when you are expecting the bubble to burst; I also believe most of you will take some of the cash off the table to pay for necessities, even for luxuries). Here, I project volatility averaging around 50 percent per cycle, which is far lower than past cycles. Even so, repeatedly selling at the cycle high and buying back at the cycle low will compound the volatility to create parabolic gains. In the scenario below, higher volatility and aggressive appreciation moving in between the Four Seasons strategy yields more than $213 million in twenty-one years, and a final buying back at the lows equals nearly 100 bitcoin. The cash appreciation is 356,426 percent by the cycle high, as well as an increase in bitcoin of 9,667.8 percent at the end of the cycle. If just 100,000 people used this strategy with one bitcoin each and the numbers played out in line with the aggressive cycle, they would end up with 9.7 million bitcoins among them (and that demand would continue to increase the price, although the volatility would surely drop).

Conservative Model *

Cycle	Cycle Sell	Cycle Buy	Multiplier	Total Cash	Total BTC
2024–2028	$160,000 (2025)	$80,000 (2026/27)	2	$160,000	2
2028–2032	$285,000 (2029)	$165,000 (2030/31)	1.72	$570,000	3.45454545
2032–2036	$490,000 (2033)	$380,000 (2034/35)	1.29	$1,692,727.27	4.45454545
2036–2040	$640,000 (2037)	$550,000 (2038/39)	1.16	$2,850,909.09	5.18347107
2040–2044	$845,000 (2041)	$790,000 (2042/43)	1.07	$4,380,033.05	5.54434564
2044–2048	$1,100,000 (2045)	$980,000 (2046/47)	1.12	$6,098,781	6.22324625

*In the charts on pages 312 and 313, the second column uses the price within 20 percent of my projected high as a recommended time to consider selling. The third column uses a price within 20 percent of my projected low for each cycle. The fourth column uses a multiplier, which is the multiple that your bitcoin will increase from the prior cycle after you sell at the top and buy back at the bottom. The fifth column is the total cash from selling 100 percent of your bitcoins at the price in column two. The sixth column is the total amount of bitcoin you will have after buying back at the bottom of the cycle. This is aligned with my prior advice to maximize cash at the end of Bitcoin Summer and maximize the number of bitcoin at the beginning of Bitcoin Winter.

Aggressive, Volatile Model

Cycle	Cycle Sell	Cycle Buy	Multiplier	Total $ (High)	Total BTC
2024–2028	$284,345	$94,000	3.025	$284,345	3.02404681
2028–2032	$435,293	$174,000	2.5	$1,316,738.17	7.56746075
2032–2036	$1,050,000	$472,000	2.22	$7,945,833.79	16.8343936
2036–2040	$1,689,000	$870,000	1.94	$28,433,290.80	32.6819435
	$2,923,000	$1,630,000	1.79	$95,529,320.20	58.6060945
2044–2048	$3,650,000	$2,190,000	1.67	$213,915,350	97.6782422

Pandora's Blocks

I originally wanted to title this book *Pandora's Blocks* and make it more about how the world and society has been fundamentally changed by bitcoin, cryptocurrency, and an expanding set of use cases for smart contracts and immutable blockchains. I still plan to write that book, but I am glad I wrote this book first, which is far more actionable. If I've done nothing more than impress upon you, the reader, that we are still early in the ultimate destiny of bitcoin and cryptocurrency, then I have succeeded. If you take action and get rich quickly or slowly, I've achieved an even higher goal. Enjoy your journey to understanding, holding, trading, and experiencing the life-changing world of bitcoin and cryptocurrency.

Endnotes

i   X (formerly Twitter), Saifedean Ammous. "The Bitcoin Standard has sold over 1 million copies in hardcover, audiobook and ebook, it's been translated into 38 different languages, and has an 80% 5-star rating on Amazon with over 7,000 reviews - if you haven't read it yet, now's your chance!" April 21, 2021. Accessed August 6, 2024.

ii   Tradingview. "BTCUSD."https://www.tradingview.com /symbols/BTCUSD/.

iii   Conte, Niccolo. "MarketsVisualized: FTX's Leaked Balance Sheet." MarketsVisualized, November 15, 2022. Accessed August 23, 2024. https://marketsvisualized.com /ftx-leaked-balance-sheet.

iv   "Monetarists Anonymous," *The Economist*, September 29, 2012, https://www.economist.com/finance-and-economics /2012/09/29/monetarists-anonymous.

v   Bitcoin Forum, June 7, 2010, https://bitcointalk.org/index .php?topic=532.msg6269#msg6269.

vi   Michael Terpin. "How Bitcoin Will Disrupt Hollywood | Michael Terpin | TEDxHollywood." YouTube video, 18:50. Posted by TEDx Talks, July 24, 2014. https://youtu.be /lM8AF2sKPT4.

vii Nigel Green, "Is Bitcoin Really Growing Faster Than the Internet?" The Digital Commonwealth, June 20, 2024,

https://www.thedigitalcommonwealth.com/posts
/is-bitcoin-really-growing-faster-than-the-internet.

viii   George Kaloudis, "Sen. Warren's 'Anti-Crypto Army' Is Just the
Beginning of Crypto's Politicization," Nasdaq, April 3, 2023,
https://www.nasdaq.com/articles/sen.-warrens-anti-crypto
-army-is-just-the-beginning-of-cryptos-politicization.

ix   VisionTrack, 2024 Institutional Hedge Fund & Venture
Report, Galaxy Digital, 2024. https://www.Galaxy.com.

x   Jesse Powell, "I will never forget the taste of that $87,000
hamburger," X (formerly Twitter), October 18, 2020, https
://x.com/jespow/status/1317873041594986497.

xi   The Motley Fool. "The Average American Household's
Discretionary Income: How Do You Compare?" October 18,
2015. Accessed August 6, 2024. https://www.fool.com
/investing/general/2015/10/18/the-average-american
-households-discretionary-inco.aspx.

xii   Daniel Kuhn, "Bitcoin's Lost Coins Are Worth the Price,"
CoinDesk, December 8, 2021, updated May 11, 2023, https
://www.coindesk.com/policy/2021/12/08/bitcoins-lost
-coins-are-worth-the-price/.

xiii   FDIC. "2021 FDIC National Survey of Unbanked and
Underbanked Households," accessed July 31, 2024, https
://www.fdic.gov/analysis/household-survey/index.html.

xiv   Michael Bellusci, "Michael Saylor's MicroStrategy Acquires
119K More Bitcoin for $786M," CoinDesk, June 20, 2024,
https://www.coindesk.com/business/2024/06/20/michael
-saylors-microstrategy-acquires-119k-more-bitcoin-for
-786m/#:~:text=This%20latest%20acquisition%20brings%20
the,each%2C%20or%20roughly%20%248.33%20billion.

xv   Research and Markets, "Remittance Market Report," accessed July 8, 2024, https://www.researchandmarkets.com/report/remittance.

xvi   YCharts. "Bitcoin Average Transaction Fee." Accessed August 23, 2024. https://ycharts.com/indicators/bitcoin_average_transaction_fee.

xvii   Chainalysis, "2024 Crypto Crime Report Introduction," accessed July 8, 2024, https://www.chainalysis.com/blog/2024-crypto-crime-report-introduction/.

xviii Jesus Diaz, "The Underground Website Where You Can Buy Any Drug Imaginable," *Gizmodo*, June 1, 2011, https://gizmodo.com.au/2011/06/the-underground-website-where-you-can-buy-any-drug-imaginable/.

xix   International Monetary Fund, "World Economic Outlook, April 2024," accessed July 8, 2024, https://www.imf.org/external/datamapper/PCPIPCH@WEO/OEMDC/ADVEC/WEOWORLD.

xx   Ayn Rand. "Money is only a tool. It will take you wherever you wish, but it will not replace you as the driver." *Atlas Shrugged*, 1957.

xxi   Oscar Wilde. "When I was young, I thought that money was the most important thing in life; now that I am old I know that it is." *A Woman of No Importance*, 1893.

xxii   D. H. Lawrence. "Money is our madness, our vast collective madness." *Pansies*, 1929.

xxiii John Dewey, *The Later Works of John Dewey, Volume 14, 1939–1941: Essays, Reviews, and Miscellany* (1988).

xxiv CoinAgenda, "CoinAgenda Global 2023," accessed July 10, 2024, https://coinagenda.com/coinagenda-global-2023/.

xxv   Warren Buffett once referred to compound interest as "the seventh wonder of the world." Quoted in *Fortune*, April 25,

2014. Accessed August 23, 2024. https://fortune
.com/2014/04/25/warren-buffett-advice/.

xxvi   Franklin D. Roosevelt, "Executive Order 6102," April 5, 1933,
accessed July 10, 2024, https://www.presidency.ucsb.edu
/documents/executive-order-6102-forbidding-the-hoarding
-gold-coin-gold-bullion-and-gold-certificates.

xxvii   Shirtoshi, "Bitcoin T-shirt Sales," X (formerly Twitter),
accessed July 10, 2024, https://x.com/shirtoshi.

xxviii   Andrew Jackson, Veto Message Regarding the Bank of the
United States, July 10, 1832. "Entertaining this opinion, and
deeply impressed with the belief that some of the powers and
privileges possessed by the existing bank are unauthorized by
the Constitution, subversive of the rights of the States, and
dangerous to the liberties of the people." Accessed August 6,
2024, from the National Constitution Center: https
://constitutioncenter.org/the-constitution/historic
-document-library/detail/andrew-jackson-bank-veto-message
-1832.

xxix   David Chaum. X, formerly Twitter, https://x.com
/chaumdotcom. Accessed 14 July 2024.

xxx   The National Archives. "Ciphers Used by Mary Queen of
Scots." The National Archives, https://www.nationalarchives
.gov.uk/education/resources/elizabeth-monarchy/ciphers-used
-by-mary-queen-of-scots/. Accessed 14 July 2024.

xxxi   U.S. Department of Defense. NCMA Artifact Catalogue.
Jan. 25, 2023, https://media.defense.gov/2023/Jan/25
/2003149564/-1/-1/0/NCMARTIFACTCATALOGUE.PDF
. Accessed 14 July 2024.

xxxii   GeeksforGeeks. "Data Encryption Standard (DES) | Set 1."
GeeksforGeeks, https://www.geeksforgeeks.org/data
-encryption-standard-des-set-1/. Accessed 14 July 2024.

xxxiii Christina Garman and Matthew Green. "ZKLedger: Privacy-Preserving Auditing for Distributed Ledgers." Lecture Notes in Computer Science, vol. 12842, 2021, 200–15. Springer, https://dl.acm.org/doi/abs/10.1007/978-3-030-90453-1_11 . Accessed 14 July 2024.

xxxiv David Chaum. "Computer Systems Established, Maintained, and Trusted by Mutually Suspicious Groups." PhD dissertation, University of California, Berkeley, 1982.

xxxv David Chaum. DigiCash. DigiCash Inc., 1989. Accessed 14 July 2024.

xxxvi David Chaum. "Ecash." DigiCash Inc., 1983.

xxxvii David Chaum. "Better Than Money." Chaum.com, 2023, https://chaum.com. Accessed 14 July 2024.

xxxviii Electronic Frontier Foundation. "John Gilmore." EFF, https ://www.eff.org/about/board/john-gilmore. Accessed 14 July 2024.

xxxix Eric Hughes. "A Cypherpunk's Manifesto." Activism.net, 9 Mar. 1993, https://www.activism.net/cypherpunk/manifesto .html. Accessed 14 July 2024.

xl Timothy C. May. "The Crypto Anarchist Manifesto." Crypto '88 Conference, 1988. Accessed 14 July 2024.

xli Wei Dai. "b-money." Weidai.com, http://www.weidai.com /bmoney.txt. Accessed 14 July 2024.

xlii Cointelegraph. "Hal Finney: The First Recipient of Bitcoin." Cointelegraph, https://cointelegraph.com/learn/hal-finney . Accessed 14 July 2024.

xliii CoinBureau. "Who Is Nick Szabo? The Mysterious Pioneer of Digital Money." CoinBureau, https://coinbureau.com/analysis /who-is-nick-szabo/. Accessed 14 July 2024.

xliv Wei Dai. "b-money." Nakamoto Institute. Accessed August 6, 2024 https://nakamotoinstitute.org/library/b-money/.

xlv   Erik Voorhees. "Bitcoin is absolutely the Wild West of finance, and thank goodness. It represents a whole legion of adventurers and entrepreneurs, of risk takers, inventors, and problem solvers. It is the frontier. Huge amounts of wealth will be created and destroyed as this new landscape is mapped out." *Forbes*, 4 Dec. 2013, https://www.forbes.com/sites/rogeraitken/2013/12/04/bitcoin-pioneer-erik-voorhees-joins-blockchain-startup-altcoinex-as-ceo/. Accessed 14 July 2024.

xlvi   Michael J. Saylor. "Bitcoin is a swarm of cyber hornets serving the goddess of wisdom, feeding on the fire of truth, exponentially growing ever smarter, faster, and stronger behind a wall of encrypted energy." Twitter, 16 Sep. 2020, https://twitter.com/michael_saylor/status/1306191153746204672. Accessed 14 July 2024.

xlvii   Roger Ver. "Bitcoin never sleeps. We need to move quickly and grow quickly and do everything sooner rather than later." Bitcoin.com, https://www.bitcoin.com/roger-ver/. Accessed 14 July 2024.

xlviii "And God said, 'Let there be light,' and there was light." Holy Bible, Book of Genesis, Chapter 1, Verse 3.

xlix   "Every new beginning comes from some other beginning's end." Seneca, Letters to Lucilius, Epistle 24.

l   "The Times 03/Jan/2009 Chancellor on brink of second bailout for banks." Satoshi Nakamoto, "The Times 03/Jan/2009 Chancellor on brink of second bailout for banks," message embedded in the Bitcoin Genesis Block, January 3, 2009, accessed July 10, 2024, https://en.bitcoin.it/wiki/Genesis_block.

li   "Running Bitcoin." Hal Finney, Twitter, January 10, 2009, accessed July 10, 2024, https://twitter.com/halfin/status/1110302988.

lii   CNBC. "Watch the Full Rant: Cramer's 'They Know Nothing.'" August 3, 2017. Accessed August 6, 2024. https://www.cnbc.com/video/2017/08/03/watch-the-full-rant-cramers-they-know-nothing.html.

liii   Bitcoin.org. Accessed August 6, 2024. https://bitcoin.org/en/.

liv   BitcoinTalk. Accessed August 6, 2024. https://bitcointalk.org/.

lv   CryptoNews. "This Man Mined 55,000 BTC—He Could Have Been a Billionaire Today" Accessed August 6, 2024. https://cryptonews.net/news/mining/20883447/.

lvi   Blockworks. "New Liberty Standard: Crypto Legacy." Accessed August 6, 2024. https://blockworks.co/news/new-liberty-standard-crypto-legacy.

lvii   Trippy. "How's this for a disruptive technology?" BitcoinTalk, July 5, 2010. Accessed August 6, 2024. https://bitcointalk.org/index.php?topic=234.

lviii   Satoshi Nakamoto. "Bitcoin P2P e-cash paper." November 8, 2008. Accessed August 6, 2024. https://satoshi.nakamotoinstitute.org/emails/cryptography/5/.

lix   Coinpaper. "Crypto Glossary: 'When Lambo?' Meme Explained." Coinpaper, August 11, 2023. Accessed August 25, 2024. https://coinpaper.com/1931/crypto-glossary-when-lambo-meme-explained.

lx   Galbraith, John Kenneth. *The Great Crash 1929*. Boston: Houghton Mifflin, 1955. https://novelinvestor.com/quote-author/john-kenneth-galbraith/

lxi   Allen, Woody. "Money is better than poverty, if only for financial reasons." *The New York Times*, December 1, 1976.

lxii   CoinGecko. Accessed August 6, 2024. https://www.coingecko.com/.

lxiii   Glassnode. Accessed August 6, 2024. https://glassnode.com/.

lxiv   CoinDesk. Accessed August 6, 2024. https://www.coindesk
        .com/.

lxv   Diego Vallarino. "The Veblen Effect on Bitcoin: Will It
        Become a Luxury Good After Halving?" Medium, May 21,
        2020, accessed July 10, 2024, https://medium.com
        /@diegovallarino/the-veblen-effect-on-bitcoin-will-it
        -become-a-luxury-good-after-halving-cf8ec7e10bc3.

lxvi   *Gizmodo.* "Silk Road." Accessed August 6, 2024. https
        ://gizmodo.com/tag/silk-road.

lxvii   CoinDesk. "Bitcoin Price Could Reach $98.5K, Say Wall
        Street Analysts." December 3, 2013. Accessed August 6, 2024.
        https://www.coindesk.com/markets/2013/12/03
        /bitcoin-price-could-reach-985k-say-wall-street-analysts/.

lxviii Business Insider. "Bitcoin Price Drops to Lowest in a Year."
        January 14, 2015. Accessed August 6, 2024. https://www
        .businessinsider.com/bitcoin-price-drop-2015-1.

lxix   Adam Hayes, "Bitcoin's Price History," Investopedia,
        December 18, 2015, accessed July 10, 2024, https://www
        .investopedia.com/articles/forex/121815/bitcoins-price
        -history.asp.

lxx   "A house divided against itself cannot stand." Lincoln,
        Abraham. "A House Divided." Speech delivered at the Illinois
        Republican State Convention, Springfield, IL, June 16, 1858.

lxxi   "We choose mania over boredom every time." Gleick, James.
        The Information: A History, a Theory, a Flood. New York:
        Pantheon Books, 2011.

lxxii   "History doesn't repeat itself, but it often rhymes." Commonly
        attributed to Mark Twain.

lxxiii Barbara A. Friedberg, "Should You Sell in May and Go Away?"
        Investopedia, May 2, 2023, accessed July 10, 2024, https

://www.investopedia.com/should-you-sell-in-may-and
-go-away-8644577.

lxxiv   Investopedia, "Santa Claus Effect," accessed July 10, 2024,
https://www.investopedia.com/terms/s/santaclauseffect.asp.

lxxv   David Zeiler, "This Bitcoin Price Prediction Sees a 2016 Rise
to $1,000," Money Morning, May 25, 2016, accessed July 10,
2024, https://moneymorning.com/2016/05/25/this-bitcoin
-price-prediction-sees-a-2016-rise-to-1000/.

lxxvi   Vinny Lingham, "A Fork in the Road," Medium, October 8,
2017, accessed July 10, 2024, https://vinnylingham
.com/a-fork-in-the-road-70288fd3c046.

lxxvii   Cointelegraph. "Hard Fork Will Slow Bitcoin Price Down,
$3,000 Target Less Likely: Vinny Lingham." Cointelegraph,
March 16, 2017. Accessed August 23, 2024. https
://cointelegraph.com/news/hard-fork-will-slow-bitcoin
-price-down-3000-target-less-likely-vinny-lingham.

lxxviii   Alex Hern, "Bitcoin Price Plunges $2,000 in 12 Hours as Year-
End Rally Fizzles Out," *The Guardian*, December 22, 2017,
accessed July 10, 2024, https://www.theguardian.com
/technology/2017/dec/22/bitcoin-price-plunges-2000-12
-hours-year-end-rally-fizzles-out.

lxxix   Mastercoin. "2nd Bitcoin Whitepaper." Accessed August 6,
2024. https://cryptochainuni.com/wp-content/uploads
/Mastercoin-2nd-Bitcoin-Whitepaper.pdf.

lxxx   TokenData. "July Had the Lowest ICO Activity in More
Than a Year." November 7, 2018. Accessed August 6, 2024.
https://research.tokendata.io/2018/11/07.
/july-had-the-lowest-ico-activity-in-more-than-a-year/.

lxxxi   YouTube, "These Teenagers Wouldn't Stop Robbing
Millionaires," uploaded by Crumb, May 11, 2024, accessed

August 7, 2024, https://www.youtube.com /watch?v=Xm2X1uKI0Sk.

lxxxii   Martin Zweig. *Winning on Wall Street*. New York: Warner Books, 1986.

lxxxiii   Ernest Hemingway. "Notes on the Next War: A Serious Topical Letter." *Esquire*, September 1935.

lxxxiv   Milton Friedman. *Money Mischief: Episodes in Monetary History*. New York: Harcourt Brace Jovanovich, 1992.

lxxxv   "Stock Market Crash of 1929," Britannica, accessed July 10, 2024, https://www.britannica.com/event/ stock-market-crash-of-1929.
"Great Depression—Stock Market Crash, Unemployment, Poverty," Britannica, accessed July 10, 2024, https://www .britannica.com/event/Great-Depression.

lxxxvi   "The National Interest." "America's Greatest Enemy Isn't China or Russia. It's $35 Trillion in Debt." Accessed July 10, 2024. https://nationalinterest.org/feature/americas-greatest-enemy -isnt-china-or-russia-its-35-trillion-debt-210525.

lxxxvii   CNBC. "Robinhood Crypto Revenue Jumped Over 45-Fold in Q2 to $233 Million." August 18, 2021. Accessed August 6, 2024. https://www.cnbc.com/2021/08/18/robinhood-crypto -revenue-jumped-over-45-fold-in-q2-to-233-million.html.

lxxxviii   Tan, Muyao Shen, and Kevin Reynolds. "Coinbase Direct Listing Gets $100B Valuation as Share Price Jumps in Nasdaq Debut." CoinDesk, April 14, 2021. Accessed July 10, 2024. https://www.coindesk.com/markets/2021/04/14 ./coinbase-direct-listing-gets-100b-valuation-as-share-price -jumps-in-nasdaq-debut/#:~:text=Coinbase%2C%20the%20 biggest%20U.S.%20cryptocurrency,press%20time%20to%20 about%20%24378.

lxxxix PYMNTS. "Bitcoin's New Headwind: ESG Investors Double Down on 'Staggering' Pollution." May 17, 2021. Accessed July 13, 2024. https://www.pymnts.com/cryptocurrency/2022 /bitcoins-new-headwind-esg-investors-double-down -staggering-pollution/#:~:text=%E2%80%9CWe%20 are%20concerned%20about%20rapidly,What's%20the%20 problem%3F.

xc BBC News. "Dogecoin price jumps on Elon Musk's tweet about using it for SpaceX mission." May 12, 2021. Accessed August 6, 2024. https://www.bbc.com/news /business-57096305.

xci CoinAgenda. "News." Accessed July 10, 2024. https ://coinagenda.com/category/news/.

xcii Moscufo, Michela. "Digital Artwork Sells for Record $69 Million in Christie's First NFT Auction," NBC News, March 11, 2021. Accessed July 12, 2024. https://www.nbcnews.com /business/business-news/digital-artwork-sells-record-60 -million-christie-s-first-nft-n1260544.

xciii Brown, Abram. "How This 30-Year-Old Musician Made $11.7 Million in 24 Hours Selling NFTs." *Forbes*, March 3, 2021. Accessed July 12, 2024. https://www.forbes.com/sites /abrambrown/2021/03/03/3lau-nft-nonfungible-tokens -justin-blau/.

xciv Warren Buffett. "Swimming Naked When the Tide Goes Out." Accessed July 30, 2024. https://money.com /swimming-naked-when-the-tide-goes-out/.

xcv CoinCodex. "What Happened to Luna?" Accessed July 10, 2024. https://coincodex.com/article/22749 /what-happened-to-luna/.

xcvi CoinDesk. "The Fall of Celsius Network: A Timeline of the Crypto Lender's Descent Into Insolvency." July 15, 2022.

Accessed July 13, 2024. https://www.coindesk.com
/markets/2022/07/15/the-fall-of-celsius-network-a
-timeline-of-the-crypto-lenders-descent-into-insolvency/.

xcvii   Investopedia. "Who Is Sam Bankman-Fried?" Accessed July 13,
2024. https://www.investopedia.com/who-is-sam-bankman
-fried-6830274#:~:text=Sam%20Bankman%2DFried%20
is%20the%20former%20CEO%20of%20FTX%2C%20
the,are%20for%20informational%20purposes%20online.

xcviii   Business Insider. "How Binance CEO Zhao Changpeng Went
from McDonald's Employee to Billionaire Crypto Mogul."
October 2022. Accessed July 13, 2024. https://www
.businessinsider.com/zhao-changpeng-binance-billionaire
-crypto-mcdonalds-fast-food-wealth-lifestyle-2022-10.

xcix   CZ. Accessed July 13, 2024. https://x.com/cz_binance
/status/1589283421704290306.

c   Investopedia. "What Went Wrong With FTX?" Accessed
July 13, 2024. https://www.investopedia.com/what-went
-wrong-with-ftx-6828447.

ci   CNBC. "Jim Cramer Urges Investors to Exit Crypto: 'It's
Never Too Late to Sell.'" December 5, 2022. Accessed July 13,
2024. https://www.cnbc.com/2022/12/05/jim-cramer-urges
-investors-to-exit-crypto-its-never-too-late-too-sell.html.

cii   Alan Greenspan, "In the absence of the gold standard, there is
no way to protect savings from confiscation through inflation.
There is no safe store of value," *Gold and Economic Freedom*
(1966), https://www.constitution.org/mon/greenspan_gold
.htm.

ciii   Herbert Hoover, "We have gold because we cannot trust
governments," quoted in *The Memoirs of Herbert Hoover:
The Great Depression, 1929–1941* (1952), https://archive.org
/details/memoirsofherbert002943mbp.

civ   Naval Ravikant, "The Internet allows any two individuals to
        transfer data without permission from any central authority.
        Bitcoin does the same for value," Twitter, January 15, 2018,
        10:23 AM, https://twitter.com/naval/status
        /952844630803730432 (post since deleted, quoted in Yahoo
        Finance, https://finance.yahoo.com/news/25-quotes-bitcoin
        -gold-201500052.html).

cv   World Gold Council, "Gold Demand Trends Full Year 2023:
        Supply," accessed July 8, 2024, https://www.gold
        .org/goldhub/research/gold-demand-trends/gold-demand
        -trends-full-year-2023/supply.

cvi   Saifedean Ammous, *The Bitcoin Standard: The Decentralized
        Alternative to Central Banking* (Hoboken, NJ: Wiley, 2018).

cvii   Nikhilesh De, "Bitcoin ETF Approval Marks Conclusion of a
        Decade-Long Journey," CoinDesk, January 11, 2024, https
        ://www.coindesk.com/markets/2024/01/11/bitcoin-etf
        -approval-marks-conclusion-of-a-decade-long-journey/.

cviii Crypto DCA Calculator, "Bitcoin Price Calendar," accessed
        July 8, 2024, https://cryptodca.io/crypto-dca-calculator
        /bitcoin/#google_vignette.

cix   Dan Morehead and Jeff Lewis. "Impending
        Bitcoin ETF…Buy The Rumor, Buy The News."
        Blockchain Letter. Pantera Capital. November 15,
        2023. https://panteracapital.com/blockchain-letter/
        impending-bitcoin-etfbuy-the-rumor-buy-the-news/.

cx   Crypto.com. "2023 Crypto Market Sizing Report." Accessed
        August 6, 2024. https://crypto.com/research/2023
        -crypto-market-sizing-report.

cxi   Naval Ravikant, "The narrative for this cycle is 'this is the last
        cycle,'" X (formerly Twitter), March 13, 2024, 10:13 PM,
        https://x.com/naval/status/1768143338929258932.

cxii   George E. P. Box, "Science and Statistics," *Journal of the American Statistical Association*, vol. 71, no. 356, December 1976, 791–99.

cxiii   Learner, Edward A. "Cyclically, We're Back to the Past." Los Angeles Times. December 6, 2006. https://www.latimes.com/archives/la-xpm-2000-dec-06-me-61818-story.html.

cxiv   Hal Borland. *Sundial of the Seasons*. Philadelphia: J.B. Lippincott Company, 1964.

cxv   B. C. Forbes. "It is only the farmer who faithfully plants seeds in the Spring, who reaps a harvest in the Autumn." *Forbes*, accessed July 10, 2024, https://www.forbes.com.

cxvi   Robert Browning. "I trust in nature for the stable laws of beauty and utility. Spring shall plant, and autumn garner to the end of time." *The Works of Robert Browning*. London: Smith, Elder & Co., 1912.

cxvii   Chainalysis, "Bitcoin Halving 2024: What It Means and Why It Matters," accessed July 10, 2024, https://www.chainalysis.com/blog/bitcoin-halving-2024/#:~:text=This%20halving%20event%20occurs%20after,are%20introduced%20into%20the%20market.

cxviii Adam Hayes, "Bitcoin Halving: What You Need to Know," Investopedia, June 24, 2024, accessed July 10, 2024, https://www.investopedia.com/bitcoin-halving-4843769.

cxix   BeInCrypto. "Satoshi Nakamoto Speculation: Is the CIA Behind Bitcoin's Creator?" Accessed July 13, 2024. https://beincrypto.com/satoshi-nakamoto-speculation-cia-bitcoin-creator/.

cxx   Nicholas Sparks. *The Notebook*. Warner Books, 1996.

cxxi   Charles Bowden. "Summertime is always the best of what might be." *GQ*, 2004.

cxxii   Jenny Han. *The Summer I Turned Pretty*. Simon & Schuster, 2009.

cxxiii   Boston Consulting Group. "Global Fintech: Prudence, Profits and Growth." BCG Publications, 26 June 2024, https://www.bcg.com/publications/2024/global-fintech-prudence-profits-and-growth. Accessed 13 July 2024.

cxxiv   Bitcoin.org. "Controlled Supply." Bitcoin.org, https://bitcoin.org/en/how-it-works#controlled-supply.

cxxv   Adrian Chen. "The Underground Website Where You Can Buy Any Drug Imaginable." *Gizmodo Australia*, 2 June 2011, https://gizmodo.com.au/2011/06/the-underground-website-where-you-can-buy-any-drug-imaginable/. Accessed 13 July 2024.

cxxvi   World Gold Council. "Gold ETF Flows." Accessed August 6, 2024. https://www.gold.org/goldhub/research/etf-flows#:~:text=But%20total%20assets%20under%20management,gold%20price%20increase%20in%202023.

cxxvii   Howard Marks. "Selling out at the bottom—and thus failing to participate in the subsequent recovery—is the cardinal sin of investing." *The Most Important Thing: Uncommon Sense for the Thoughtful Investor*, Columbia University Press, 2011.

cxxviii Bill Stewart. "My dad used to say that every once in a while, the market has to shake out the grocery clerks." *Forbes*, 1989.

cxxix   Erik Voorhees. "The value of Bitcoin is astronomical, but the price goes all over the place as a million buyers and sellers try to figure out what that value is and how likely it is to manifest." Twitter, 2017.

cxxx   Albert Camus. "In the depth of winter, I finally learned that there was in me an invincible summer." *Return to Tipasa*. 1952.

cxxxi Warren Buffett. "Be fearful when others are greedy, and greedy when others are fearful." *The Essays of Warren Buffett: Lessons for Corporate America*. Edited by Lawrence A. Cunningham, 3rd ed., The Cunningham Group, 2013.

cxxxii Nathan Rothschild. "Buy when there's blood in the streets, even if the blood is your own." Quoted in *Forbes*, 1986.

cxxxiii Ray Kurzweil. *The Singularity Is Near: When Humans Transcend Biology*. Viking, 2005.
Ray Kapor. "Technology advances at exponential rates, and human institutions and societies do not. They adapt at much slower rates. Those gaps get wider and wider." *Wired*, 1998.
Albert Allen Bartlett. "The greatest shortcoming of the human race is our inability to understand the exponential function." *The Essential Exponential! For the Future of Our Planet*. Center for Science, Mathematics, and Computer Education, University of Nebraska–Lincoln, 2004.

cxxxiv Milton Friedman. "Inflation is Taxation Without Legislation." Shortform. "Inflation Is Taxation Without Legislation: Was Friedman Right?" Accessed August 6, 2024. https://www.shortform.com/blog/inflation-is-taxation-without-legislation/.

cxxxv Cato Institute. "Routledge Handbook of Major Events in Economic History: World Hyperinflations." Accessed August 6, 2024. https://www.cato.org/sites/cato.org/files/images/troubled-currencies-project/routledge-handbook-of-major-events-in-economic-history-world-hyperinflations.pdf

cxxxvi International Monetary Fund. "World Economic Outlook Report." April 2024.

cxxxvii Saifedean Ammous (@saifedean), "The Bitcoin Standard has sold over 1 million copies in hardcover, audiobook, and ebook, it's been translated into 38 different languages, and has an 80% 5-star rating on Amazon with over 7,000 reviews - if you haven't read it yet, now's your chance!," Twitter, June 12, 2024, 12:00 AM, twitter.com/saifedean /status/1800785142094430617.

cxxxviii PlanB (@100trillionUSD). "Creator of the stock-to-flow (S2F) model." Twitter, 13 July 2024, https://x.com/100trillionusd ?lang=en.

cxxxix CoinDesk. "Cathie Wood Sees Bitcoin Price Reaching $1.5M by 2030 After ETF Approval." January 11, 2024. Accessed August 6, 2024. https://www.coindesk.com/markets/2024 /01/11/cathie-wood-sees-bitcoin-price-reaching-15m-by-2030 -after-etf-approval/

cxl Robert Greene. "Mastery is not a function of genius or talent. It is a function of time and intense focus applied to a particular field of knowledge." *Mastery*. Viking Adult, 2012.

cxli Chef Jiro Ono. "You must immerse yourself in your work. You have to fall in love with your work. You must dedicate your life to mastering your skill. That's the secret of success." *Jiro Dreams of Sushi*. Directed by David Gelb, Magnolia Pictures, 2011.

cxlii Charlie Munger. "The big money is not in the buying or selling, but in the waiting." *Poor Charlie's Almanack: The Wit and Wisdom of Charles T. Munger*. Donning Company Publishers, 2005.

cxliii CoinGecko. "Bitcoin (BTC)." CoinGecko, https://www .coingecko.com/en/coins/bitcoin. Accessed 14 July 2024.

cxliv Budki Vineet. X, formerly Twitter, https://x.com/vineetbudki. Accessed 14 July 2024.

cxlv Trade The Pool. "Wyckoff Method: The Law of Effort and Result." Accessed August 6, 2024. https://tradethepool.com /wyckoff-method/#:~:text=price%20and%20volume.-,The%20 law%20of%20effort%20and%20result,the%20result%20 on%20price%20action.

cxlvi   Vitalik Buterin. "Bitcoin is great as a form of digital money, but its scripting language is too weak for any kind of serious advanced applications to be built on top."

cxlvii   Inevitable ETH. "World Computer." Accessed August 6, 2024. https://inevitableeth.com/en/home/ethereum/world-computer.

cxlviii   Steve Jobs, Interview with *BusinessWeek*. Accessed July 21, 2024. Steve Jobs Quotes.

cxlix   Vitalik Buterin, Twitter. Accessed July 21, 2024. Vitalik Buterin on X, formerly Twitter.

cl   Vitalik Buterin. "A Next-Generation Smart Contract, and Decentralized Application Platform." January 14, 2014. Retrieved from ethereum.org.

cli   Zerocap. "Virtual Machines, Turing Completeness, and Infinite Computation." Zerocap Research Lab. Accessed July 21, 2024. https://zerocap.com/insights/research-lab /virtual-machines-turing-completeness-infinite-computation/

clii   *Forbes*. "Solana Price Prediction." Accessed August 6, 2024. https://www.forbes.com/advisor/au/investing/cryptocurrency /solana-price-prediction/#:~:text=The%202022%20bear%20 market%20was,sharp%20decline%20in%20SOL's%20value.

cliii   Kauflin, Jeff. "How Did Sam Bankman-Fried's Alameda Research Lose So Much Money?" *Forbes*, November 19, 2022. https://www.forbes.com/sites/jeffkauflin/2022/11/19/how-did -sam-bankman-frieds-alameda-research-lose-so-much-money /. Accessed July 21, 2024.

cliv   Stephen R. Covey. "I am not a product of my circumstances. I am a product of my decisions." *The 7 Habits of Highly Effective People, 1989*.

clv   Wayne Gretzky. "You miss 100% of the shots you don't take."

clvi   Thomas Jefferson. "I'm a great believer in luck, and I find the harder I work, the more I have of it."

clvii   CoinGecko. Accessed August 6, 2024. https://www.coingecko
.com/.

clviii   CryptoAtlas. "BTCD." Accessed August 6, 2024. https
://cryptoscope.cryptoatlas.net/BTCD.php

clix   LCX. "Layer 1 Blockchain Explained." Accessed August 6,
2024. https://www.lcx.com/layer-1-blockchain-explained/

clx   Oscar Wilde. "It is better to have a permanent income than to
be fascinating." *The Model Millionaire*, 1887.

clxi   George Foreman. "The question isn't at what age I want to
retire, it's at what income." BrainyQuote. Accessed July 19,
2024. https://www.brainyquote.com/quotes/george
_foreman_634547.

clxii   Errol Flynn. "My problem lies in reconciling my gross habits
with my net income." BrainyQuote. Accessed July 19, 2024.
https://www.brainyquote.com/quotes/errol_flynn_136357.

clxiii   Alyze Sam. "Stablecoin History: The Master of All Altcoins."
HackerNoon. Accessed July 19, 2024. https://hackernoon
.com/stablecoin-history-the-master-of-all-altcoins.

clxiv   Kraken. "What is Compound (COMP)?" Accessed July 19,
2024. https://www.kraken.com/learn/what-is-compound
-comp.

clxv   DeFiLlama. "Home." Accessed July 19, 2024. https://defillama
.com/.

clxvi   Aave. "Markets." Accessed July 19, 2024. https://app.aave
.com/markets/?marketName=proto_mainnet_v3.

clxvii   Satoshi Nakamoto. "Bitcoin: A Peer-to-Peer Electronic
Cash System." Accessed July 19, 2024. https://bitcoin.org
/bitcoin.pdf.

clxviii   DeFiLlama. "Uniswap V3." Accessed July 19, 2024. https
://defillama.com/dexs/uniswap-v3.

clxix   Warren Buffett. "Risk comes from not knowing what you're doing." *The Essays of Warren Buffett: Lessons for Corporate America*. Edited by Lawrence A. Cunningham, 2001.

clxx   Mark Zuckerberg. "The biggest risk is not taking a risk. In a world that's changing really quickly, the only strategy that is guaranteed to fail is not taking risks." Interview with Y Combinator's Jessica Livingston, 2011. Accessed July 19, 2024. https://www.youtube.com/watch?v=upbTqB-aue0.

clxxi   Babe Ruth. "Yesterday's home runs don't win today's games." *The Babe Ruth Story*. By Babe Ruth and Bob Considine, 1948.

clxxii YouTube. "MMCrypto." Accessed August 6, 2024. https://www.youtube.com/channel/UCBkGMys0mYl3Myxh3CTsASA.

clxxiii CoinDesk. "JPMorgan Wants to Bring Trillions of Dollars of Tokenized Assets to DeFi." June 11, 2022. Accessed August 6, 2024. https://www.coindesk.com/business/2022/06/11/jpmorgan-wants-to-bring-trillions-of-dollars-of-tokenized-assets-to-defi/.

clxxiv Ordiscan. "Inscription 47254695." Accessed July 19, 2024. https://ordiscan.com/inscription/47254695.

clxxv   Bitcoin.com. "Study: Ordinals and Runes Reach $1 Billion Market Cap." Accessed July 19, 2024. https://news.bitcoin.com/study-ordinals-and-runes-reach-1-billion-market-cap/.

clxxvi Frederick Douglass. "The thing worse than rebellion is the thing that causes rebellion." Accessed July 21, 2024. https://www.goodreads.com/quotes/60156-the-thing-worse-than-rebellion-is-the-thing-that-causes.

clxxvii Nick Hanauer. "You show me a highly unequal society, and I will show you a police state. Or an uprising. There are no counterexamples. None. It's not if, it's when." Accessed July 21,

2024. https://www.goodreads.com/quotes/812821-you-show
-me-a-highly-unequal-society-and-i-will.

clxxviii Mahatma Gandhi (attributed). "First they ignore you, then
they laugh at you, then they fight you, then you win." Accessed
July 21, 2024. https://www.goodreads.com/quotes/103701
-first-they-ignore-you-then-they-laugh-at-you-then-they.

clxxix Mark Cuban. "Being rich is a good thing. Not just in the
obvious sense of benefiting you and your family, but in the
broader sense. Profits are not a zero-sum game. The more
you make, the more of a financial impact you can have."
Accessed July 29, 2024. https://www.goodreads.com/
quotes/785785-being-rich-is-a-good-thing-not-just-in-the.

clxxx Patrick M. Byrne. "How high can bitcoin go? The real question
is, how low can the dollar go?" Accessed July 29, 2024. https
://www.goodreads.com/quotes/105308-how-high-can-bitcoin
-go-the-real-question-is-how.

clxxxi Confucius. "When prosperity comes, do not use all of it."
Accessed July 29, 2024. https://www.goodreads.com
/quotes/47853-when-prosperity-comes-do-not-use-all-of-it.

Acknowledgments

This book was truly a community effort, both with the people who worked with me closely to add ideas, proofread, and design the book, as well as the industry giants who set me on the path of bitcoin understanding and knowledge, and who continue to inspire me today.

First, to my proofreading crew led by author and BitAngels global director Alyze Sam, who tirelessly kept up with my changes and was responsible for all of the footnoting, you have my deep respect and thanks. Taking their turns making sure nothing was missed were my inner circle of critics (and I mean this in a good way), including my head of research, David Lathrop, who additionally keeps my world together as I'm traveling the globe, and fellow author Monica Profitt, who kept me encouraged as the chapters rolled by. Major thanks to our incredible designer Dave Ravin of Form-u.la Creative, who besides contributing ideas was fully responsible for the wonderful cover art and meticulous charts and graphics; you're an amazing talent and ardent bitcoiner. And, of course, the remarkable Joyce Chow was the final person to touch everything, doing her usual great job of herding cats and conducting the carnival.

The list of mentors who have both inspired and informed me is long, but I'll try to do my best. First, Brock Pierce introduced me to bitcoin and has been a great friend and inspiration to keep pushing and achieving more as fast as possible. I want to thank Bruce Fenton for his vision and friendship as founder of the Satoshi Roundtable; Charlie Shrem, whose foreword didn't quite make the publisher deadline; Nick Spanos, who is a tireless voice for bitcoin and an amazing friend; Enzo Villani, my partner in an evolving array of businesses since his early days at NASDAQ, which only accelerated when he let me drag him into the world of crypto; and Cypher Capital managing director Vineet Budki for contributing his wisdom and graphs. Thanks to Glassnode and Look into Bitcoin for letting me republish their charts.

Many thanks to the leaders who I also count as friends who have informed me immeasurably, as well as challenged me, including Binance chairman Gabriel Abed, who is the quiet glue keeping the world's top bitcoin and crypto thinkers in constant discussion; MicroStrategy executive chairman and cofounder Michael Saylor, who has been a graceful host to the top bitcoin leaders at his remarkable home; BTC Media founder David Bailey, for pushing bitcoin onto larger and larger stages; David A. Johnston, for continually seeing what is next; Erik Voorhees, the most eloquent speaker and profound thinker in bitcoin; Dan Held, who first popularized the idea of a bitcoin supercycle; Max Keiser and Stacy Herbert, for being right for so many years; Jim Lowry, for his impeccable timing and patience during all bitcoin cycles; Ray Youssef, who is busy changing the world for the Global South, one new bitcoiner at a time; Anthony Di Iorio and Vitalik Buterin, for introducing me to the world of Ethereum and allowing me to break the story to the world; BitPay cofounder Stephen Pair (who first got me thinking about $1 million bitcoin . . . in 2013); Alan Meckler and Stewart Quealy, who gave me my first international speaking roles; Arthur Hayes, for his brilliant real-time analysis of bitcoin and the world; Liam Robertson, for riding the parabolic waves with me as managing director of Alphabit Fund; Ran Neuner, for first dubbing me the Crypto Godfather and staying in the loop with me now that's he's one of the world's top crypto influencers; Benjamin "Into the Cryptoverse" Cowen, Carl "the Moon" Runefelt, Davinci Jeremie, and Chris "MM Crypto" Jaszczynski for their daily insights and personal guidance; Dr. Marwan Alzarouni for introducing me to the new world crypto capital of Dubai; Jordan Feintech, for his friendship, collaboration and for supercharging my education on memecoins (along with Marcie Jastrow, Shytoshi, and the Shib Nation); Jim Blasko, who programmed several early projects with me and educated me about the inner workings of proof-of-work; William Quigley, for his great vision as one of the most intuitive investors in crypto; and Mark Jeffrey, who is a constant source of inspiration and education on what's new in defi, decentralized AI, and whatever is new and exciting in crypto. If I've left you out by name and you belong on this list, I still acknowledge you, but I ran out of time . . .

Speaking of time, I want to sincerely thank the entire crew at Skyhorse Publishing, especially founder and CEO Tony Lyons and my editor Michael Campbell and agent Marco Vicenzino for their patience as I had to extend the publishing date, first to accommodate my unexpected eye surgery, then to incorporate some important industry landmarks by deadline. The book will be greater because of your patience!

Finally, many thanks to my teams at Transform Ventures, BitAngels, Alpha Transform Holdings, Blockchain Wire, OpenCarbon, Tokenize! and Transform Group, as well as my advisory clients and current investments for providing me the ability to disappear long enough to write this book. And to my Puerto Rico crypto crew, who I get to bounce ideas off of constantly and who kept encouraging me all summer as I slowly closed out the writing and editing of this book, including Scott Walker, Jeff Mcdonald, Mitchell and Chin Dong, Carly Howard, as well as the global community of my friends and advocates who have encouraged me throughout. I hope you enjoy the book and what comes next.

About the Author

Michael Terpin is one of the earliest thought leaders, investors, and entrepreneurs in bitcoin and crypto, earning him the moniker "Crypto Godfather" from CNBC in 2018. He has worked on more than four hundred crypto projects as an advisor, investor, and media strategist, including the launches of Ethereum and Tether, as well as the first ICO (Mastercoin) and largest funding (Eos). Projects he has advised have raised in excess of $8 billion. He has been an advocate for the enduring value of bitcoin as a powerful investment since early 2013, when he started the BitAngels investor network.

Bitcoin Supercycle is the culmination of more than a decade of research on what Terpin calls "the Four Seasons of Bitcoin," the unmistakable cycles that have propelled bitcoin and crypto forward from a miniscule value to the multitrillion-dollar asset class it is today.

Terpin is founder and CEO of Transform Ventures, a blockchain advisory firm and venture studio, which incubated Blockchain Wire, the pioneering crypto newswire, and OpenCarbon, a blockchain-based carbon offset marketplace. In early 2013, he founded Transform Group, the oldest and most prominent media strategy firm in the crypto world. In 2014, he founded CoinAgenda, the longest-running crypto investor conference, which has been relaunched as Tokenize!

Conferences to better serve the diverse tokenized digital asset ecosystem of founders, investors, and thought leaders.

Terpin is an active investor in crypto projects, both as an angel investor and through his funds. He cofounded with David A. Johnston one of the earliest crypto venture funds, the BitAngels Fund 1 (also known as the Dapps Fund) in March 2014, which invested in the Ethereum ICO and other prominent early projects. He is currently a general partner at Alpha Transform Holdings and at Tradecraft Capital, as well as a limited partner and advisor to Alphabit Fund and Project Richport, and a limited partner in Asian-focused crypto venture firm, OP Crypto.

Prior to crypto, Terpin was a successful serial entrepreneur in tech and media. He founded Internet Wire (now Globe Newswire), securing funding from Sequoia Capital and Hummer Winblad, then selling it in 2006. The company is now a $500 million division of Apollo Global Management (NYSE: APO). He also founded and sold his first PR firm, The Terpin Group, which was a leader in new media marketing and PR in the 1990s, launching the Motley Fool, Earthlink, and America Online Greenhouse, among others. He sold the firm into a roll-up that is now part of FTI Consulting (NYSE: FCN). He also cofounded DirectIPO, one of the first equity crowdfunding companies, in 1996.

Terpin received a dual-degree BA from Syracuse University's prestigious Newhouse School of Public Communications, where he went on to serve on the school's board of advisors since 2000 and has been recognized on its Wall of Fame. He also holds a master's degree in creative writing from SUNY at Buffalo.

Michael lives in San Juan, Puerto Rico, with investment property secondary homes in Miami and Las Vegas. In 2016, he was the first person from the crypto world to receive an investor decree from Puerto Rico under its Act 20/22 incentive program, earning him the nickname "the Messiah" of the Puerto Rico crypto movement, which now counts more than 1,000 new residents from the crypto industry who permanently moved to the island. He also cofounded the Caribbean Blockchain Association with crypto icons Gabriel Abed (Barbados) and Roger Ver (St. Kitts).

Terpin has been a frequent speaker on bitcoin and crypto investing throughout the world, including six times at the Consumer Electronics Show (CES), which awarded him as a pioneer in the field. He has also spoken at the leading events in crypto, including the Bitcoin Conference, Bitcoin Foundation Conference, Consensus, Inside Bitcoins (Berlin, Chicago, New York, Hong Kong), Korea Blockchain Week, and many others.

Index